Reading William Kennedy

 Sanford Sternlicht, *Series Editor*

Other titles in Irish Studies

Harp Re-strung: The United Irishmen and the Rise of Irish Literary Nationalism
   Mary Helen Thuente

Ireland's National Theaters: Political Performance and the Origins of the Irish Dramatic Movement
   Mary Trotter

Irish Literature: A Reader
   Maureen O'Rourke Murphy & James MacKillop, eds.

Modern Irish-American Fiction: A Reader
   Daniel J. Casey & Robert E. Rhodes, eds.

New Plays from the Abbey Theatre, 1996–1998
   Judy Friel and Sanford Sternlicht, eds.

Reading Roddy Doyle
   Caramine White

Real Lace
   Stephen Birmingham

Seamus Heaney, Poet of Contrary Progressions
   Henry Hart

Textures of Irish America
   Lawrence McCaffrey

Women Creating Women: Contemporary Irish Women Poets
   Patricia Boyle Haberstroh

Writing Irish: Interviews with Irish Writers from
   The Irish Literary Supplement
   James P. Myers, Jr., ed.

Yeats and Artistic Power
   Phillip L. Marcus

Reading
William Kennedy

MICHAEL PATRICK GILLESPIE

 Syracuse University Press

First Edition 2002
02 03 04 05 06 07   6 5 4 3 2 1

The paper used in this publication meets the minimum requirements of
American National Standard for Information Sciences—Permanence of Paper
for Printed Library Materials, ANSI Z39.48–1984.∞™

Library of Congress Cataloging-in-Publication Data

Gillespie, Michael Patrick.
　　Reading William Kennedy / Michael Patrick Gillespie.—1st ed.
　　　　p. cm.—(Irish studies)
　　Includes bibliographical references and index.
　　ISBN 0-8156-2929-X (alk. paper)—ISBN 0-8156-0724-5 (pbk. : alk. paper)
　　　　1. Kennedy, William, 1928—Criticism and interpretation. 2. Albany
　　(N.Y.)—In literature. 3. Irish Americans in literature. I. Title. II. Irish
　　studies (Syracuse, N.Y.)
PS3561.E428 Z67 2001
813'.54—dc21　　　　　　　　　　　　　　　　　　　　2001049511

Manufactured in the United States of America

To Jeoffrey Miller and Christopher Pape,
two good friends

Michael Patrick Gillespie is the Louise Edna Goeden Professor of English at Marquette University. He has published books on the writings of James Joyce and Oscar Wilde. He has also written essays on a range of topics related to Irish and British literature.

Contents

Acknowledgments

I am grateful to many people who have at various points in this project offered timely advice and encouragement. Listing them does not adequately attest to the deep impact each has had on my work, but I do hope it conveys my sense of debt and deep regard: Annie Barva, John Boly, the Rev. Thaddeus Burch, S. J., Amy Farranto, A. Nicholas Fargnoli, Don Faulkner, Benedict Giamo, Susanne Dumbleton, Paula Gillespie, Thomas Hachey, Vivian Valvano Lynch, John McCabe, Tim Machan, Robert Mandel, Christian Michener, Albert Rivero, and Neila Seshachari. Their help and insights have greatly enriched this work.

My deepest gratitude goes out to two people who have not had a hand in the material production of this work but whose generosity, confidence, and enthusiasm have made it possible. Sara Cohen recommended me to Syracuse University Press as someone who might write this book. She introduced me to William Kennedy, and she gave me a sense of the importance of this project. William Kennedy has overturned my narrow-minded belief that an author's charm and grace vary inversely with his talent. He has shown me the profound beauty of the Irish American experience, and he has trusted me to write about his work in a fashion that does it justice. I cannot say whether I have lived up to the expectations of these two fine individuals, but I can say that this book is a much better work for their patience, goodwill, and faith.

Introduction

Despite the reassuring sentiments of *"e pluribus unum,"* one of the official mottos of the United States, in literature at least multiplicity remains the dominant form. From the time that writers on this continent began to see themselves as something other than European authors, American fiction has self-consciously drawn attention to the localized milieu from which it has emerged. In a nation distinguished by its pluralism, this interest in the cultural mores of a specific locale or of a particular group inevitably accentuates paradoxes inherent in the larger social institutions that form the American consciousness, and apprehension of these dichotomies underscores the disruptive nature of American fiction.

The works of any number of writers, from James Fenimore Cooper to Bobby Ann Mason, provide evidence of the often uneasy pluralism that resides within the canon of American literature: fiction in the United States over the past two hundred years has consistently emphasized the highly structured and vastly different features of the diverse communities that exist—often in turbulent tension—within the broad configuration of our culture. In consequence, the most insistently American writers have forged a sense of identity from religious, regional, ethnic, or class traits that distance various groups from the rest of society.

This fascination with the way closely constructed and conflicted environments mold the consciousnesses of literary characters poses very particular interpretive challenges for William Kennedy's readers. A highly determined cultural atmosphere forms the characters, shapes their experiences, and lays down the protocols for judging conduct in Kennedy's writing. Even a cursory review of his books will underscore their close association with the occupations and roles that formed his life—as newspaper reporter, literary and film critic, and long-time resident of Albany, New York. Any analysis that seeks a full understanding of his fictional world must grapple with the idiosyncracies of this ambiance.

Indeed, because of the overt shaping force of the Albany environment, coming to an interpretive sense of Kennedy's world stands as much more important for readers than for readers of authors such as John Updike, Norman Mailer, or Saul Bellow. Although characters emerging from the ambiences created by these authors strive to define themselves against the strictures of a hegemonic culture that reflects a generalized version of American society, figures in Kennedy's writing contend with the highly particularized and unique milieu of working-class, ethnic Albany. In fact, this ethos seems to mimic so cannily the community in which Kennedy himself grew to manhood that in reading his work one encounters an insistent impression of the intertwining of his imaginative and material worlds. Compositions of place, cadences of language, clusters of themes—all of these narrative features enforce the idea that the Albany of Kennedy's childhood and youth, and for that matter the city of his parents and grandparents, formed his creative consciousness and continues to manifest itself through his writing.[1]

These conditions give his fictional renderings of upstate New York between the world wars an interpretive importance to his readers equal to that held by turn-of-the-century Dublin for James Joyce's audience. By the same token, Kennedy no more deserves the label of regionalist than does Joyce. Rather, both stand as artists writing out of themselves, using particular experiences and specific locales to evoke any number of broad reactions.

Reading William Kennedy entails a great deal more than matching places and events in his life with the incidents and settings he features in his novels. A more useful approach takes into account the imaginative context surrounding the production of his writing while leaving ample room for the evolution of personal readings. Like the works of Joyce and those of the magic realists, Kennedy's books facilitate repeated and diverse imaginative engagements, and they militate against fixed, mechanistic methods of interpretation.

As for any writer of marked talent, identifying the characterizing features of Kennedy's canon will clarify one's sense of the artistic purpose that fuels and sustains its development. Such a recognition will not, however, inevitably lead to a narrow or one-sided exposition of his writing. Quite the contrary: Kennedy's habits of introducing diverse characters, employing distinct stylistic frames, and ranging across a broad historical spectrum work against any effort to apply formulaic readings to his books. Through the incorporation of vastly divergent concepts into an increasingly sophisticated prose format, the discourse of each novel moves forward with complex explorations of the natures of ostensibly simple characters, who are always at the forefront of the author's efforts.

Whatever imaginative concerns animate Kennedy's books, a clear and engaging prose style informs all of them and facilitates a reader's involvement in his work. This trait stands as particularly gratifying given the uniqueness of Kennedy's world. Anything like the Albany that emerges from his narratives has long disappeared, and even lifetime residents might feel hard-pressed to remember the city outlined in his descriptions. Further, the individuals that populate his books, though commonplace in their own right, exude an idiosyncratic aura that distinguishes each of them from anyone that a reader might know personally. The events and experiences chronicled in the novels, though part of a quotidian existence, feature personalized elements that make them equally distinct.

At the same time, Kennedy enables us to identify the terrain, to become familiar with the individuals, and to picture the incidents of his fiction by distinguishing each element through precisely articulated particulars that provide near instantaneous identification. One does not need to be a gangster, a pool hustler, or a vagrant to comprehend the worlds of Jack Diamond, Billy Phelan, or Helen Archer. One needs only to remain attentive to Kennedy's rich descriptive language.

Clarity makes such enlightenment possible. Nothing superfluous encumbers Kennedy's narrative style. His writing features only the details needed for one to comprehend the essence of his descriptions, and he highlights only the essential in a manner both deft and assured. James Joyce once boasted that if Dublin were destroyed, one could rebuild it from the information found in his novel *Ulysses*. One would never attempt to re-create stone by stone the material Albany as described in Kennedy's works. Far too many significant gaps in the picture occur. At the same time, as with Joyce's fiction, one has no difficulty creating an imaginative representation of the world of Kennedy's novels, for so many relevant markers distinguish it for us.

The ease with which readers can construct their own versions of the Albany milieu relates directly to Kennedy's love of language. Time and again his prose offers ample evidence that the creative act, the skillful manipulation of words in a fashion that invites thoughtful responses, stands itself as a source of genuine pleasure for him. His writing does not emerge as a solipsistic effort producing an opaque discourse that inhibits the transmission of his ideas. Rather, it reflects the endeavors of someone conversant with the diversity of rhetoric and respectful of the power of individual words to convey subtle and shifting meanings.

Just as a comprehensible yet sophisticated vocabulary distinguishes the formal structure of Kennedy's canon, a core of recognizable central themes punctuates his process of composition. Over the course of the Albany cycle, in generation after generation, characters face the same issues. More often than not, each handles these problems in a unique fashion that outlines for us Kennedy's complex conception of this seemingly simple society. Further, the recurrence of these familiar topics draws together diverse narrative strands to make the most complex stylistic efforts comprehensible to the reader. Although it may seem simplistic to say that Kennedy teaches us how to understand his works, we can clearly see how a growing awareness of common creative patterns in his narratives facilitates our response to his writing.

A number of structuring elements function within Kennedy's canon to establish the representative dimensions of his thematic concerns. The relation of the past to the present shapes the imaginative development of characters within all of his novels, for he presents time as more than a concept of measurement. It exerts a transformative force that both disrupts the conventional movement of individual lives and unifies seemingly unrelated experiences through its patterns of repetition and renewal. Kennedy's narratives capture time's elasticity while enforcing its cyclical, predictable qualities. The progress of events, set up in a clear (though not always linear) chronology, asserts the mutability of human endeavor, even as this operation circumscribes individual lives with the stabilizing regularity of seasonal rhythms.

Place, for Kennedy, occupies a role as significant as time, and the very term *Albany cycle* underscores most directly the importance of understanding the evocative function of location within the author's work. As graphically described in both his fiction and nonfiction, the city of Albany takes on a status equal to that of a major character. The nature of Kennedy's hometown emerges through traits that both mark it and testify to its ongoing formative influence on the figures who appear in the various narratives. Kennedy's men and women stand as strikingly different from citizens of New York City or of western New York State. They function as a breed apart, unique in their attitudes and distinct in their world view. Further, they effectively engage the reader's imagination as individuals because the environment that has formed them remains so singular. The communal Albany, amorphous and evolving, continually commands attention even as it resists easy categorization.

At the same time, although the prominent traits of an urban locale circumscribe and define Kennedy's narrative context, the subtle features of individuality exert a shaping influence. Throughout the Albany cycle, his writing highlights the complexities and contradictions in human nature, and in the process these descriptions infuse singularity into the most ordinary of lives. Kennedy underscores our awareness of the uniqueness of the figures in his works by having many of those characters relentlessly strive for a full comprehension of their own natures. In some cases, as with Jack Diamond, a character's identity remains fixed throughout the novel, yet that character develops nonetheless through the process of discerning the consequences of living the life dictated by his or her temperament. In other instances, an individual such as Edward Daugherty strives, over the course of several works, to evolve a disposition in harmony with the moral universe even while endeavoring to comprehend the parameters of an ethical system he does not fully believe exists.

In every instance, the narrative does not privilege a static or intransigent consciousness, but rather gives primacy to an impulse that brings unity to diverse attitudes. Francis Phelan personifies this creative feature, but others—most notably Katrina Daugherty, Orson Phelan, Marcus Gorman, Martin Daugherty, Helen Archer, and Molly Phelan—also reflect this ability to produce stability from antinomy. Like figures found throughout American fiction, especially in the last century, most of Kennedy's characters lead mundane lives circumscribed by predictable events, but each one's fierce humanity reminds us of the power of even the most trivial-seeming experiences to imbue individual existence with transformative significance. In the Albany cycle, neither education nor breeding counts so much in the formation of a character as does the flexibility and resilience that the character displays across a range of experiences.

Adaptability depends to a large degree on self-awareness, and memory plays a crucial role in the process of coming to this understanding. Memory acts as the force bridging time, place, and identity, and it mediates the diverse and often conflicting impressions that each of these phenomena generate. For all of Kennedy's central characters, recollections become the means to negotiate and to reconcile the contrasting urges and demands of their worlds. By observing individual characters struggle to comprehend the evolution of their lives by recollecting the events that formed them, readers come to understand how memory informs perception throughout Kennedy's work.

Various social institutions facilitate the way characters order this relationship of past events to current lives, but none does so with a clarity and precision equal to that of politics. Though its immediate impact on city life appears most evident in Kennedy's nonfiction work *O Albany!* politics emerges as a major force throughout his writing. *Billy Phelan's Greatest Game* demonstrates most overtly the strengths and the weaknesses of the political machine that runs Albany, yet one finds traces of its influence in a number of other novels. In *Legs*, politics for a time allows Jack Diamond to operate with impunity and then brings about his demise. As *Ironweed* details, politics can intrude in a forceful fashion even on the life of someone as alienated as Francis Phelan. In *The Flaming Corsage*, politics enforces a muted but insistent influence on the Daugherty family from the time of Edward's early courtship of Katrina. And politics stands at the heart of Kennedy's most recent work, *Roscoe* (scheduled for publication in January 2002), with its detailed look at the McCall machine from the perspective of Roscoe Conway, the secretary of the Albany Democratic Party during World War II. Throughout the Albany cycle, politics acts in a way analogous to gravity: it is an ever-present, regulating force, rarely acknowledged but impossible to escape.

Politics occupies a particularly important position in interpreting Kennedy's fiction because its structure provides a useful gauge for understanding the compulsive rule breakers who proliferate in his writing. Not surprisingly, religion occupies a similar though less easily defined role. Roman Catholic dogma colors almost every moral decision in Kennedy's works, but a broad, more diverse ethical system than that articulated in *The Baltimore Catechism* informs the ethical universe of his writing. Most of Kennedy's characters link themselves either closely or loosely with the Catholic Church, but they also practice an idiosyncratic expression of belief that continually reevaluates the moral world in which each of them operates. This is not to diminish the importance of standard ethical systems within Kennedy's writings. Rather, it underscores the tensions that naturally arise between rigid public ritual and evolving personal belief.

The final social institution informing so many of the actions, attitudes, and perceptions within Kennedy's writings—the family—emerges only through the uneasy equilibrium of individual desire and group cohesiveness. In a clannish fashion, his families rise out of a cultural memory. They function as social units both joined and disrupted by blood ties that retain strong links to the heritage bequeathed by their ancestors. However, the bonds of marriage and the generation of children, although essential aspects of the institution, do not set the boundaries of Kennedy's families. Rather, the most successful families deftly avoid the suffocating parochialism of single-perspective, tribal identity and instead assume more malleable characterizing forms that acknowledge their heritage while remaining responsive to society at large.

One best sees this responsiveness in the way individuals successfully or unsuccessfully negotiate the movement between the close-knit society in which they were raised and the broad, amorphous world that surrounds it. Many of Kennedy's protagonists emerge from an environment self-reflexively similar to the Irish American society that conditioned the author's own upbringing, and the mores of that group assume an important characterizing role. At the same time, Irish American Albany does not take on an archetypal status in Kennedy's narratives. Alternative groups, such as the Taylors and the Staats, show the profound impact of the English and the Dutch cultures on the Albany families of his fiction. Overall, no single social group defines the world in which his characters live, yet the consistent influence of the culture of the city makes it every bit as significant as politics or religion in shaping those characters within the Albany cycle.

The complex effects of identity, place, time, and urban social institutions, all stimulated by memory, coalesce within the figures that animate Kennedy's writing. From *The Ink Truck* to *The Flaming Corsage*, unique personalities dominate his narratives. In consequence, the bulk of this study seeks to illuminate the natures of individuals such as Jack Diamond, Francis Phelan, Helen Archer, Katrina Daugherty, and others as a means of understanding the key features of Kennedy's fictional world. To explain such a compositional strategy, it might be useful to end this introduction by outlining the critical assumptions I have applied throughout this study.

Let me begin, contrarily, by noting what I do not do. A great many other critics—among the most prominent, J. K. Van Dover (1991), Vivian Valvano Lynch (1999), Benedict Giamo (1996), and Christian Michener (1995, 1998)—have made fine use of Kennedy's opinions on his writing in their own interpretations. And Neila C. Seshachari (1997) has edited a valuable collection of interviews with Kennedy. I have benefited greatly from their work. Nonetheless, although the remarks I have already made underscore my sense of the importance of the environment out of which Kennedy wrote, I have endeavored to separate his process of composing that context from his retrospective responses to what he has created. Consequently, in a self-conscious fashion, I have avoided quoting Kennedy's views on his own writing in all but a few instances.

My interpretations instead put emphasis on the other side of the exegetic process by drawing attention to the alternative strategies that may inform a reader's response to Kennedy's writing. This means concentrating on efforts to discern meaning through procedures that accommodate an individual's subjective perspective, but also working within the structure of each novel as presented in Kennedy's discourse. My approach rests on the belief that the strength of Kennedy's writing lies in the discursive fashion he follows in conveying information. The best way of responding to this discursiveness lies in a willingness to highlight the ambiguities he creates. His characters come alive through the narrative's ability to reflect a number of complex and even contrasting points of view, so foregrounding one interpretation over all others can never get to the heart of his work. Rather, the most satisfying interpretations of Kennedy's writing come from reconciliations of the antinomies that characterize each of his books.

Thus, I seek to foreground the role of the reader, tracing the ways that key elements of the discourse contribute to the impressions that shape an individual's comprehension of the work. This aim makes it more important to focus on options for interpretation than to privilege a particular meaning. Because every reader will come to a sense of the text in a slightly different fashion, a book of this sort becomes most beneficial when it focuses attention on the way that the process takes place rather than on how one articulates particular responses. Toward this end, this volume seeks to facilitate understanding of how one finds meanings in the works. (Readers familiar with the methods employed by Wolfgang Iser [1978], Hans Robert Jauss [1982], or Roland Barthes [1977] will recognize similar patterns in my criticism. However, I do not believe it necessary for readers to consult their work to understand my approach.)

At the same time, I have tried to make this study an introduction for those readers not completely familiar with Kennedy's work. In keeping with this goal, I have balanced within the chapters a measure of synopsis and speculation, offering my summary of what occurs in each work and elaborating on that outline with my impression of its significance. In a symbiotic fashion, these overviews of the central events and principal characters in all of Kennedy's published fiction highlight an individual's imaginative engagement with his narrative.

This approach emphasizes the central concern of my study: the diverse opportunities for interpretation inherent in Kennedy's writing. For an author such as Kennedy, a single interpretation, no matter how accommodating, cannot capture the complexity of his writing. Rather, each effort has imbedded within it the invitation to begin again the process of imaginative engagement. Thus, what follows is intended to be neither the first word on Kennedy's writings nor the last. Instead, it seeks to serve as a guidebook for facilitating the process of reading his canon again and again.

Part One

Apprenticeship

 CHAPTER ONE

William Kennedy's Albany

As the Viking-Penguin copy editor tells us in a note tucked discreetly within the inside papers of *Riding the Yellow Trolley Car,* "William Kennedy is a novelist who began his writing career as a journalist." This designation has a matter-of-fact tone that makes the conjunction between the two professions seem perfectly obvious. Nonetheless, as Kennedy implies throughout this collection, one should not assume that the transition came about in the easy fashion suggested by such a brief description. Indeed, in essays and interviews, he goes to some pains to underscore distinctions between the two occupations, and at several points in *Riding the Yellow Trolley Car* he invokes the words that Ernest Hemingway employed to differentiate the output of journalists from that of creative writers. Hemingway asserts that the

> newspaper stuff I have written . . . has nothing to do with the other writing which is entirely apart. . . . The first right that a man writing has is the choice of what he will publish. If you have made your living as a newspaperman, learning your trade, writing against deadlines, writing to make stuff timely rather than permanent, no one has any right to dig this stuff up and use it against the stuff you have written to write the best you can. (qtd. in Kennedy 1993, 6)

The positioning of this quotation in *Riding the Yellow Trolley Car* implicitly invites us to enlarge on these remarks to see that the two practices act in diametrically opposed fashions. At the same time, Kennedy takes care neither to disassociate himself from his journalistic work nor to suggest that it stands as a body of writing of which he is ashamed. Instead, he plays the dual card of invoking Hemingway's prohibition and then of qualifying it through a loophole that permits selective publication: "Of course you have the right to do this yourself" (1993, 6).

Needless to say, the fact that Kennedy has gone to the trouble of sifting through and reprinting (or in some cases publishing for the first time) the essays that appear in *Riding the Yellow Trolley Car* suggests at the very least his tacit endorsement of their worth. Further, although the author's opinions may not completely establish for the skeptical reader the significance of these essays, more objective interpretive standards mitigate against any inclination to dismiss as hack work the pieces that appear in *Riding the Yellow Trolley Car* and *O Albany!* No matter what one's opinion of the connections or differences between journalism and fiction, both the technical precision and the revelatory analysis of the essays compel our attention. These self-contained reflections capture Kennedy's attitudes toward his family, his heritage, his city, his artistic likes and dislikes. Anyone seeking an enhanced sense of the cultural, intellectual, and imaginative consciousness from which Kennedy's fiction emerges will be very glad to have the opportunity to read these pieces.

The very term *Albany cycle*—a designation that appears in an interview with Peter Quinn reprinted in *Riding the Yellow Trolley Car* (Kennedy 1993, 44)—labels Kennedy's fiction as work steeped in the world that surrounded him from childhood to young adulthood. Like the work of one of the authors whom he most admires, James Joyce, Kennedy's writing repeatedly returns to the same setting even as it succeeds in creating that ethos anew within each novel. In the 1930s, Joyce explained the logic behind returning in his fiction to a familiar venue. "For myself, I always write about Dublin, because if I can get to the heart of Dublin I can get to the heart of all the cities of the world. In the particular is contained the universal" (qtd. in Magalaner 1959, 19). As subsequent chapters of this study illustrate, that same rationale informs Kennedy's approach: a careful exploration of familiar territory inevitably produces fresh insights. Nonetheless (as surely is the case with readers of Joyce), for readers to understand how Kennedy is able to "get to the heart" of Albany, they must acquire a great deal of background information before going on to comprehend that city as a microcosmic representation of the universal.

Joyce scholars have devoted an enormous effort to compiling reference works that gloss the cultural, geographic, and psychological allusions in that author's canon and to rediscovering book reviews, nonfiction essays, and offhand remarks recorded in biographies, memoirs, and letters that illuminate, even imperfectly, Joyce's artistic dispositions. *O Albany!* and *Riding the Yellow Trolley Car* anticipate that process with regard to Kennedy's work. In each book, Kennedy has collected a great deal of the fundamental information necessary for readers striving to identify the landmarks that delimit the Albany of his novels and hoping to comprehend the aesthetic standards that shape his imaginative work. Using *O Albany!* and *Riding the Yellow Trolley Car* to form a sense of Kennedy's social and artistic milieu enables readers to approach the canon with an enhanced comprehension of that context and with a greater confidence to ground their own interpretations. Reading the nonfiction with this in mind is not the same as linking Kennedy's imaginative and factual worlds to suggest that every novel functions as a roman à clef. Rather *O Albany!* and *Riding the Yellow Trolley Car* give readers the information necessary to comprehend more fully the settings from which his fictional material emerged. This understanding, in turn, leads to insights into the aesthetic aims and values informing Kennedy's novels. (Susanne Dumbleton's "William Kennedy: Telling the Truth the Best Way I Can" [1996] provides an excellent general introduction to the potential of these two works.)

With the possible exception of responses to *The Ink Truck*, no interpretation of Kennedy's fiction can be quite the same after one has gained the vivid sense of the complexities of the neighborhoods and people chronicled in *O Albany!* This collection begins with a series of ostensibly disconnected observations that in fact provide an overview of Kennedy's complex association with his city. Succeeding chapters anatomize the town from personal, geographic, and ethnic perspectives. The narrative then goes on to highlight Albany's political intricacies and ends with a series of personal anecdotes that reveal as much about the writer as they do about his city. One might argue in fact that *O Albany!* stands as no less fanciful a representation of the town than do the fictional descriptions that appear in any of the novels. From the subjective perspective that Kennedy very happily imposes on his recollections, that seems a fair comment.

Distinctions between the fictive and the real, however, remain entirely beside the point. *O Albany!* illuminates the rest of Kennedy's writing because it presents a judicious sampling—so necessary for a reader being introduced to Kennedy's town for the first time—of the environment that shapes the natures of all of his characters. J. K. Van Dover is surely correct in calling it "the best introduction to the Albany of William Kennedy" (1991, 25), for nothing else has so clearly captured the social milieu and the cultural memory that continues to inform Kennedy's canon.

Part of the emotive power of this collection comes from an unflagging determination to celebrate, in language that moves perilously close to the hyperbolic vocabulary of a booster, what an observer lacking Kennedy's ardor might characterize as the drab features of an undistinguished urban setting. Few readers will doubt that Kennedy believes most sincerely in the uniqueness of Albany, and his skill at evoking what he perceives as its very special ethos comes from his instinctive ability to blend his enthusiasm for the world that he has experienced with a marvelous openness to the diverse influences of the people and neighborhoods of his hometown. Kennedy deftly translates this flair for recognizing and articulating the traits that make Albany so distinct and so interesting for him into the compelling images that underpin so much of his fiction. Because the two cities—real and imagined Albany—so closely resemble one another, the elaborate delineation of these features in his nonfiction provides a useful outline for understanding the interplay of his narratives.

Kennedy begins *O Albany!* with a chapter entitled "Albany as a State of Mind." It presents a very neat summary of the impressions that formed his conceptions of the city as he grew to adulthood, and it establishes an informative contrast between the consciousness of the young man who first engaged this world and that of the experienced writer who now transmutes his recollections to satisfy his creative aims. With disarmingly straightforward charm, Kennedy sums up in a few sentences feelings that capture the attitude of any intellectually precocious individual who chafes at the perceived limitations of a world that he believes he understands all too well:

> I once thought I loathed the city, left it without a sigh and thought I'd gone for good, only to come back to work and live in it and become this curious cheerleader I now seem to be. But I'm fond of things beyond the city's iniquity. I love its times of grace and greatness, its political secrets and its historical presence in every facet of the nation's life, including the unutterable, the unspeakable, and the ineffable. (Kennedy 1983b, 4)

These lines offer us a clear description of the lyrical point of view and accommodating temperament that dominate the essays that follow in the book, yet their sharp delineation of the writer's evolving attitudes also encourage us to assess that consciousness in a manner that few other authors would dare invite. With the aplomb of an unapologetic insider, Kennedy here announces his loyalty and promises glimpses of the features of Albany that so fascinate him. With equal confidence, he leaves it to his readers to determine the validity of these enthusiasms.

"Legacy from a Lady" seems to continue the autobiographical tone of the opening piece by beginning as a charming commemoration of a precocious schoolboy's fascination with the local library. In relatively short order, however, the essay shifts its interest to highlight Albany's social history from the late nineteenth century to the mid-twentieth century as seen through the eyes of Huybertie Pruyn Hamlin, a descendant of one of the original Dutch governors of the demesne of Rensselaerwyck, the initial European settlement that eventually became the city of Albany. (Readers already familiar with Kennedy's canon will see in Huybertie's background analogues to that which formed Hillegond Staats, a prominent character in *Quinn's Book*.) Huybertie's insights into a powerful, status-dominated world that Kennedy himself could only glimpse from a distance nicely underscore the complexity of urban life and provide us with a useful paradigm for understanding the compositional multiplicity that characterizes Kennedy's writing. Her recollections highlight the complex ethnic structure that extends well beyond the conventional contemporary conceptions of clashes between Eurocentric views and those of other cultures: "Legacy from a Lady" illustrates, literarily and metaphorically, that perceived social distinctions are never as clear as black and white. In the Albany of living memory, descendants of the Dutch colonists see the offspring of seventeenth-century English settlers as Yankee interlopers. Likewise, to certain individuals, Irish Americans remain intruders, even as some of the Irish in turn marginalize representatives of other groups.

Kennedy's narrative acumen reiterates the mercurial nature of this pluralistic view of the city throughout *O Albany!* "The Romance of the Oriflamme," for example, turns on a canny sketch of how civic institutions inevitably come to reflect individual egos. In this chapter, Kennedy discusses the rise and fall of the city's railroad terminus, Union Station (incidentally resurrected as an office building since the publication of *O Albany!*). Here, in deft sketches that nicely catch petty vanities and foibles, Kennedy fleshes out the picture of the class of people to whom Huybertie alluded in the previous chapter. His assessment is not mean-spirited. Rather, it has a stabilizing effect, serving as a reminder of the way mundane events have a far greater impact on the city's life than do the ambitions or machinations of particular individuals, no matter how powerful they seem.

Kennedy describes his own roots with a feeling of nostalgia but not sentimentality in "North Albany: Crucible for Childhood." The sophisticated perspectives and straightforward vocabulary of this essay present a deceptively simple view of the environment that recurs throughout his novels. On the one hand, one can see in this account examples of individuals with the eccentricities and idiosyncracies that distinguish characters from *Legs* to *The Flaming Corsage*. On the other, the undercurrent of this chapter explains much about Kennedy himself as it outlines the life of a much loved and pampered only child. The net effect can only enhance one's admiration for the way Kennedy has taken the raw material of his childhood and refashioned it into the gritty Albany of his creations. At the same time, as one comes away from this sketch with a sense of the influences shaping Kennedy's world view, one also recognizes the need to avoid reading the fiction as if it were autobiography.

Kennedy led a life carefully sheltered from the harshness seen by his fictional counterpart Danny Quinn, son of Peg Phelan Quinn and nephew of Billy Phelan. (A photograph of a nine—or ten-year-old Bill Kennedy on page 470 of *Riding the Yellow Trolley Car* shows a determined young batter in full baseball uniform facing a world from the yard of his family home with a self-confidence blessedly free of the suspicion or apprehension that a similarly aged Danny Quinn shows in *Billy Phelan's Greatest Game*.) Kennedy can speak blithely of neighborhood violence marked by bloody noses and chipped teeth without evincing a real concern for his own safety, and he can evoke the anti-Irish, anti-Catholic sentiments of the American Protective Association without any apprehension regarding the impact that such a group might have on his life. At the same time, his colorful relatives gave the young Bill Kennedy, even then, a vague awareness of the night world that he would come to chronicle later in *O Albany!* and again in his fiction. Thus, the chapter neatly conveys, in the understatement typical of Kennedy's discourse, the realization that he led a Norman Rockwell-like childhood, which he could embellish to fit a Studs Lonigan-like background whenever he chose.

In the final chapter of this opening section, "The Democrats Convene, or, One Man's Family," Kennedy expands on the Irish American world of the city of his youth (while playing on the title of a soap opera popular in his youth) by touching on its distinguishing component, machine politics. Kennedy evokes this institution with a deftness that goes well beyond stereotypical representations, transcending mere comprehension of the way it works. His depiction of what makes the O'Connell clan, and in particular Dan O'Connell, so powerful succeeds where so many smug pundits fail because Kennedy never lost his fascination with the way that power asserts itself in his city. With a tone never overborne by moralizing or cynicism, Kennedy explains in direct and unambiguous terms why machine politics plays such an important role in the lives of ordinary, working-class people. Throughout the process, he assumes the role neither of apologist nor of censurer, for he refuses to be seduced by the vitality of the machine or by the self-righteousness of its detractors.

Kennedy writes so well about machine politics because he understands its rites, rituals, and dogmas in a way few observers besides Mike Royko have. Kennedy acknowledges the excesses of political bosses such as the O'Connells, but as he traces his own family's ties to their machine, he also demonstrates the important role that the party organization played in alleviating much of the misery that dogged the lives of the constituents who proved so loyal to it. Kennedy reminds us—underscoring the point so often forgotten in simplistic views of machine politics—that, for those routinely excluded from many forms of employment and social services because of religion or ethnicity, the patronage system was not simply a viable alternative to other ways of making a living. It was often the only option.

The next section of the book, "The Neighborhoods," begins the complex process of tracing the social development of Albany through the demographic features of the city. Many of Kennedy's novels traverse the streets and alleys of the central sections of his city, and this 120-page section offers pungent accounts of life in the Downtown, the South End, Arbor Hill, and other locations. In essence, it provides the gazetteer for the Albany cycle of fiction that some scholar would surely have felt the need to compile had *O Albany!* not been written.

Kennedy fittingly begins his account with the Downtown area because its Broadway, Pearl, and State Streets anchor so much of the action in his fiction. One of the important features in understanding the center of Albany emerges in this description: from the city's inception throughout the periods depicted in Kennedy's novels, "Downtown remained partly residential despite all the commerce" (1983b, 60). This determinedly domestic component has leavened the harsh and sometimes coarse world of gamblers, hustlers, and gangsters who have exerted a profound influence on the tone of that part of the city. Although the Downtown, like analogous areas in most other American cities, became the jumping off point for residents determined to move up the rungs of the economic ladder, its residential component has had a continuing, stabilizing force on the rest of the city.

Kennedy recounts the history of the South End through a series of colorful individuals and places. He has a knack for singling out eccentrics such as the nineteenth-century landlord Lackey Doherty and striking locations such as the Albany Penitentiary. Throughout the twentieth century, this portion of town experienced a fairly steady economic decline, but Kennedy eschews the predictable chronicle of urban blight. Instead, he affects thumbnail sketches, no less loving for their brevity, of the people whose lives have given character to this section of Albany. He has a wonderful eye for detail. He knows how to draw out a story without letting it become tedious, and, at the same time, he can convey a very full impression in a few select paragraphs. Deploying these skills in this chapter highlights the traits that made Kennedy a good journalist and that continue to sustain him in whatever mode of writing he adopts.

That is not to say that Kennedy shies away from detailing the harsher realities of inner city life. His chapter on Arbor Hill in fact turns on the idea that what was a lovely nineteenth-century neighborhood inexorably became a twentieth-century slum. Because this area forms the setting for so much of his fiction, this record of its rise and fall stands as particularly useful background information for readers. Nonetheless, in perhaps a telling testament of Kennedy's own feelings, the chapter describes at length the pleasant times of the nineteenth-century neighborhood and leaves the details of its decline to the reader's imagination.

The remaining essays in this section follow the pattern laid down in the surveys of the Downtown, the South End, and Arbor Hill. They are part of a series on neighborhoods (with some expansion for this volume) that Kennedy wrote in the 1960s for the *Albany Times-Union*. Although these pieces give one a good overall sense of the city and highlight areas that appear sporadically in the novels, they have a broader benefit, for they reinforce one's sense of Kennedy's deep love for Albany and of his acceptance of its myriad contradictions and shortcomings. As in the other chapters, the dominant figures of this overview remain the individuals who catch Kennedy's imagination and whose idiosyncracies provide the inspiration for so many of his characters, though at times the fictional counterparts needed to be toned down to sustain believability.

If "Neighborhoods" describes fully the physical makeup of the Albany that Kennedy cherishes, the next portion of the book, "Nighttown" (a term borrowed from Joyce's *Ulysses*), gives a detailed account of the sources of the psychological world of his fiction. The chapter "Sports and Swells" delineates the subtle gradations within a group that has made games of chance not a recreation but a livelihood. He neatly distinguishes between the types of gamblers who give the chapter its title: "Swells tend not to go broke. Sports are broke as often as they're flush. Swells tend to pick up only their own checks, and they hate to lose. Sports think like Nick the Greek, who said that after gambling and winning, the thing he liked most in the world was gambling and losing" (1983b, 179). Kennedy fleshes out this distinction through a synopsis of the gambling life as it existed during the time between the world wars (which he could have learned about only secondhand). He talks of picking numbers, playing poker, and shooting craps. He describes the atmosphere of places such as barbershops and hotels that catered to the men who gambled. As Kennedy sketches the environments inhabited by these men who loved to win and by the ones who simply loved to play, attentive readers develop a clearer sense of Billy Phelan, George Quinn, and other fictional characters who live by a combination of luck, skill, and resignation.

Gambling inevitably leads to more serious crimes, and in a chapter that might stand as a reference guide for the novel *Legs*—"Prohibition: It Can't Happen Here"— Kennedy traces the rise of Dutch Schultz, Jack Diamond, and other Depression-era gangsters. The story is a familiar one: insufficient law enforcement resources attempting to uphold an unpopular statute in the face of numerous criminal organizations that are generating massive amounts of money through illegal operations. Nonetheless, the details of Jack Diamond's life offered in this essay give one a sense of the creative process by which Kennedy transformed that information into a powerful work of fiction, *Legs*. The following chapter—"The Death of Legs Diamond"—might serve as an epilogue to that novel, offering an educated guess, supported by hearsay, as to who was involved in the death of the noted gangster, a topic that recurs in both Kennedy's play *Grand View* and his latest novel, *Roscoe*.

The next full section of *O Albany!*—entitled "Some of the People"—highlights in successive chapters Kennedy's impressions of Jewish, Italian, German, and African Americans. None of this material relates directly to Kennedy's fiction, nor does it build on the reader's sense of the Albany that such fiction evokes. It does, however, say a great deal about Kennedy's moral nature, especially his social conscience. In the bigoted world of urban America, Kennedy succeeds in writing about diverse racial and ethnic groups without a trace of bias or a hint of reductivism. He neither glorifies nor degrades the ethnic people he describes. Rather, he celebrates each group's humanity even as he accepts its inherent flaws. The English and the Dutch have no chapters in this section, presumably because they represent the majority world of the city. Likewise, no chapter is given to the Irish, though of course they appear everywhere in Kennedy's writing. However, one might argue that the absence of the Irish in this section reflects Kennedy's view that the Irish have achieved positions of prominence that make any perception of them as minorities wrongheaded and naïve.

Anyone doubting this theory would do well to look carefully at the next section, "Long-Run Politics: Wizardry Unbound." It carefully chronicles how the O'Connell and Corning families, respectively Irish and English by descent, successfully wielded political power in Albany through most of the twentieth century. (The Dutch elite, represented by Nelson Rockefeller, also appear, described in terms no more flattering or deferential than those applied to the others.) This section complements the earlier one on the O'-Connell machine, and, as in that section, it offers a far more sophisticated view of big city politics than one usually encounters. Kennedy understands how power and money function within the political world, and he deftly shows how machine politics works across ethnic differences not because of the high-mindedness of political leaders but because power and money exert a much greater shaping force on the principals' behavior than mere racial prejudice ever could.

Kennedy begins with the Irish. "They Bury the Boss: Dan Ex-Machina" uses as its organizing image the funeral of Daniel O'Connell, last surviving member of the Irish family that dominated Albany politics for nearly six decades. (Though Kennedy does not call our attention to the fact, the name ironically evokes images of the great nineteenth-century Irish politician Daniel O'Connell, who did so much in the efforts to achieve Catholic emancipation from British domination.) With the passing of the great man as the chapter's theme, anecdotes from Dan O'Connell's life illustrate how he gained power and how he kept it. Kennedy neither ignores the corruption within the machine nor wastes time moralizing about it. Instead, he offers a detailed account of how a political organization such as the one set up by the O'Connells functions—both positively and negatively—and then he leaves the final judgment to his readers. What the chapter does most clearly is show the connection between money and power and the trade-off demanded. As Mike Royko opined three decades ago when analyzing the regime of Mayor Richard J. Daley of Chicago (1971), in politics one must decide whether one wants money or power, for it is impossible to have both. Kennedy shows how the O'Connell machine, embodied in Dan's career, lasted for so long because so much of the money that it accumulated went back into the process to ensure its retention of power. Kennedy sums it up succinctly: "Tammany and money: a winning combination" (Kennedy 1983b, 293).

The partnership between power and money, however, does not operate exclusively within Irish political systems, and Kennedy wonderfully illustrates this fact in the next chapter, "The South Mall: Everything Everybody Ever Wanted." He recounts the story of how construction of the new state capital complex came about through the cooperation of the English mayor of Albany, Erastus Corning, and the state's Dutch governor, Nelson Rockefeller, because each had something to gain from its completion. The project, stalled for months, quickly became a reality only when Rockefeller, who saw the buildings as a way of memorializing himself, gave Corning's political allies access to the lucrative sources of funds associated with construction. As with any political endeavor, the details of featherbedding and cost overruns seem all too familiar. What distinguishes the essay is Kennedy's insight into the way machine politics works no matter what the ethnicity of its participants.

"Erastus: The Million-Dollar Smile" parallels the life of Erastus Corning and the chronicle of Dan O'Connell's rise to power. The backgrounds of the patrician Erastus Corning and the plebeian O'Connell could hardly have been more different. Kennedy also contrasts the personality of the affable and gregarious Corning with that of the gruff, even shy O'Connell. In the end, however, Kennedy reconciles these differences and shows the more profound similarities between the two through an elaboration of the keen understanding that both men had of the world in which they existed and of the rules by which it operated. Ultimately, their complementary abilities to adapt to the complexities of Albany politics made both men exemplary figures in what they chose as their profession.

O Albany! ends with a potpourri of observations in a section entitled "Closing Time." This series of recollections and remarks evinces a fragmented quality, but nonetheless has an evocative coherence for those familiar with the characters and neighborhoods of Kennedy's fiction. It sums up the book as a detailed and at times rambling description of the world from which the author emerged, one that will serve readers to the varying degrees that they consider such extratextual material important to their own interpretations of Kennedy's fiction.

Riding the Yellow Trolley Car complements and extends *O Albany!* As noted earlier, although the latter collection of essays traces the physical environment from which the author emerged, the former presents an overview of the imaginative ethos that shapes his work. In the opening chapter of *Riding the Yellow Trolley Car*, Kennedy himself presents an ambitious outline of its features:

> This book, in a way, is a writer's oblique autobiography (of his taste, if nothing else). It is the tracking of a writing style as it develops. It is about reading, and it can stand as a chorale of contemporary voices, also a chorale of my own assumed voices. It is a historical chronicle of what some of the world's best writers were writing in the decades the book spans, and it is an analysis of how fiction is written: writers talking of their craft, their ideas. (1993, 6)

Riding the Yellow Trolley Car certainly fulfills all of these aims by collecting a representative survey of the journalistic work that Kennedy did over a nearly forty-year span from the mid-1950s to the early 1990s. Like many volumes made up of occasional pieces, *Riding the Yellow Trolley Car* has a good amount of repetition, and in consequence some readers will find the discourse at times plodding. Nonetheless, revisiting familiar topics allows one to see both Kennedy's intellectual development and the subtlety of his aesthetic position. Additionally, selected articles give tremendous insight into his artistic consciousness. Numerous pieces exemplify his imaginative range. And, overall, the book collects a great deal of useful commentary—such as the revelation of Damon Runyon as "my earliest writing hero" (1993, 13)—from which to construct a conception of Kennedy's aesthetics.

Time and again we can find in Kennedy's remarks on his writing insightful guidelines for our interpretive judgments. These comments are not glosses for particular works he has written. Rather, they outline, through tracing the reading habits of a highly accomplished individual, a keen sense of the beauty of literature, and they help us come to an understanding of the power of the written word.

Admittedly, we might too easily miss these fine points, for they occur offhandedly, almost in passing. Nonetheless, they carry no less weight for their brevity or even lack of specificity. Perhaps the most useful appraisals grow out of Kennedy's inclination to celebrate the mystery of the creative process. Describing what infuses life into a work of fiction, for example, Kennedy can speak only in generalities: "There must be a transformation of the material, of the characters, of the age, into something that is intriguingly new to the writer" (1993, 34–35). In the end, however, the fact that he never indicates precisely what that newness entails stands as far less important than the relentless assertion of his belief in the artist's power to recognize that quality:

> The writer, when he is functioning as an artist, understands when this power is at hand, and he knows that it does not rise up from his notepad but up from the deepest part of his unconscious, which knows everything everywhere and always: that secret archive stored in the soul at birth, enhanced by every waking moment of life, and which is the source of the power and the vision that allow the writer to create something never before heard or seen on earth. (1993, 35)

One might easily succumb to the temptation to dismiss such a locution as evidence that Kennedy does not really understand what makes his writing good. That assumption, however, would be akin to dismissing Monet for failing in attempts to describe with any degree of oral precision why his haystack paintings are beautiful. What one sees in passages like this is a moving testament to the author's faith in art, a belief in it as a mystical experience (much like those experiences described in the lives of saints that Kennedy remembers studying in his religious education classes).

In an interview conducted by Peter Quinn and reprinted in *Riding the Yellow Trolley Car,* Kennedy elaborates in a telling fashion on an intuitive author's feeling of how a particular piece of writing functions. Coming from a man devoted to words, his description remains maddeningly vague, yet its very generality becomes the key to a fairly specific comprehension:

> With *Legs,* I began to understand writing a little more clearly. . . . I knew I wanted to say something, thought I knew what I wanted to say—I had all the material, but nothing would come together. I couldn't figure out what to do or how to do it. But after those long hours, I would begin to write, and feel very good about what I'd achieved by the end of the day. I

came to understand in those days that writing itself was what was
important. (1993, 41)

Kennedy articulates a faith in the practice of his profession every bit as profound and mysterious as a religious commitment, and he anchors that faith
in a communal relationship integral to all of his writing. He views his audience as equals and invites them to participate with him in the creative
process: "I write for people like me who used to appreciate Damon Runyon
sentences. I write for people who appreciate writing first, who understand
the difference between an ordinary sentence and a real sentence that jumps
off the page at you when you read it" (1993, 55).

In most instances in this book, however, Kennedy's remarks about the
art of writing take the form of far more oblique statements, with the onus on
the reader to intuit meaning from the wide-ranging comments about others
in the craft. An essay on attending a James Joyce conference in Dublin, for
example, articulates Kennedy's reverence for Joyce and qualified respect for
those who serve as his critics. A piece on Malamud verges on hero worship.
One on Hemingway shows a wonderful sensitivity to that author's strengths
and a humane tolerance for his weaknesses. With a fine ironic touch, a report of a J. P. Donleavy reading becomes an indictment of pretension, although several accounts of Saul Bellow (who was fully capable of as much or
more pretension as Donleavy evinced) demonstrate a profound respect for a
master of the craft. Like most of us, Kennedy shows himself at his best assessing writings of those authors for whom he feels a measure of ambivalence. Strong likes or dislikes often go undeveloped and in consequence
often unexplained for readers who do not share those views.

Ultimately, *Riding the Yellow Trolley Car* stands as more reflective of
Kennedy as a reader than of Kennedy as an author. This rather eclectic volume gives us a broad sense of Kennedy's aesthetic likes and dislikes. He has
a passionate love of jazz, but seemingly narrow tastes. He finds intellectual
cruelty almost intolerable, yet he can ignore it when manifested by artists
whose work he deeply admires. He champions iconoclasts who do not
threaten his own viewpoints. In short, he reveals himself as a man made up
of the sorts of contradictions that characterize most of us.

Does that help us when we turn to his fiction and seek a model for structuring our own readings? The answer can only be yes and no. Understanding the complexities of Kennedy's nature helps us give meaning to his
fiction. That is to say, our reaction to *Riding the Yellow Trolley Car* tells us how

we wish to react to Kennedy's other books. It does not prescribe our readings, and indeed I suspect that Kennedy would not wish it to do so. Rather,
it helps us understand how we will derive those readings, and in that fashion
it gives us a clearer sense of both what and how we read.

At its heart, *Riding the Yellow Trolley Car* traces the imaginative life of a
hardworking author who takes his art but not himself very seriously.
Kennedy does not write to articulate profound ideas on complex subjects.
Indeed, he makes no attempt to present himself as a deep or sustained
thinker. I most certainly do not mean this assessment as a disparagement of
Kennedy or of his work, for I can think of very few truly good writers who
attempt to assume this position. (Is Shakespeare, for example, a deep
thinker, or is he rather someone who facilitates our efforts to think deeply
about ourselves? For me, he must be the latter, or his writing would not have
sustained the interest that it has for more than four centuries.) Kennedy is,
however, without question a man with a deep commitment to his craft, and
this commitment emerges throughout his discourse and engages our imaginations. He stands out as a man with a profound trust in his art and in his
readers. He grounds his approach to writing on perseverance and opens his
work to the scrutiny of his audience. If Kennedy's nonfiction tells us anything about interpreting his fiction, it is that we should trust him, for he
clearly trusts us.

CHAPTER TWO

The Ink Truck as Prelude

The books that make up the Albany cycle have done so much to establish William Kennedy's literary reputation that one may feel an understandable temptation to ignore *The Ink Truck*. It is his earliest published fiction and in many ways functions as an apprentice piece.[1] *The Ink Truck* admittedly does not demonstrate the level of imaginative creativity that one finds in Kennedy's subsequent writing, and discussing it often leads one to critiques of his writing not at all applicable to his later works. Nonetheless, examining it remains a useful exercise for anyone seeking to comprehend the forces shaping Kennedy's artistic development.

Just as the essays of *O Albany!* and *Riding the Yellow Trolley Car* give readers a sense of the cultural background and the aesthetic values that always function in Kennedy's writing, *The Ink Truck* introduces, in inchoate form, the thematic concerns, aesthetic values, and stylistic patterns that recur throughout his subsequent work: its regional structure, its exploration of the concept of redemption, and its struggle with the definition of self offer early versions of the imaginative features that will frame all subsequent fiction. Likewise, the predilection in *The Ink Truck* for punctuating seemingly naturalistic accounts with surreal descriptions only loosely related to the story, its integration of elements from diverse genres into a metanarrative that becomes a commentary on the work itself, and its penchant for nonlinear exposition establish a form of writing that will become the hallmark of Kennedy's fiction. These efforts do not exhibit the same level of creative skill that one finds in later works, but they clearly outline artistic inclinations that will dominate Kennedy's writing.

At the same time, if one wishes to make a serious comparison of *The Ink*

Truck to Kennedy's other fiction, one must keep in mind the significant contextual and stylistic variations that distinguish this first novel from his later writing. Its narrow narrative structure is perhaps the primary difference. In *The Ink Truck,* Kennedy does not attempt to introduce a fully articulated cultural tradition to serve as a framework for contextualizing both actions and characters within the discourse. Novels in the Albany cycle (from *Legs* through *The Flaming Corsage*), although remaining self-contained, anchor their narratives by tracing and retracing events that span generations in the lives of close-knit (though not always loving) families who live in a world made comfortably predictable by clannish loyalties, a shared heritage, and a common ethical system. Kennedy's habit of reiterating descriptions of key incidents within books of the Albany cycle produces broader understanding through multiple perspectives, and a reader's consequent and increasing familiarity with those events brings a richness and complexity to what at first might seem the most ordinary of incidents.

In contrast, the isolated, episodic structure of *The Ink Truck* cannot sustain any system that features wide-ranging incidents and closely linked individual histories. Figures in its narrative lack a sense of connection to the past, and they operate seemingly without any awareness of the communal bonds that so effectively guide the behavior of characters in Kennedy's subsequent novels. (Perhaps the most straightforward illustration of the shaping impact of the community comes in *Billy Phelan's Greatest Game.* When the McCalls blackball Billy from the action of Broadway, his life, temporarily at least, comes to an end. See chapter 4 for further discussion of this novel.) As a result, the discourse of *The Ink Truck* lacks the social depth, the communal distinctiveness, and the historical continuity afforded by chronicles that can recall events and provide motivations for the behavior of the Phelan, Daugherty, Quinn, and McCall families over the course of a century of life in the city.

Instead, Kennedy's first novel undertakes a much less ambitious narrative approach. By emphasizing individual rather than communal experiences, Kennedy limits the novel's scope to an isolated event, the chronicle of one man's reaction to the final stages of an unsuccessful, twelve-month-long strike by newspaper workers. Because the strikers lack the solidarity characteristic of workers in successful labor movements, the narrative foregrounds disengaged individuals whose only real links to one another come from their participation in the same job action.[2] Even that association proves to be fairly flimsy, for their bond does not enjoy the cohesion provided by shared values or a real sense of community. This deficiency becomes all the more evident when compared with the commitment of figures who appear in later novels: the gamblers, gangsters, politicians, and hoboes of the Albany cycle acknowledge the shaping force of the ethical systems and the specialized societies that give definition to their world. In *The Ink Truck*, no two characters hold the same set of beliefs or subscribe to the same moral code, and no two inhabit the same community. In consequence, anarchy inevitably comes to dominate the action of the novel because every response retains the potential for being unpredictable and idiosyncratic.

A narrative style that focuses most of the descriptive attention on a single figure further narrows the dimensions of the work: over the course of the novel, the personality of Bailey, the idealistic but deranged central character who has moved from newspaper columnist to militant striker, dominates the action. Unfortunately, he always behaves in an unpredictable fashion that does little more than establish a quixotic nature. With little space given to the workings of his mind, readers never develop a clear sense of the motivation behind the erratic shifts in his demeanor. Other characters—Bailey's wife Grace, his friend Rosenthal, his mistress Irma, his employer Stanley—do little to expand our sense of this world, for they remain fixed as types and take their significance exclusively from their relations to Bailey. As a result, although each possesses some distinguishing trait, presented with Kennedy's characteristic mastery of seemingly trivial detail, none emerges as a fully developed character: Grace does little more than play the part of a bitter, lonely housewife who does not understand Bailey's complexities; Rosenthal stands out chiefly as a doctrinaire labor activist without a sense of humor who serves as a foil for Bailey's zaniness; Irma never progresses beyond the role of a promiscuous and good-hearted girlfriend (it is likely that the cinema-loving Kennedy took this name from the good-natured prostitute played by Shirley MacLaine in *Irma la Douce*); and the psychotic Stanley, the mastermind of the newspaper's efforts to destroy the strike and the strikers, appears as a cartoonish nemesis with a mother fixation.

Despite his thematic emphasis on Bailey, however, Kennedy already knows his craft too well to allow a predictable, linear exposition to dominate his novel's discourse. In fact, a cheerfully disjointed rhythm punctuates its narrative development. Admittedly, this format can at times succumb to its own resistance to order, privileging anarchy for anarchy's sake. Nonetheless, the stylistic shape of *The Ink Truck* shows Kennedy's willingness to take formal risks, even as it demonstrates his sense of the need to avoid programmatic writing.

Kennedy breaks up *The Ink Truck* into six major sections, with each in turn subdivided into short chapters. This narrative configuration neatly complements the fragmented form of the novel's discourse. As the plot unfolds, one sees that the author does not feel the need to impose a tightly choreographed scheme on the action. Instead, in much the same way that James Joyce uses gaps in the narrative in his novel *A Portrait of the Artist as a Young Man*, Kennedy truncates descriptions without fully resolving events, leaving it to the reader's imaginative response to complete the meaning of the passage.[3]

In an even more overt nod to Joyce's influence, and with an oblique acknowledgment of his own journalistic background, Kennedy introduces a measure of metatextuality into the novel's discourse. Newspaper-like headlines announce the beginning of each of the major sections of *The Ink Truck*, grabbing reader attention by parodying some subsequent element of the narrative.[4] To enhance this effect, epigraphs extend, explicate, and in some instances counterpoint initial impressions created by these headlines. The first three epigraphs—taken from Robert Benchley's *Maxims from the Chinese*, Victor Appleton's *Tom Swift and His Undersea Search*, and Don Marquis's *Archy and Mehitabel*—prefigure the irreverent humor of the first three sections. The second three—from Joseph Campbell's *The Hero with a Thousand Faces*, W. B. Yeats's "To a Friend Whose Work Has Come to Nothing," and William Saroyan's "For My Part I'll Smoke a Good Ten Cent Cigar"—signal an attitudinal shift within the novel, for they highlight a growing pessimism that blunts the humor of the final three sections. All in all, these obliquely vatic passages bracket major divisions in the novel, announce a willingness to employ chronologic disruption, and presage Kennedy's inclination for widespread formal experimentation that will become a feature throughout his novels, albeit usually in a more restrained fashion.

The title of the novel's first section signals the freewheeling imaginative associations that emerge as the dominant style of the narrative discourse: "A Bizarre Bolly Follows Ink Carrier. What's a Bolly? People Ask." By taking up the invitation to answer that question, one finds that the *Oxford English Dictionary* defines a bolly as a hobgoblin. Looking at the Benchley epigraph that appears below the title, one sees a passage that sardonically equates radicalism with the lack of a soul. Together these two markers suggest to readers the forces alternately tormenting and motivating Bailey. His fragmented, distracted, and contradictory comprehension of his environment produces in him a sense of conflicted apprehension. Bailey's scarred perception of the world around him fosters an attitude that searches for meaning by rejecting conventional assumptions but achieves only imperfect cognizance because it lacks clear standards for judgment. The opening of this section suggests that either approving or disapproving of Bailey's quirky behavior remains a secondary issue. The contradictions that inform his nature dominate the discourse and leave the reader obligated to form a unified picture.

Within *The Ink Truck*, Kennedy's process of composition remains narrowly focused, with all elements geared toward setting off this central character. To this end, immediately following the introduction of Bailey, the narrative brings his counterpart into the discourse. Rosenthal is a friend and an idealistic striker whose character seems perpetually on the point of degenerating into caricature. Kennedy neatly finesses this possibility by introducing an ironic point of view that makes Rosenthal aware of the same problem: "From the closet he took his black cape off its hook, put on his Tyrolean hat with a fat red feather in its band and grabbed his swagger stick from the shelf. Bailey said he dressed like a sartorially confused British jewel thief. But he had pursued a specialized image ever since Shirley, his wife, said he had none" (Kennedy 1969, 7). As the narrative subsequently affirms, Shirley is right. Rosenthal has little to offer on his own account, but the inherent drabness of his temperament highlights Bailey's picaresque demeanor. Further, although Rosenthal's forced eccentricity may seem like labored humor to many readers, these idiosyncracies take on a deeper significance for both Bailey and Rosenthal. In the harsh world of the novel, their self-absorptions have become a necessary defense against the grinding reality that confronts them every day that the strike continues. To a degree, they operate with the obliviousness of Laurel and Hardy and other comedic teams of Kennedy's youth: they survive through a fierce naïveté that relentlessly resists the numbing realities of their environment.

Unlike Kennedy's subsequent works, *The Ink Truck* generally underplays the significance of specific Albany locations. Instead, the contextual underpinning of the work comes from an emphasis on an undistinguished, unrelenting gray atmosphere—evoked by both the weather and urban decay—that threatens to engulf the characters. The dreary milieu becomes a goad that spurs Bailey and Rosenthal's quixotic dedication to the Guild (the newspaper union) and stokes their determination to continue their walkout. Both men see the strike as a way of countering the hopelessness of their environment. Paradoxically, the strike also enforces the futility of their position. When Irma—Bailey's sometimes paramour and one of the few remaining strikers actually dedicated to the work action—resigns from the Guild, she becomes "the 247th defection, leaving only eighteen members" (13). In fact, with a strike effort led by Jarvis, the ineffectual union chief, Rosenthal and Bailey have fallen into a degraded routine that involves little more than wandering between the Guild office and Fobie's bar, making crank phone calls, and fulminating against the unjust attitudes of newspaper management. The strike itself is a parody, with desperate individuals such as Rosenthal and Bailey attempting to use it to counterfeit a sense of community.

Although Kennedy does lend a measure of dignity to the actions of these men, he refuses to take their idealism too seriously. Instead, his narrative elaborates on an impulse toward farce, balancing the sketch of a public life informed by depressing circumstances with a description of the equally unsatisfying conditions that inform Bailey's private life. When Bailey invites Rosenthal home for lunch, for example, the chaos of his household and his uneasy relations with his wife Grace emerge through a series of shattered images.

> Rosenthal looked around the living room, captured immediately by an enormous poster of Mrs. Bailey in a roller-derby costume, coming at the viewer with skates skyward, buttocks forward, about to land with a fracturing thump. . . . Beneath the photo a large printed message suggested:
>
> DROP IN
> & see
> GROOVY GRACE
> The Toughest Broad on Wheels
> —Queen Of The Camden Bloomer Busters—
> Madison Square Garden
> Tuesday, Dec. 4, 1943
> 8 P.M.
>
> On another wall Rosenthal recognized bits of Bailey's taste: a magazine cartoon sketch by Ronald Searle of a decapitated James Joyce climbing down the rocks beside the Martello Tower with his eyepatched head under his left arm clutching his ashplant with his right hand; and above

him a screaming hawk flying off with a copy of *Ulysses* in its claws. Beside
the sketch was a framed Playbill from the Abbey Theatre, and below
these, three composite photos, each with a head superimposed on Bailey's
torso. (17–18)

The icons in Bailey's household represent his ideé fixe as the unfulfilled desire to form a unified and unambiguous identity. The outlandishness of the
images on his wall play on the contradictions in his life: marriage informed
by sex and violence; imagination as a compound of aesthetics and adrena-
line; and art as contested by the formal and the kitsch. Although James
Joyce haunts Bailey's consciousness, he still cannot settle on the person
whom he wants to be. Unfortunately, despite a promising beginning
through the unconventional aura surrounding these depictions, Bailey fails
to develop beyond these associative images. Consequently, too often his
subsequent actions seem contrived because he cannot convey to readers
anything of interest in his solipsism.[5]

In a gesture that foregrounds this failure, the narrative offers a sample of
the sort of column that Bailey writes in syndication. Filled with non se-
quiturs that try to pass off disruptions in logic as cleverness and with images
fascinating only to its author, it reveals much more about Bailey's temperament than it does about his ideas.

Then from this flows the understanding that the ego is so knotted up with
itself that it becomes incapable of extending sympathy, friendship or
pooka toward another. Then follows the pooka to apologize for this failing and the wish to explain it away by admitting self-pooka. And all this
oddly, is accompanied by a glorious sense of pooka, for this is life intensi-
fied, new pooka. But then it turns black pooka, and you see it as oppor-
tunistic cheap, battening on your own suffering pooka. (19)

Invoked throughout the column in a near incantatory rhythm, the concept
of a *pooka*—a trickster creature from Irish mythology—seems so forced as to
be akin to the secret language of children. As a result, although the image of
the *pooka* as a spirit inhabiting the house as Bailey's ally and Grace's nemesis
recurs throughout the novel, its significance goes undeveloped. The column
in general shows how the deftness of Bailey's mind conflicts with the undis-
ciplined quality of his nature to prevent him from exploiting his brilliance. It
stands more as a cry for help than as a declaration of independence.

The narrative counterpoints Bailey's piece with a love letter purportedly written to Grace by the local butcher but in fact authored by her to provoke Bailey's jealousy. Just as Bailey's column reveals through indirection how he has come to see himself, Grace's spurious missive reflects her desperate sense of the most important aspects of her life. Like so many elements in the narrative of *The Ink Truck*, the column and the love letter suggest the sort of devices that Kennedy will use well in his later writing. At this stage, however, the technique simply produces awkward sentences and remains rather underdeveloped. The violence that ends the section serves as little more than a convenient way to bring to an end what has become a fairly tedious and predictable squabble.

Bailey's ties to his mistress, Irma, serve as a contrast to his relations with his wife. Though the attraction that Irma feels for Bailey remains unexplained, this gesture of introducing analogous characters in parallel scenes stands out, for it will become a staple technique in Kennedy's subsequent narrative efforts, emerging as an important device for illuminating the complexity seemingly buried within the psyches of many of the figures in his works. In *The Ink Truck*, however, he has not yet developed the full sense of characterization that will make these sequential descriptions resonate so powerfully for his readers.

By this point, the narrative has established a familiar pattern. The action unfolds in a fairly predictable fashion, and it moves at a pace that easily allows the readers to form a clear idea of the novel's milieu. Clarity, however, does not always lead to aesthetic satisfaction. When, for example, the discourse describes the pivotal event of the novel—a confrontation on the picket lines and a fire that leads to the death of the gypsy queen and transforms the nature of the strike—the scene has an arbitrariness that many readers might find disquieting.

The incident does stand out, however, because it captures the ineffectual efforts that typify the actions of characters in the novel. Indeed, the strikers' inept and frustrated attempts to stop the ink delivery serve as a microcosm for the entire job action. Bailey strives to sabotage the truck, but cannot find the valve that will release the ink onto the pavement. As guards and gypsies—whom the newspaper has hired to intimidate the strikers—beat up the others, Bailey, in frustration, sets fire to the building where the gypsies have been living, which is near the newspaper. One sees in the episode the same inclination toward mindless chaos popular in many books written in the 1960s—Thomas Pynchon's *The Crying of Lot 49* comes immedi-

ately to mind as an example—but neither the paranoia nor the anarchic glee
that animates other novels informs the action here. Instead, a mixture of resentment and confusion circumscribe Bailey's behavior.

Kennedy clearly senses this awkwardness, for, having created a scene of
high dramatic consequence, he sets out to undermine its seriousness as a
way of maintaining the comic edge of the narration. He begins most dra-
matically with the punning title to the next section—"Missing Striker May
Be Victim of Foul Plague. Black Spots May Be Sore Points." Combined with
the epigraph from Victor Appleton's *Tom Swift and His Undersea Search*, the
opening of this section relies on flippancy to deflate the serious consequences of what is unfolding.

The narrative shifts to a hospital emergency room, where a farcical
chaos dominates the action. The gypsy queen, Putzina, has been badly injured in the fire, and, when she dies, the gypsies begin an elaborate mourn-
ing ritual that they film in the hopes of selling to a local TV station. As with
the slapstick comedies of the silent film era, Kennedy uses gestures that ex-
aggerate and burlesque normal human behavior to blunt the reader's sense
of the consequences of the suffering that the discourse describes. However,
although the narrative reduces the level of violence to cartoon mayhem, it
does not seem to have a clear idea of how seriously it wishes to treat the social issues introduced by the strike. As a result, the tone becomes muddled.

When the narrative turns its attention from the gypsies to the strikers, it
continues to send mixed signals. It recounts Rosenthal's prosaic dreams,
under the influence of painkillers, of rising in the Guild ranks to become a
local leader. In contrast, a fully alert Jarvis, with a far less idealistic attitude,
shows only concerns for appeasing the newspaper in the aftermath of the
fire Bailey set. The disarray of the Guild, comically represented in the first
section, becomes painfully apparent in this portion of the narrative.

From the disintegration of institutions around individuals, the novel
turns to the physical, intellectual, and moral fragmentation of characters
themselves. Bailey is kidnapped from the hospital by company guards and
taken to a dilapidated barn, where he is abused by a variety of characters.
Although it may seem unfair to make such comparisons, the awkwardness of
this scene becomes immediately apparent to any readers who recall the
powerful episode in the 1988 *Quinn's Book* describing young Daniel's discovery of a badly beaten Dirck Staats in a rundown barn. In that novel,
Kennedy shows he has learned to combine economy of language with
graphic detail to evoke horror and to direct the discourse toward the devel-

opment of the plot. In the *Ink Truck* barn scene and in those that immediately follow, violence and menace degenerate into predictable, heavy-handed plot devices.

In three successive locations, Bailey is subjected to torture and proselytizing. The gypsies beat him as a reflexive action while berating him as insensitive. Later, in a seedy apartment, Skin, a defector from the Guild who now has returned to the paper and works to break the strike, continues the polemic by subjecting Bailey to a rambling disquisition on metaphysics that quickly degenerates into meandering self-justification cloaked in homespun mysticism. Although the hypocrisy is clear enough, this blatant representation makes one wonder why Kennedy belabors the point.

Sex fares no better. Bailey eventually finds himself in the apartment of Miss Blue, a company secretary and "one of a long line of Stanley's concubines" (97), where sadism elides into bondage, which moves to eroticism. Miss Blue draws Bailey into a ménage involving machines that replicate the copulation of bulls and cows. "It's got two parts. The toro machine and the cow frame. You play toro, and guess who I play?" (103). The allusions to the classical Greek myth of Queen Pasiphae and the bull are fairly obvious, though the relevance remains open to interpretation. The erudition displayed here will continue in later novels, but the purposefulness of such allusions will be much more apparent in the Albany cycle.

The next section—"Guild Members Beset by Weirdness. A Big Mystery It Seems"—begins with a quote from Don Marquis's *Archy and Mehitabel* that gives an account of ants seeking meaning in a shattered world. The title and the epigraph set the stage for Bailey's response to the confusion unfolding around him as he attempts to find a balanced environment within his chaotic world. Searching for stability, he discovers change in every place to which he goes—the Guild offices, Rosenthal's home, his own apartment, even his uncle Melvin's house. Bailey increasingly inhabits an unfamiliar world with few reference points to guide his acts or offer him support.

In the Guild office, Popkin, one of the "exalted leaders of the International Guild" (111), has visited the local. He has instituted a number of sweeping policy changes, all reflecting an overt desire to appease the newspaper. The most egregious of these gestures is a demand that Bailey go to the newspaper offices to deliver an apology for the violence that took place around the ink truck. The resulting confrontation with Stanley evolves like a case study in abnormal psychology. Although Bailey and Stanley talk about the strike, all of Stanley's insecurities and neuroses, including a mother obsession, come to the surface. Representations of Stanley's sadism, viciousness, and prurience make him seem buffoonish rather than menacing. His revelations call to mind Hannah Arendt's thesis about the banality of evil, but his buffoonish tone simultaneously makes it difficult for one to take him and his threats seriously. This contradiction becomes another disillusionment for Bailey: even his archenemy lacks the dignity and menace of a worthy adversary. Rather, Stanley comes across as simply a nagging, whiny neurotic.

The narrative underscores the pervasiveness of this erosion of sensibility when it shifts perspective to Rosenthal's consciousness and begins to describe his initial reactions to the scene in his apartment after the gypsies vandalize it: "Rosenthal knew that he had done this himself. When you are in a war, even a guerrilla war, even a passive war of attrition, the enemy respects only force and he shows his respect with counterforce. Why shouldn't Rosenthal have expected this, and worse?" (129). This paragraph comes at a good time for readers who have become restive with the plot. It reminds them that although *The Ink Truck* is in fact Kennedy's first novel, he already possesses sophisticated technical skills. The move to free indirect discourse, a narrative form that employs the dual perspectives of first—and third-person points of view, allows the reader to see Rosenthal's subjective feelings while sustaining the objective perspective of the omniscient narrator.[6] In a narrative so overshadowed by Bailey's presence, this approach allows the reader to get a fuller sense of the other characters and yet continue to follow the dominant tone of the discourse. These moments of alternative perspectives, of course, punctuate rather than redirect the narrative, and the discourse returns relatively quickly to description influenced by Bailey's point of view.

The destruction of Rosenthal's apartment parallels Bailey's arson attack on the gypsies' building, and the ambivalent presentation of these acts of violence underscores efforts in *The Ink Truck* to establish a form somewhere between parody, satire, and naturalism. This struggle is similar to the reader's efforts to sustain a cohesive discourse in the face of such conflicting impulses. Like other American authors writing in the 1960s—Thomas Pynchon, William Gaddis, and Joseph Heller, to name just three—Kennedy follows an impulse to heighten the bizarre features of the world that he already perceives from a sardonic and alienated point of view. The result is a reality analogous to one a reader would recognize yet profoundly more intense than that encountered by the reader in daily life. The representation of that reality is alternately tinged with comedy and menace so that the reader must struggle to determine what weight to give to the events unfolding in the discourse.

The chaos in Rosenthal's flat stands as emblematic of the anarchy that has come to dominate Bailey's world. Even the strike has lost the rhythmic routine that offered a form of security through its regularity and predictability. As Bailey and Irma work with Rosenthal and his wife to clean the place, the catalog of destruction recounted in the narrative makes it clear that such security has vanished for Bailey and the others. Rosenthal's wife Shirley sums up the despair that she now feels in a stuttering anecdote told to prove that "God is against us": "I was sitting at a drugstore counter and a w-woman next to me was t-t-tearing paper napkins into strips. I w-w-watched her awhile and she looked at me and threw the napkins in my f-f-face. 'You're no good,' she said. 'You w-w-wear three sweaters. You'll never be any g-good.' She knew. They all know" (131). This sort of summation by a minor character at a central point in the narrative will become a trademark technique in Kennedy's later fiction. For now, it beautifully captures the feelings of despair that every individual in the Rosenthal flat confronts at that moment.

Having seen the erosion of the ordered existence that the strike had temporarily imposed on his life, Bailey responds by beginning the process of severing ties to all of the institutions that have heretofore shaped his behavior. A brief but vindictive exchange with Grace confirms the predictable rupture in the marriage, with the narrative bias making Grace seem unreasonable despite Bailey's philandering. This split fits the pattern of shattered institutions and relationships that dominates this section of the narrative, but in fact it leaves Bailey free to go on doing whatever he wishes without the burden of guilt that continuing ties to Grace might produce.

The next section—"Pigs Are Where You Find Them Outlaw Decides. Soul Is a Pork Chop, He Discovers"—opens at a point representing Bailey's spiritual nadir and marks a sharp shift in the action. (The change in the tone of the epigraphs, with a more somber reference from Joseph Campbell's *The Hero with a Thousand Faces*, further establishes the point.) This portion of the novel stands as an important document for those interested in the long-term impact of Kennedy's writing because here the narrative breaks, at least temporarily, from the rather predictable cycle of zaniness that has begun to pall by this point. It also shows how with proper discipline Kennedy can in fact integrate to good effect the preternatural into an otherwise realistic narrative.

After his expulsion from the Guild as a result of his confrontation with Stanley, Bailey takes a job at the State Library sorting and shelving books. The solitude of the position insulates him from the dissolution of the Guild, and the library's archival resources enable him to retreat into his own mind by researching gypsy lore and acquiring an understanding of the curses that the gypsies flung at him. Additionally, he finds time to indulge in fantasies derived from his casual reading of the books that he sorts. All this obviously provides Kennedy with the opportunity to use exposition to flesh out the plot, but it does more as well.

The narrative tone here exemplifies the extent to which Bailey has changed through a dialectic that he conducts with a disembodied voice emanating from somewhere in the stacks. Their discussion focuses on Bailey's decision to discard the old way of life, and he offers an example of his "apparently incomprehensible thought" (164) in the form of a newspaper column reflecting his search for order. The column, in Blakean tones, unfolds a fragmented account of a society desperately seeking direction through appeals to Gokki, the great unknowable. Like the syndicated piece that Bailey shows to Rosenthal early in the novel (19), this column mixes homegrown philosophy and self-generating myth. Although the questions raised in the piece have validity, Kennedy has yet to learn the knack of integrating such discussions into the overall discourse.

Similarly, in an extended reverie, Bailey conjures up an Albany of one hundred years earlier very similar to the one that Kennedy will evoke in *Quinn's Book*. With a nod toward Mark Twain's *A Connecticut Yankee in King Arthur's Court*, this section propels Bailey back to the mid-nineteenth century, and it gives a more effective outlet for Kennedy's bent toward magic realism than one finds anywhere else in the novel. Perhaps most strikingly, it provides Bailey with a reference point for the concept of the cyclical nature of suffering. Scenes of the cholera epidemic of the 1840s enable him to imagine the anguish and despair endured—and to a degree surmounted—a century prior to the Guild struggles. This contrast in turn offers Bailey an alternative to the pessimistic dismissal of any effort to struggle against adversity. Although no happy ending uplifts his recollection of the epidemic, the continuing growth of Albany refutes any sense that such a disaster marks the end of everything.

The section that follows—"Famine Can Be Fun Boardwalker Tells Friends. And Necessity Turns Out to Be a Mother"—brings the narrative

back to the distinctive discourse established earlier in the novel and insti-
gates a leisurely denouement. The epigraph for this section, from Yeats's "To
a Friend Whose Work Has Come to Nothing," provides a note of bittersweet consolation and sets the stage for the movement toward a form of resignation, if not toward the resolution of the issues that have dominated the
action. Bailey has undergone a period of exile, and now he returns to confront the disparities between idealism and reality.

As shown in so many of Kennedy's works, any sort of resurrection begins with a woman. In this case, Irma literally drags Bailey away from his
reveries in the State Library to face the changes that have taken place since
the beginning of his self-imposed exile. Bailey, in the role of secular re-
deemer, now begins to try to sort out the mess into which the Guild has
fallen. Matters at first seem no better than they were when he first buried
himself in the stacks of the State Library, as he discovers himself cut off from
those who had formerly participated in the drama of his life. Just the act of
taking stock of the situation, however, relieves the sense of helplessness that
pervaded earlier sections. The meager coterie that until now has supported
Bailey is dissolving, forcing him to confront his nature directly, perhaps for
the first time. Paradoxically, as he is compelled to become more self-reliant,
his solipsism diminishes.

Unfortunately, as the plot moves to its resolution, a tendency toward
the melodramatic begins to set the pace of the action. Bailey responds to the
unbroken string of labor defeats chronicled in the narrative by going down
to the newspaper, beginning to picket on his own, and combining a hunger
strike with his marching. While he is walking the picket line, the lack of
food begins to take effect, and he starts to hallucinate. He imagines meeting
with Terence MacSwiney, the lord mayor of Cork, who died in 1920 while
on a hunger strike protesting British rule in Ireland. The exchange consists
of Bailey's fawning attempts to express his admiration to an indifferent Mac-
Swiney. The hallucination ends abruptly with an image very similar to those
appearing in the Circe chapter of Joyce's *Ulysses*: MacSwiney moves backward through a concrete wall while offering some very simple advice, "Try
very hard to . . ." (226, author's ellipses). The truncated salutation evokes
the lack of closure in Bailey's life, but offers little direction for anyone trying
to comprehend the movement of the narrative in these closing episodes.

Bailey finally ends his picketing when another ink truck attempts to
make a delivery at the newspaper. Although he is now hallucinating as he

walks, he still makes an effort to prevent the delivery. He is able to get under the truck, and before being apprehended by guards, he turns the tap, and the ink begins to drain from the truck onto the snowy ground. In a continuance of the theme of the ambiguity of perception that has dominated this section, Bailey is beaten into unconsciousness before he can tell whether the events he set in motion in fact lead to the emptying of the truck.

The next section—"Rowdy Is Ousted As Last Trolley Goes Clang, Clang. And the Boon Is on the Spoon"—takes a tone of nihilism from the epigraph from William Saroyan's "For My Part I'll Smoke a Good Ten Cent Cigar," but a slapstick mentality makes the narrative seem more silly than satirical or profound. The episode begins, without a backward glance, with Bailey awakening at Stanley's mansion, leaving the reader unaware of how the scene at the ink truck was resolved. Downstairs, at the end-of-strike party thrown by Stanley to celebrate the destruction of the Guild and attended by participants from both sides of the struggle, guests consume more and more drink and food, and their behavior becomes increasingly bizarre. When Bailey joins the bacchanal, he assumes that guests are being doped. Nonetheless, he rather quixotically decides to give up his hunger strike and join in.

From there, the pace of events accelerates, and the narrative moves toward a conclusion that suggests that Kennedy simply wishes to end things as quickly as possible. Random violence serves as the force that brings closure: the chaos in the party mounts, and abruptly Bailey fires the pistol that Irma has been hiding. Stanley's guards respond by throwing them both out of the party. Bailey goes on to telephone Rosenthal, who agrees to meet him at Fobie's for a drink. At the bar, Bailey and Rosenthal get into a fight with the bartender, and they leave. They go to the Guild office and find a notice that the local has been dissolved and the office emptied. They have a desultory conversation, which includes Irma, who has joined them; then "[a]fter a long silence they got up and left the room" (178), and the book ends.

The abrupt conclusion certainly fits the anarchic impulse of the entire novel. Nonetheless, it seems more a cessation than a resolution of any of the aesthetic or intellectual issues Kennedy has introduced. It is, at the same time, a mistake to judge *The Ink Truck* a failure simply because it does not match Kennedy's later work. In fact, as noted at the beginning of this chapter, this novel stands as an apprentice piece, and many of the elements that characterize its narrative hold the promise of what will come when its author learns to deploy the full effect of his talent. The imaginatively powerful narratives of the later fictions will grow out of the author's developing sense of the creative frames that best suit his abilities. Like his characters, Kennedy needs the supportive structure of the Irish American, Albany milieu, and in his next novel, *Legs,* he begins to invoke that world to shape the context of his writing.

Part Two

Independence

 CHAPTER THREE

Legs and the Pursuit of Knowledge

By the time William Kennedy published *Legs* in 1975, his writing effortlessly demonstrated the technical control and imaginative sophistication that would stand as the hallmark of the rest of his work. In fact, as the initial novel in the Albany cycle, *Legs* introduces readers to the refined structural features—thematic and stylistic—that establish Kennedy as one of America's foremost contemporary writers. Here one encounters for the first time the deft amalgamation of language, setting, and characterization that give a uniqueness to his writing and an enduring quality to his reader's experiences.

As in the two books that immediately follow it in order of composition—*Billy Phelan's Greatest Game* and *Ironweed*— the action of *Legs* unfolds primarily in upstate New York between World Wars I and II. In this novel, the recklessness and the violence of the Prohibition era complement the despair and bitterness brought on by the Great Depression. Together these elements form the dominant force driving the narrative and place a menacing and hopeless self-indulgence, emblematic of the times, at the center of many of the characters' lives. It is equally important to note that the significance of community never completely disappears from the discourse, for the perspective of the narrator, Marcus Gorman, evokes the tribal milieu of Albany that dominates the society at the heart of all of Kennedy's writing.[1] Thus, in *Legs*, one sees Kennedy articulating the dynamics between the representation of individuality and the development of a communal understanding. This affiliation continues to evolve as an important relationship throughout the Albany cycle.

Nonetheless, distinctive compositional decisions set *Legs* apart from other works in the Albany cycle. Unlike Kennedy's subsequent novels, which take an overtly parochial and communal approach to the composition of identity, *Legs* focuses attention on the development of an isolated, nomadic individual. Jack Diamond in fact matures outside the regionalized influence of the Albany environment, away from the clannish attachments of the extended Irish American families who range through the ensuing novels. He exists in the tightly defined world of bootleggers, thieves, and murderers, but he operates on the margins even of this milieu. Indeed, Jack functions as a loner whose relation to a particular city, to its culture, and to its history turns more on chance than on disposition.[2]

Further, even the action surrounding Jack Diamond remains secondary to the way his personality unfolds. Although events remain an important feature of the novel, it is the individual and not society that measures their significance. The opening chapter, set nearly half a century after the events recorded in the rest of the book, begins with a gruesome recollection of the scene of Jack's murder and a thumbnail sketch of his rise and fall as a gangster. This summary makes the central events of Jack's existence seem anticlimactic as the story unfolds. The opening announces a shift in emphasis away from plot development—early on, the downward spiral of Jack's life becomes apparent to readers through repeated allusion to his demise—and toward characterization; it invites readers to consider not so much what happened as what sort of individual drove the action.

From the start, the narrative provides ample evidence of the importance of Jack Diamond's nature to the significance of what has occurred and to understanding the makeup of other central figures in *Legs*. In that first chapter, for example, Marcus Gorman struggles to form an epitaph for Jack and ends up describing the enduring and disturbing effect that Jack had on him.

> [H]e was an original man and he needs an original epitaph, even if it does come four and a half decades late. I say to you, my reader, that here was a singular being in a singular land, a fusion of the individual life flux with the clear and violent light of American reality, with the fundamental Columbian brilliance that illuminates this bloody republic. Jack was a confusion to me. I relished his company, he made me laugh. Yet wasn't I fearful in the presence of this man for whom violence and death were well-oiled tools of the trade? (Kennedy 1975, 14)

This fixation suggests how the gangster's personality dominates people throughout the narrative and why, because of their recollections, his story never quite achieves a sense of closure.[3]

This sense of open-endedness does not come about because of a lack of information about Jack. Throughout *Legs*, Marcus Gorman, the well-connected attorney with political ambitions, provides a running commentary on the central incidents in the gangster's life. His account ranges from 1908 to mid-1976, highlighting Diamond's impact on the lives of a variety of people who appear in the novel. At the same time, although Marcus talks about a series of pivotal incidents—from the 1929 shooting at New York City's Hotsy Totsy Club to Jack's 1931 death in an Albany boarding house—he makes no attempt to give primacy to any event. Further, despite his fairly detailed knowledge of Jack's life and his keen eye for motivation, he seems little inclined to judge Jack's behavior or, for that matter, his own. Indeed, the tendency to downplay the seriousness of the brutality informing Jack's life at first seems incongruous (perhaps even delusional) coming from a veteran criminal lawyer. In consequence, although a series of vivid accounts anchor his development of Jack's story, Marcus gives the reader little direction for interpreting them. Rather, we each come to our own sense of Jack Diamond independent of Marcus's or anyone else's opinion.

That is not to say that the narrative does not provide ample evidence for understanding Jack's effect on those he encounters. The combination of admiration and envy that unmistakably tinges Marcus's recollections helps to explain Jack's hold on people. As an enigmatic figure whose behavior often seems unmotivated and unpredictable, Jack embodies a way of life both foreign and fascinating. The prospect of knowing Jack (in the sense of understanding him as well as of making his acquaintance) is what draws Marcus into the events recounted in the book. It becomes quickly apparent, however, that full comprehension will require a far more complex series of operations than either Marcus or the readers initially realize.

The book's title—the nickname created and popularized by newspapers yet used by none of Jack Diamond's friends—emphasizes from the start how the sharp divergence between public perceptions of Jack and the views of those close to him shapes the narration. Joe Fogarty—Jack's driver, erstwhile bodyguard, and sometimes confidant—says as much to Marcus Gorman on their first meeting. "Nobody who knows him calls him anything but Jack" (32). Late in the novel—in a manner characteristic of Kennedy's inclination to offer information early while withholding the full explanation until much later—the narrative presents an account of how Jack acquired the nickname, in the public mind at least: "O'Donnell explained that Eddie Diamond [Jack's younger brother] was once called Eddie Leggie ('Leggie,' a criminal nickname out of the nineteenth-century slums) and that somehow it got put on Jack. Cop told a newsman about it. Newsman got it wrong. Caption in the paper referred to Jack as Legs. And there was magic forever after" (245). The exchange with Fogarty marks the stark contrast between those who know Jack and those who do not, and it immediately precedes Marcus's first meeting with Diamond at a farm owned by another gangster: " 'God's country?' . . . 'Fogarty told me Jimmy Biondo owned this place' " (35). After a joke about coming to the Catskills straight from an Albany Police Department Communion Breakfast, Marcus joins Jack and Jack's wife Alice at target shooting with a machine gun. The incongruity of it all does not escape Marcus, and his inference of an inherent difference between the gangster and his attorney rings a bit hollow: "Altar Rosary Society Member [a reference to Alice] attends machine-gun outing after mass, prods lawyer to take part. What a long distance between Marcus and Jack Diamond. Millenniums of psychology, civilization, experience, turpitude. Man also develops milquetoasts by natural selection" (40).

Marcus's sense of irony nicely subverts any inclination to see his descriptions as self-aggrandizing. Nonetheless, even at this early stage in the novel, both the reader and Marcus sense that the putative distance between the gangster and the lawyer is not as great as the latter would like to believe. In this apparently offhand fashion, the episode underscores Kennedy's overall approach to characterization, first employed in The Ink Truck but already taking a much more sophisticated form: he introduces individuals by contrasting them with their ostensive opposites and then through gradual revelations shows the striking similarities that obtain beneath the superficial differences.

Like any fictional account of a real person, the narrative of Legs unfolds with the principal events of Jack Diamond's life already set and presumably familiar to many readers. In consequence, revealing what happens becomes a matter of less importance than identifying the forces that shape events and the patterns that emerge from the action. With this in mind, Kennedy's narrative plays off descriptions of Jack's propensity for unmotivated violence against intimations of what will occur. This omniscient awareness of the future imposes a measure of order on Jack's world without diminishing its anarchic potential: "Fogarty was the only man I ever met through Jack who wasn't afraid to tell me what was really on his mind. There was an innocence about him that survived all the horror, all the fear, all the crooked action, and it survived because Jack allowed it to survive. Until he didn't allow it anymore" (33).

An equally important feature of Kennedy's work, an attitude that recurs throughout his fiction, emerges relatively early in the narration: the banality of evil. The decor of the farm that Jack and Alice are occupying when Marcus first meets them offers a neat overview of their petit bourgeois surroundings.

> He did let Alice pick out the furniture, for the hot items he kept bringing home clashed with her plans, such as they were. She'd lined the walls with framed calendar art and holy pictures—a sepia print of the Madonna returning from Calvary and an incendiary, bleeding sacred heart with a cross blooming atop the bloody tapestry, a souvenir from Jack's days as a silk thief. Three items caught my eye on a small bookshelf otherwise full of Zane Grey and James Oliver Curwood items: a copy of Rabelais, an encyclopedia of Freemasonry, and the Douay Bible sandwiched between them. (43)

Art, religion, superstition, and secular ritual struggle against the mundane, overlaid with kitsch. The objects around the room outline the tastes of profoundly ordinary characters with limited education and circumscribed imaginations. A veneer of cynicism covers an insipid yet anxious ignorance. As the titles of the books that capture Marcus's attention suggest, Jack makes some effort to go beyond the cultural boundaries of the world that he has always known. Ultimately, however, only the mayhem that punctuates his own life and that of his associates distinguishes their otherwise banal existence.

Indeed, naked force quickly becomes the distinguishing feature in Marcus Gorman's account of the world that Jack Diamond inhabits. Although the narrative repeatedly refers to Jack as a thief, raw violence and brute sensuality, not larceny, stand out as his dominant characteristics. Predictably, mayhem and gratification manifest themselves in the coarsest and most reflexive manner imaginable, for Jack's sensibilities are neither those of a cultivated epicurean nor those of a self-conscious sadist. Rather, his feelings function on the instinctual level, lacking any imaginative refinement. At times, of course, Jack can adopt a sophisticated veneer, but the effect is short-lived and often only serves to point up the shallowness in the efforts of others. Indeed, stark brutality consistently defines his personality, and it stands as the trait that so fascinates the more sophisticated, if no less ruth-less, lawyer.

The narrative makes their affiliation eminently clear in episodes where Marcus and Jack follow roughly parallel patterns of behavior. For example, near the opening of *Legs*, Marcus first appears reading Rabelais (15–16). Ini-tially, this seems to set him apart from the more earthy Diamond, yet a few days later Marcus describes Jack casually skimming his own copy of the book: "I said I knew the book, but avoided mentioning the coincidence of Rabelais being here and also in the K. Of C. library, where I made my deci-sion to come here, and in the additional fact that a lawyer had given the book to Jack" (43). Marcus may choose not to mention the coincidence to Jack, but as narrator he ensures that readers make the connection. Kennedy himself does not let the link rest on a simple replication in taste. Instead he uses the parallel first to suggest an association between the two men and then to underscore their differences. For Marcus, the Rabelais volume at-tests to a refinement in taste that he chooses to downplay at the Knights of Columbus Hall and to conceal completely from Diamond. For Jack on the other hand, the book represents not a powerful literary tradition but an ex-ample of someone able to flout public standards. Reading aloud a passage that describes Gargantua urinating becomes a way for Jack to chafe Alice and by extension to play the naughty boy who can shock adults by his risqué behavior (44).

Kennedy's development of the literary allusion, however, does not stop there. By the end of the episode, the invocation of Rabelais has become a striking example of the way that Jack draws on a variety of weapons to as-sault humanity. Marcus's appreciation of the same book now faces the sug-gestion of being less sophisticated and more juvenile than it at first appeared. In a trend that runs throughout the novel, Jack's behavior contin-ues to undercut that of other characters. The accumulation of similarities be-tween Jack and Marcus, for example, wears down the facade of cosmopolitanism that Marcus endeavors to maintain over the course of the narration. It becomes clear not that the gangster is as refined as the attorney but rather that both men are subject to equally coarse behavior (despite Marcus's ability to mask his true character with an affectation of refinement).

The narrative sets out to develop further connections between Jack Di-amond and Marcus Gorman through their mutual fascination with brutality. Even before the two meet in the Catskills, the action of the novel begins to unfold with an account of a violent confrontation in 1929 at the Hotsy

Totsy Club in New York City. The fight that takes place between Jack and his friends on one side and the Reagan brothers on the other grows out of a drunken ethnic slur that demeans the ability of the prize-fighter Benny Shapiro. The escalation of violence progresses from insults to shooting in a ridiculously short amount of time, and it culminates in the most pointless act of all, the murder of Tim Reagan, the man who has striven to act as the peacemaker throughout the exchanges leading up to the fight.

> Jack Diamond, rising slowly with his pistol in his hand, looked at the only standing enemy, Tim Reagan, who was holding Saul's pistol. Jack shot Tim in the stomach. As Tim fell, he shot a hole in the ceiling. Standing then, Jack fired into Tim's forehead. The head gave a sudden twist and Jack fired two more bullets into it. He fired his last two shots into Tim's groin, pulling the trigger three times on empty chambers. Then he stood looking down at Tim Reagan. (27–28)

Jack's brutal, instinctual response marks the final stage in a series of acts that cause the senseless murder of two men, and it offers an unflinching portrayal of the ruthless, thoughtless violence that stands as a central feature of Jack's nature. Although its implications become evident only retrospectively, this outburst leads to Jack's virtual expulsion from New York City, and it marks the commencement of a self-destructive cycle that ends with Jack's own death two years later.

The notoriety of the killings forces Jack to shift his operations to the Catskills. There he specializes in bootlegging and beer distribution, existing in a fashion that indicates both the range and the limitations of his character. Jack Diamond lives a detached life with seemingly no regard for the consequences of his acts and little apparent thought given to long-term plans. His behavior remains stuck at the reflexive level, and violence predominates as his immediate response to any situation that presents unforseen difficulties.

It is only through mimicry that Jack ever advances, albeit only temporarily, beyond living by his instincts. His desire to imitate his mentor and sometime antagonist, A. R. Rothstein, for example, leads him to contact Marcus Gorman about becoming his lawyer on retainer. This gesture emerges as a crucial feature for the structure of *Legs*, by introducing into the action the perfect chronicler of Jack's life: a man without any scruples of conscience yet someone guided by the prudence to know which risks are not worth taking. Although Marcus feels drawn by many of the same animal appetites that shape Jack's behavior, he also manifests a lawyerly awareness of the need to acknowledge the force of societal conventions and of the imperative for exerting some sort of control on one's life by organizing it according to some plan. He understands what society will abide and what it will not endure, and he shapes his life accordingly, though he remains careless of what society will think.

Thus, the visit Marcus makes to Jack in the Catskills on an ostensibly tranquil summer Sunday serves to lay out the diverse concepts that inform the novel, and it marks the onset of a series of events that recast (and in Jack's case end) the lives of both men. For Marcus, it starts a relatively brief association that remains a fixture in his consciousness for the rest of his life. In particular, the casual brutality that dominates Jack life also captivates Marcus's imagination, forcing the lawyer to confront his own inclinations to live in an uncivilized manner. Midway through the novel, Marcus sums up his views of Jack in a strikingly perceptive assessment: "He was a liar, of course, a perjurer, all of that, but he was also a venal man of integrity, for he never ceased to renew his vulnerability to punishment, death, and damnation. It is one thing to be corrupt. It is another to behave in a psychologically responsible way toward your own evil" (118).[4] This disposition, as much Marcus's as Jack's, reflects an attitude very different from the ordinary mendacity of other men. It does not merely identify a willingness to break the law. Patsy, Bindy, and Matt McCall—the bosses who control politics and gambling in Albany during most of the period in which Kennedy's novels are set—all break the law, and to some degree they are called to account for it. In Kennedy's next book, *Billy Phelan's Greatest Game,* for example, readers not only discover that Patsy McCall did "six months [in prison] for contempt in the baseball-pool scandal," but also learn that all clippings of the event have been removed from the files of the *Albany Times-Union* newspaper (Kennedy 1978, 44–45). In the need to create such absences lies the distinction between the lawlessness of Jack and Marcus and that of the rest of society. The McCalls understand the importance of hiding their felonious behavior. Jack by his actions and Marcus by his associations openly declare their willingness to operate outside the limits set down by society. For the lawyer, such an assertion ensures that he can never follow his political ambitions, and for the gangster this declaration means that he will die in a peremptory and violent fashion.

The Catskill meeting also marks more immediate changes in the lives of both men. This first visit between Jack and Marcus establishes a competitive yet fraternal association. Marcus's unexpected proficiency with a machine gun (shooting at a target designated as Dutch Schultz, Jack's rival at the time) and his sexual attraction both to Alice, Jack's wife, and to Marion "Kiki" Roberts, Jack's girlfriend, introduce an understated rivalry. At the same time, Jack admires Marcus's polish and intelligence in much the same way that Marcus reveres Jack's recklessness and courage. They amuse one another. It seems only natural then, shortly after this first meeting, for Jack to invite Marcus on a trip to Europe.

Despite Jack's vagueness regarding purpose, it soon becomes clear to Marcus that the aim of the trip is to buy heroin for a drug distribution scheme that Jack and another gangster, Jimmy Biondo, are undertaking. For Jack, the trip takes on an added imperative to escape the consequences of a falling out over beer distribution he has had with fellow gangster Charlie Northrup. Efforts by Jack's gang to intimidate Northrup have gotten out of hand and have precipitated Northrup's brutal murder by Murray "the Goose" Pucinski, one of Jack's henchmen. Local interest in what might have happened to Northrup has made it unwise for Jack to remain in the Catskills.

Throughout Jack and Marcus's trip across the Atlantic, the disappearance of Charlie Northrup insistently insinuates itself into the narrative, and the ambiguity about Jack's involvement in the Northrup case has a corrosive effect on relations between the two men. Additionally, the publicity generated by the disappearance and the assumed killing follows Jack wherever he goes in Europe. The scrutiny that it produces prevents any possible drug purchase, and it creates such notoriety for Marcus that it dooms his chances of ever becoming the Democratic Party candidate for the Albany area congressional seat.

Not surprisingly, none of this has any effect on Jack's demeanor. On the trip, he behaves in the same ad hoc fashion that has governed his actions throughout the novel. Indeed, the narrative very neatly underscores the way that violence surrounds Jack, even when he takes no direct part in it. During the opening stages of the ocean voyage, an incident with a crazed dog illustrates the point.

> The fox terrier: He appeared as I stood on the sports deck near the rail, while Jack was shooting skeet. I saw nothing chasing the dog, which came at me in a blur of brown and white, but there must have been some-

thing, for he was panicky or perhaps suddenly maddened. He took a corner at high speed, dead-ended into a bulkhead, turned around, and leaped
through the rail, flailing like a crazy-legged circus clown falling off a
tightrope into a net. I saw him surface once, go into a wave, bob up again
and then vanish. I doubt anyone else saw it.

A man finally came toward me at a brisk pace and asked if I'd seen his
dog, and I said, yes, I'd just seen it leap overboard.

"Leap overboard?" the man said, stunned by the concept.

"Yes. He leaped."

"He wasn't thrown?"

"Nobody threw him, I can tell you that. He jumped."

A dog wouldn't leap overboard like that."

He looked at me, beginning to believe I'd killed his dog. I assured him
I'd never seen such a thing either, but that it was true, and just then he
looked past me and said, "That's Legs Diamond," the dog instantly forgotten, the man already turning to someone to pass along his discovery. In a
matter of minutes a dozen people were watching Jack shoot. (Kennedy
1975, 83)

The scene encapsulates the primary features of Marcus's consciousness: his
gravitation toward violent action—in this case skeet shooting—strains
against a preference to observe rather than to participate. At the same time,
he cannot hold himself aloof indefinitely—he tells the man in this instance
what happened to the dog, although by his own admission the event seems
highly unlikely. This inevitably produces a kind of confrontation that lets
him rely on one of his strengths, talking. As with so many scenes in the
novel, however, it is the presence of the gangster rather than the ability of
the attorney that gets the latter out of a tough spot.

In an interesting formal flourish, the passage quoted above shifts from
indirect to direct address, underscoring the emotional fluctuation that characterizes the exchange. It deftly charts the rising level of tension, suggesting
that Marcus has become too excited to translate the discourse into narrative. Like any clever oral antagonist, he wants to mask his own apprehension
while exploiting that of his adversary. Nonetheless, by shifting from narrative to a more direct presentation of events, he reveals the intensification of
his own feelings without having to articulate them. Conversely, as Jack Diamond captures the dog owner's attention, the narrative returns to indirect
address.

Thus, despite sporadic narrative moments of close scrutiny of Marcus's life, Jack never slips far from the center of the discourse. Whenever Jack re-acts to a situation, his propensity for direct and brutal behavior rivets atten-tion on everything that he does. One sees this in his casual shipboard affair that leaves the young librarian from Minneapolis angry and humiliated. "You turn women into swine" (85). At the same time, however, instinctual brutality stands as only one element within a complex, interconnected pat-tern of motives for Jack's aberrant behavior. In describing to Marcus his first killing, Jack traces the links between status, violence, and behavior: "Maybe I wouldn't have killed [Wilson] if [Rothstein] didn't say that about the hair-cut, make me feel I was such a bum. I knew I was a bum, but I didn't think it showed so much. With the four grand I wasn't such a bum anymore. I bought a new suit and got a haircut at the Waldorf-Astoria" (95).

Jack goes on to recount his steady rise as a gangster. Within a short time after his first killing, he has gained prominence as a bootlegger by highjacking liquor from other criminals. As a predictable consequence, he makes enemies, and blood feuds result. The account of the death of Billy Blue, to which Jack alludes and on which the prostitute Flossie elaborates, underscores both Jack's viciousness toward his enemies and the general bru-tality that characterizes his approach to the world. As Flossie tells Gorman, "I saw Jack quite a lot. He was our protector. That's what they called him anyway. Some protector. It was him and his guys beat up Loretta and Mar-lene—the bastards, the things they could do and then be so nice" (103). This behavior neatly fits the pattern of Jack's life, which Marcus succinctly sums up early on in the narrative: "He'd failed at [burglary] as a teenager and graduated to the activity that conformed to his talent, which was not stealth but menace" (92).

Violence, however, has reciprocal effects, and over the course of his Eu-ropean trip Jack feels keenly the repercussions resulting from being linked to the criminal brutality of the bootlegger's world. Even a continent away, the search by U.S. law enforcement authorities for Charlie Northrup creates insistent disruption in Jack's life. The relentless publicity in the press regard-ing Northrup's disappearance causes Jimmy Biondo to pressure Jack to call off their drug deal. It also makes Jack a persona non grata in every country—Britain, Belgium, and Germany—he tries to enter. Although the action itself seems predictable in the light of his growing reputation as a thug, it marks an important turning point in the narrative. The consequences of his behavior begin to impose limits on him that mere violence cannot overcome.

Predictably, Jack fails to recognize this change, so he continues to apply the same form of brutality that has always served as his response to any situation that confronts him. In Berlin, for example, Weissberg, the playwright nephew of Jack's German lawyer, unconsciously exposes the banality that informs Jack's world by linking their two lives. Jack's terrifying rejoinder—firing a pistol at a spot on the floor between the legs of the young braggart—forces Weissberg to confront exactly the sort of mindless violence that he boasts of celebrating in his writing. Nonetheless, the problem inherent in such a gesture, made clear through the commentary of Marcus Gorman, is that all of Jack's actions have an isolated, episodic quality. His humiliation of Weissberg produces immediate satisfaction, but it only confirms the opinions of those who judge him unfit to remain in Germany. He acts like a gangster, and then he feels outrage when European authorities respond by expelling him from the continent.

The savageness that conditions Jack's behavior intrudes even when his consciousness moves toward a different reaction to the world around him. Returning to America on the freighter *Hanover*, for example, Jack becomes enthralled by the sight of the forty-five hundred Hartz Mountain canaries traveling to the United States on the same ship. Though clearly moved by the birds' beauty, he has difficulty expressing that fascination in any way that does not reflect a struggle for control, and this awkwardness in his relation with these birds evokes for readers his response to the two pet canaries, Alice and Marion, kept in his farm in the Catskills. After Jack's wife learns that the birds are named for her and for his current lover, a fight ensues, and each kills a bird as a way of affirming their violent passion and possessive love for one other.

> When Jack said nothing, Alice wrung the bird's neck and threw it back in the cage. "That's how much I love you," she said and started past Jack, toward the living room, but he grabbed her and pulled her back. He reached for the second bird and squeezed it to death with one hand, then shoved the twitching, eyebleeding corpse down the crevice of Alice's breasts. "I love you too," he said. (54)

As with his pets in the Catskills, Jack treats the birds that he encounters on the ship roughly, but they respond in a far less passive and far more complex manner: "Jack opened a cage to gentle one of the birds. It pecked once at his knuckle. He lifted the bird out and saw it was dead. He put it in his pocket and opened another cage. That bird flew out, silently, and perched on top of the highest stack of cages, beyond Jack's reach unless he used the sailor's ladder. The bird twisted on its tail and shat on the floor in front of Jack" (112). Although Jack shows a natural interest in the canaries, he finds himself unsure how to pursue it. In consequence, his response reflects his usual brutality, but lacks the assurance that he so readily demonstrates in other situations. When his clumsiness kills one bird, another responds with the avian equivalent of reciprocal aggression. Within the narrative, such suggestions of entropy recur with ever-increasing frequency, placing Jack in a bigger world, one that he can no longer control. Unfortunately, he has never cultivated the ability to read the significance of such incidents and in consequence moves forward with a fatalism derived from ignorance rather than from courage.

Within a world view dominated by menace, the limitations to negotiate successfully with exigencies of the unknown become increasingly apparent in the reception Jack receives when he returns to America. From the moment he walks off the gangplank in Philadelphia, the narrative offers recurring evidence that he can no longer direct the events going on around him. The paradigm for which Jack had shown so little concern all of his life has shifted. The world that he has taken for granted for so long no longer exists, and a new environment offers challenges he does not know how to recognize, much less meet. In consequence and with no conscious assent on his part, the way that he lives begins to change because of the cumulative effects of his violence.

Philadelphia gives Jack the same treatment meted out to him in Europe. Local police arrest him as the boat docks. While being taken away into custody by the authorities, he has a pierside exchange with one of his cousins that underscores the depth of his isolation:

> "Ah shit, Will, have you got anything to tell me? How's Aunt Elly?"
> "She's fit."
> "Does she need anything?"
> "Nobody needs anything from you."
> "Well. It was nice seeing you, Will. Give my regards to the worms."
> "We know who the worm in this family is, cousin." (119)

After Jack has spent twenty hours in a Philadelphia jail, a local judge bluntly orders him to leave town: "I speak for the decent people of this city in saying that Philadelphia doesn't want you any more than Europe did. Get out of this city and stay out" (120). On the ride from Philadelphia to New York, Jack consumes most of a bottle of rye whiskey, slipping into a drunken stupor that acts to anesthetize the pain that grows out of the disdain that has met him since his return to the United States.

Back in New York City, the cycle of violence escalates, even as Jack's control over the world around him deteriorates. Jimmy Biondo, Jack's erstwhile partner in the failed European drug deal, attempts to intimidate him into returning the money advanced for the purchase of drugs. When that fails, a gang war begins. Images of violence from the past resurface as Jesse Franklin, the man who runs Jack's still in the Catskills, gives Marcus Gorman just enough information for the attorney to know that Charlie Northrup is truly dead. Later, Fogarty fills in the details, explaining that Murray the Goose killed Northrup against Jack's wishes.

At this point in the novel, certain disparities in the interpretations of the events that have formed the narrative become impossible to ignore. From the opening pages of *Legs*, Marcus has acted as an interpretive mediator, serving as a barometer roughly analogous to the reader's impressions of Jack's nature. Repeated incidents have shown Jack responding violently when confronted. Like Marcus, the reader has become only gradually aware of the full range of Jack's viciousness. Even after the account of the Northrup killing, however, Marcus continues to downplay the horror of events through his deadpan account of Jack's behavior, which perhaps reflects the kind of popularity Jack enjoys. Nonetheless, as examples of the vicious element in Jack's nature mount, this inclination toward brutality steadily challenges any sympathy readers might feel for Jack and makes them aware of the need to judge him with a detachment and a rigor that Marcus seems incapable of exerting.

The death of Northrup functions as the immediate cause of the unraveling of Jack's world. Although the narrative does not make his motives clear (indeed, as noted above, lack of any sort of forethought or long-range planning stands as a central feature of Jack's character), Jack has Murray the Goose shot, presumably for killing Charlie Northrup. This effort to kill Murray fails, however, and that leads inevitably to further mayhem. On the surface, such a reaction stands in perfect harmony with all of Jack's other escapades: brutality provokes a savage response. One simply answers violence in kind. Jack, unfortunately, does not see the consequences of any act beyond its immediate result, and for this reason he often sets events in motion that produce results completely unforeseen by him. In addition to high-lighting his inability to learn from experience, this sort of behavior under-scores a pervasive lack of faith in the future. For Jack, everything of significance resides in the moment, and he sees any effort to look beyond that moment as a futile gesture. Kiki captures this attitude, in her own unre-flective manner, as she offers her version of the feeling surrounding their lovemaking: "We were killing the empty times, and then we'd die with them and wake up and kill them again until there wasn't anything left to kill and we'd be alive in a way that you can never die when you feel like that because you own your life and nothing can ruin you" (145).⁵ Even in descriptions of what one might expect to be some of Diamond's most pleasurable experi-ences, the images of violence and desolation persist. They point up not a heightened awareness of life but rather numbness, even apathy. When Kiki strives to find a metaphor for the cycle of their lovemaking, she cannot go beyond the concept of "killing the empty times." The isolation and reac-tionary desperation that underscore Kiki's recollections of their lovemaking do more than sketch the brutality of the world that Diamond made for him-self. They throw into relief the pointlessness of his life. Sex for Kiki serves as a way of affirming existence and as a means of holding the reality of the world at bay. For Jack, it amounts to little more than an interruption. The stark contrast in their views becomes clear when, later in the narrative, she asks for his assurance that "[w]e'll make love even when you're seventy-five." Jack cannot conceive of such longevity: "No, kid. I'm not going to live to be seventy-five. I didn't expect to make it to thirty-three" (151).

Such pessimistic views coincide with another period of accelerated vio-lence. Jimmy Biondo has Jack shot. As if to underscore the significance of Kiki's previous description of her love life with Jack, the description of the attempt on his life unfolds from Kiki's perspective in the "silk cocoon" of their love nest, and with the assistance of Madge, another showgirl, she struggles to make sense of what happened (149–59). Imbedded within this depiction is a brief exchange between Kiki and a foppishly dressed old man at Broadway and Forty-seventh Street. As the old man sums up his assess-ment of the devastation evident in Kiki's demeanor, the image of the ca-naries again insinuates itself into the discourse: "Forgive me for speaking so freely, but you look to me like a bird wounded in the heart, the brain, and between the legs, and we in the Audubon Society do what we can for the wounded. My card" (156). When Kiki identifies herself as "Jack Diamond's girl," the old man quickly perceives the menace that surrounds her. He exchanges the first card for a second bearing the bland rationalization of his own indiscretion: "There is no good and bad in the elfin realm" (156).[6]

When neither Murray the Goose nor Jack dies in the initial attempts on each other's life, the Goose begins to hunt Jack with a methodical savagery. Presumably, revenge motivates him, but again the narrative does not articulate a specific reason. Instead, readers find themselves drawn, to an even greater degree than before, into the act of completing the narrative, of bringing order to a world that still operates on the instinctual level.[7]

While Jack recuperates from his gunshot wounds, the final phase of the cycle of violence that has structured the narrative, and indeed Jack's life, begins. As a result, the interpretive demands made by Kennedy's writing in the second half of the novel change, and the discourse makes readers increasingly aware of Marcus Gorman's pivotal role. He does not simply act as the impartial chronicler of a particularly seamy element of American society. By taking the trouble to record and reflect on the events of Jack's life, Marcus confers a measure of dignity and significance on that life that Jack's efforts alone could never have achieved. When he visits Jack in the hospital, for example, he is bemused by Jack's sudden religious enthusiasm. Marcus gives readers a new insight into Jack's character by suggesting, in an unvoiced critique, that Jack has a certain culpability in his own shooting: "Could it have happened without your approval? You saw them alone, you know what they were. I know what such go-betweens can be, and I'm not even in your business. And you never had any intention of turning over that money. You asked for exactly what you got" (165). The observation further highlights the divergent roles of the narrator and the readers. Marcus has not ventured a moral judgment, but rather has offered a practical one. As such distinctions recur, we as readers become increasingly aware of the interpretive responsibilities laid on us. Like so many of Kennedy's characters, Marcus Gorman stands well outside the limits of conventional morality, and if we accept his views, we must realize that we are seeing the world from a perspective hardly unlike Jack Diamond's.

On the next page, Marcus presents us with the interpretive crux of the novel: "I've often vacillated about whether Jack's life was tragic, comic, a bit of both, or merely a pathetic muddle" (166). This observation provides readers with useful interpretive insights. At the same time, in terms of their significance to Marcus, the distinctions might have greater import if the lawyer had articulated a set of values—whatever that might entail—that rose above mere pragmatism. Instead, he has come to use his mind the way Jack uses his muscle, as a means of generating an immediate, episodic response to whatever he encounters, seemingly unrelated to a broader world view. He cannot find a label for Jack's life because both Jack and he lack an ethical system against which to measure it. However we as readers choose to resolve the series of options Marcus outlines for us will depend on our own values and will set the tone for how we interpret the remainder of the narrative.

As a prelude to returning to bootlegging in the Catskills, Jack asks Marcus to see if the local political organization will assume an accommodating or at least a disinterested attitude toward these illegal operations. With this in mind, Gorman visits Warren Van Deusen, a friend from law school whose practice encompasses Jack's area of criminal operations. Van Deusen makes it clear that people in the Catskills would not welcome Jack's return, but he does not offer a clear idea of how they will react. The vague sense of a growing resentment against Jack's tactics does not produce an immediate response in Marcus, but it signals to the reader that societal values—manifest through a series of protocols that Jack has never taken the trouble to comprehend—are now exerting pressure to take action against the gangster.

Readers can follow this change through the novel's presentation of communal institutions, such as the family, that Jack never completely accepts or fully understands. Unlike the modernist writers whose works were coming to maturity at the same time that Jack was achieving notoriety, Jack has no clear awareness of the scope or institutional power of the conventional family even as he tries to overcome the limitations imposed by that institution.[8] Accounts early in *Legs* of the close ties between Jack and his brother Eddie seem initially to reflect Jack's efforts to sustain some version of family life, but on closer inspection their relationship lacks the clannish complexity so evident in other families in the Albany cycle—the Phelans, the Daughertys, the McCalls. Rather, the brothers' affiliation comes more to resemble the behavior of a boy with a favored pet. Eddie's tuberculosis allows Jack the opportunity to make material demonstration of his affection, and that sickness underscores Eddie's loyalty when he comes back to New York from his convalescence to help Jack during the uproar over the Hotsy Totsy shootings. After Eddie dies, Jack hires Fogarty, who is recovering from tuberculosis, as an unofficial replacement. "Jack used him as a driver but also trusted him with money and let him keep the books on beer distribution. But his main role was as Jack's sidekick. He looked like Eddie. And Eddie had died of TB" (34).

Throughout the discourse, the narrative affirms the sense that Jack's alienation rests directly on his inability to understand the institutions of the world he inhabits. One sees specific evidence of this in his relations with women. In her own fashion, his wife Alice has tried mightily to provide a family life for Jack. During his extended convalescence after being shot by the men trying to recover Jimmy Biondo's drug money, she comes close to succeeding. Once Jack has recuperated, however, a restlessness seizes him, and he resists the stability of the routine that Alice has established. Instead, in an effort to accommodate both wife and mistress, Jack brings Alice and Kiki together under the same roof in an ill-fated attempt to turn a ménage into a family. He follows such a course of action not out of a desire to outrage society but rather out of a fetching naïveté regarding what one might do. He does not realize that peccadillos always remain at the level of salacious gossip as long as one keeps them private. Any attempt to regularize such behavior, however, is doomed to failure because of its confrontational nature. The society in which he seeks to exist has neither the means nor the desire to support such enterprises. Instead, as he moves closer to the time of his death, evidence of the banality of his life mounts.

The narrative skillfully juxtaposes this social vapidness with Jack's inherent brutality, effectively distancing readers from him and from all of the other characters associated with him. As always, violence propels us to judgment. One evening, coming home from dinner with Kiki, Jack encounters Streeter, a local bootlegger. Jack and his henchman Fogarty abduct Streeter and a young helper, and they torture Streeter to make him reveal the location of the still. Streeter does not, and as a consequence of these actions Jack is arrested and put on trial. The mindless brutality of the incident, recounted in great detail (197–205), has a dual effect. Textually, it provides the excuse to act for those men in the Catskills looking for an opportunity to arrest Jack. Metatextually, it invites readers to assess on an elemental level the full implications of Jack's brutal nature. Although violence has always punctuated the course of the narrative, Jack's reaction to Streeter's stubborn refusal to give up information presents readers with an extended view of Jack's turbulent and bestial nature.

The savage abuse of his rival throws into relief Jack's fundamental human limitations. He cannot articulate emotions, nor can he interact with others as equals. Once the facade of aloofness or good humor is stripped away, he has only menace to convey his feelings and achieve his desires. His treatment of Streeter reminds readers of the events surrounding the murder of Jack Northrup, of the actions that precipitated the shootings at the Hotsy Totsy Club, of Jack's murder of the card cheat Wilson, and indeed of all of the other examples of violence that run through the novel. The very fact that his torture of Streeter, brutal as it is, fails to get the man to give up any information underscores the fundamental ineffectualness of Jack's sadistic nature. He is not the romantic outlaw that one might have assumed him to be. Rather, he is simply a thug and not a very efficient one. He is someone of interest only because of the way that art transforms him: first in the shoddy accounts of tabloid headlines and then in the more reflective prose of the narrative discourse of Marcus Gorman.

After the abduction of and unsuccessful effort to intimidate Streeter, events in Jack's life move rapidly toward closure. Franklin Delano Roosevelt, then governor of New York, orders a grand jury investigation of Jack Diamond. Murray the Goose continues to prowl the Catskills, presumably seeking revenge after Jack's attempt to have him killed. When Jack is ambushed at a roadhouse and other members of the gang, including Fogarty, are arrested, previous sources of money dry up. Simply getting enough to sustain himself on a day-to-day basis becomes a challenge for Jack.

By now even the gangster's trademark menace seems to have deserted him. Without the power that it conveys, Jack finds himself at a loss as to how to deal with others. In an Albany restaurant with Alice, Kiki, and Marcus, he finds himself accosted by strangers and insulted by waiters.

A voluptuous woman in a silver sheath with shoulder straps of silver cord paused at the table with her escort.

"This one here is Legs," she said to the escort. "I'd know him anywhere, even if he is only a ridiculous bag of bones."

.   .   .

The waiter leaned over and spoke into Jack's face so all could hear. "They tell *me* you've got the power of ten thousand Indians."

Jack picked up his butter knife and stared at the waiter, prepared to drive the blade through the back of that servile hand. He would take him outside, kick him down the stairs, break his goddamn snotty face.

"Where do they get these people?" Jack asked. But before anyone could respond, the waiter's voice carried across the room from the kitchen,

"A tomato surprise for the lady killer," and the room's eyes swarmed over Jack in a new way. (245–47)

Though still infamous enough to attract attention, Jack Diamond no longer commands the fear that had previously brought respect and profound courtesy. Now he has become a figure of derision, a wounded animal to be teased and ridiculed by turns.

More pivotal and public demonstrations of his vulnerability match the loss of respect Jack has suffered socially. Though Marcus succeeds in the summer of 1931 in winning an acquittal for him on state charges of kidnaping Streeter, Jack cannot escape a federal conviction in Manhattan on bootlegging charges. Plans to merge forces with other mobsters fall through when New York police arrest most of the gang. The state authorities prepare to retry Jack in December on the charge of kidnapping Streeter, and Murray the Goose continues to stalk him.

Jack has by now lost so much stature that he has regressed to the level of venality that he occupied when he first made the move from petty thief to gangster: he must deliver his own bootleg liquor in a frantic effort to acquire the capital he needs to support himself. Not only does this necessity represent a fall in status, it also exposes Jack's physical vulnerability. While dropping off a load of beer at Packy Delaney's saloon, Jack discovers that Murray the Goose and several henchmen are waiting in ambush outside the building, presumably planning to shoot him when he emerges. Rather than confronting the ambushers, Jack and Marcus, accompanied by Flossie the prostitute, hide in an abandoned peanut butter factory connected to the tavern as they wait for the police to come and chase the Goose away.

Though Jack, a man with little inclination toward introspection, seems unaware of the change that has occurred, the reader cannot fail to miss it: Jack now must hustle beer to get spending money; he must depend on the police to protect him from his enemies; and he has lost his aura as a sexual force (it is Marcus, not Jack, who has intercourse with Flossie in the abandoned peanut butter factory). Marcus sums up the situation succinctly: "It was a very long, very hot summer for all of us, but especially Jack, like the predator wolf pushed ever farther from civilization by angry men, who was learning the hard way how to die" (253). The image of the wolf reflects Marcus's inclination to romanticize Jack, but even from this perspective his remarks underscore the pathetic aspect of Jack's isolation.

In the closing pages of the novel, Jack faces retrial on state kidnapping charges, and his reduced circumstances have become all too evident. As Jack enters the courthouse in Troy, New York, he suffers two indignities: a pigeon defecates on his coat, and a young thug taunts him. He remains oblivious to the first incident (which recalls his shipboard experience on his return from Germany), but he feels outrage over the second, not because of the implied threat but because of the person who delivered it. "He looked like a hundred-dollar pay killer. Too green to be in the big money. . . . *They send punk kids after me*" (280, author's emphasis). In keeping with the diminution of Jack's stature, the account of his quick acquittal takes on an almost incidental tone.

By this point in the novel, one cannot ignore Jack's palpable deterioration. Weariness and chaos permeate the closing pages of the work. Following Jack's acquittal, the discourse adopts the crosscutting pattern of cinema montage. As the third-person narrative fast-forwards to describe Diamond preparing for bed (and for his own death) at the end of a long day, it intersperses the details of his last moments with accounts of current news events.

> From Buffalo the hunger marchers began their walk toward Washington. John D. Rockefeller, in Ormond, Florida, told newsreel microphones that "better times are coming," and he wished the world a Merry Christmas. In Vienna a grand jury unanimously acquitted Dr. Walter Pfrimer and seven other Fascist Party leaders of charges of high treason stemming from an attempted putsch. A speedy recovery was predicted for Pola Negri. (291)

An aura of valediction suffuses the victory celebration Jack gives for himself following his acquittal of the Streeter kidnapping charge. The party's array of unlikely guests serves to underscore just how alienated he is from society: "Pair of cops toasting Jack's glorious beswogglement of law and order. Hah! And alongside them the priest and the screwball" (290). It also produces Marcus Gorman's pompous congratulatory toast, ironically dissected and reproduced over a dozen pages (288–99), that serves as a counterpoint to the dejected image of the gangster sitting alone in his boardinghouse room.

A world weariness now dominates the narrative. Sterility, exhaustion, and even boredom characterize Jack's final tryst with Kiki. "Jack erected, Marion lubricious, they could have danced all night. But Jack wearied of the effort and Marion ran out of her capacity to groan with pleasure" (297). By the time Jack is shot to death by unknown assailants in an Albany boardinghouse in the early morning hours of the day following his acquittal, he has become a figure drained of all energy and potency.

The behavior of Jack's women immediately after his death puts much of his life into perspective. Both Kiki and Alice capitalize on his notoriety and on their associations with him by going on stage. The tawdriness of these gestures underscores the sense that we have of a life inflated by tabloids and fickle public interest. The women themselves quickly lose their importance in part because Marcus, like the rest of the country, has no real interest in them apart from their association with Jack Diamond. He mentions that Alice is murdered in her apartment in Brooklyn, but does not even bother noting the date. He sees Kiki in 1936 and then loses track of her.

Nonetheless, Marcus remains faithful to the tasks of illuminating Jack Diamond's world and giving it a significance it previously lacked.

> Didn't I, like everybody else who knew him, end up on a barstool telling Jack's tale again, forty-three years later, telling it my own way? . . . The magazines never stopped retelling Jack's story either, and somebody put it out in book form once, a silly work, and somebody else made a bum movie of it. But nobody ever came anywhere near getting it right, and I mean right, not straight, for accuracy about Jack wasn't possible. His history was as crooked as the line between his brain and his heart. (309–10)

Despite Marcus's own preoccupation with the details of Jack's life, however, the events that he narrates make that life far less fascinating than he realizes. Rather, it is his willingness to take an interest in Jack, one that extends beyond the normal attorney-client limits, that suggests a significance in the story not immediately apparent to readers.

Jack Diamond's aura of importance emerges not so much in what he does, which never rises above the level of the behavior of a rather unimaginative thug who associated with shallow, amoral men and women, rather, his significance lies in the way his life takes hold of the imagination of Marcus Gorman, the man who tells the story. Marcus's accounts have an ancient mariner quality, with an undertone of compulsion punctuating every reminiscence: "Brother Wolf, are you listening?" (285). As he goes on to tell of Jack Diamond, the narrative outlines a world that in turn defines the individual. It becomes an account made important by the act of telling.

The penultimate chapter of the work makes this ineluctably clear. The scene returns to that which opened the novel, the reunion in the Kenmore

nightclub arranged by Marcus Gorman because of the feeling that Jack Diamond "needs an original epitaph, even if it does come four and a half
decades late" (14). As the novel has already shown, however, no single
image of Jack exists from which to form such a tribute. One sees how jum-
bled impressions have become when Flossie makes reference to Jack's "tan
collie," and Tipper corrects her, calling it "a black and white bull terrier
named Clancy." And Packy tells a story—interrupted time and again by
Flossie—about the dog, "a white poodle," who fails to fetch a sweater that
Jack has requested because it has been "sewin' on a button that was missin'
off the pocket" (310–11). Each has a different sense of the dog just as each
has a different sense of Jack.

A three-page coda closes the novel. It recounts Jack Diamond's ruminations in the first few moments after his death. Perhaps most significantly, it
ties Jack to Marcus in the final lines, in which Jack echoes a view that Marcus expressed three hundred or so pages earlier in the opening lines of the
novel: "I really don't think I'm dead" (317).

A number of unanswered questions stand insistently before anyone attempting a final interpretation of the work. Once readers recognize the features of the world that Jack Diamond inhabits, what interpretive options lie
open to them? How do they judge Jack Diamond? What values should they
invoke to make such a judgement? The narrative of *Legs* concludes without
providing hard and fast answers to such queries. Rather, it compels readers
to assess the assumptions that shape the way they find meaning in the text.
Such an exercise not only clarifies their response to *Legs*, but also prepares
them for the equally subjective reaction evoked by issues important in
Kennedy's next novel, *Eddie Phelan's Greatest Game.*

CHAPTER FOUR

The Emergence of Self in *Billy Phelan's Greatest Game*

As in *Legs*, coming to grips with the individuality of the central character plays an important role in understanding *Billy Phelan's Greatest Game*. Nonetheless, readers cannot fail to note that setting assumes a more prominent role in the way that they comprehend the structure of the latter work. In *Legs*, the city serves primarily as a place holder, a reference to a geographic location set vaguely between New York City and the Catskills. In *Billy Phelan's Greatest Game*, Albany no longer occupies the position of a nondescript metropolis best defined as not New York. Instead, it evinces a temperament of its own, one clearly delineated by readily identifiable attributes that exert formative influences on its citizens. Billy Phelan's plight late in the novel illustrates the degree to which the city or at least portions of it have come to form an integral part of many individuals' natures. When the Mc-Calls deny him access to the bars and gambling houses of downtown Albany, Billy finds himself struggling to maintain a clear sense of who he is.

Of course, characterization rather than plot still dominates the development of Kennedy's narratives. At the same time, the discourse of *Billy Phelan's Greatest Game* establishes the notion that place exerts a force of near equal significance to that of intrinsic attitudes in forming the evolving natures of diverse individuals. In *Legs*, as previously noted, a static and narrowly defined milieu circumscribes the action. Jack Diamond's nature remains unchanged over the course of the narrative. His isolation poses a significant impediment to his prospective growth. Lacking social affiliation or a genuine sense of community, he experiences neither the motivation nor the guidance toward maturation that society offers. Beginning with *Billy Phelan's Greatest Game*, however, place and community are crucial in defining identity, and recognizing this fact is singularly important for those seeking an overview of thematic concerns in Kennedy's work. With this in mind, this chapter builds on the ideas of identity introduced in chapter 3, but it puts a greater emphasis on exploring the characterizing relationship between individual and place.[1]

Of course, given Kennedy's skill at evoking a psychological ethos through deft descriptions of the natures of key figures, characterization always remains a dominant aspect in all of his narratives.[2] Characters who in themselves live relatively mundane if ethically marginal existences—such as Billy Phelan, his father Francis, Martin Daugherty, and a range of minor figures—come forward as sharply defined and profoundly interesting individuals because of the complexity of their consciousnesses. Indeed, although the pace of their lives proves to be far less frenetic than that of the flamboyant Jack Diamond, characters in *Billy Phelan's Greatest Game* stand out as more sharply attuned to the subtleties of the world around them. Through the elaboration of this sensitivity to environment, Kennedy shows that he does not need sensational events to make the world of this subsequent novel interesting to observe.

Legs derives its appeal, despite being founded on what I have characterized as an exploration of the banality of evil, from a story line that captivates the reader's attention. We see Jack Diamond succeeding as a criminal through his reckless application of violence, a habit of behavior no less fascinating because it remains quite foreign to most of us. The sheer scale of Jack's brutality sets him and his world apart from what most of Kennedy's readers would conceivably know, yet its dynamism holds their attention.

By contrast, *Billy Phelan's Greatest Game* operates at the opposite narrative extreme. It shows how events and concerns that normally occupy a position of marginal importance in the lives of ordinary men and women become the animating features of the world inhabited by most of the characters in the novel. Games and gaming provide more than mere diversion, more even than excitement designed to enliven dull lives. They validate one's existence. Indeed, without the ability to play games—bowling, cards, pool— Billy Phelan loses his reason for living. In the next book of the Albany cycle, *Ironweed* (Kennedy 1983), Kennedy continues to explore this condition, albeit in a more subtle and more sophisticated fashion, when he assesses the professional baseball career of Billy's father, Francis Phelan. Nonetheless, *Billy Phelan's Greatest Game* lays the groundwork by examining the fundamental issues of how sports and the sporting life define a man.

As the opening chapter illustrates, ordinary recreation takes on a life-and-death importance for the men of the novel.[3] (This book is unambiguously a novel of men. Angie Velez, Billy's girlfriend, and Melissa Spencer, a woman involved with both Martin Daugherty and his father, play important parts in advancing the action, but they never occupy roles central to one's comprehension of the narrative, as figures such as Helen Archer, Maud Fallon, Giselle Marais, and Katrina Daugherty do throughout the remainder of the Albany cycle.) The discourse begins by describing Billy's near-perfect game bowling against Scotty Streck, and—through the account of the contest, descriptions of the men who watch it, and intimations of the protocols governing play—it outlines a microcosm of the society of the novel.[4]

Like much of the action throughout the novel, minor events in the bowling alley have a snowball effect, contributing to an increasing tension that extends well beyond the results of the game. The match begins with a five-dollar bet at Scotty's instigation: "He'd been nicknamed Scotty for his closeness with money, never known to bet more than five dollars on himself" (Kennedy 1978, 5). As side bets escalate, they serve to underscore for the men in the room the seriousness of what is transpiring: "The bet between Charlie Boy and Morrie had begun at one hundred dollars. . . . [W]hen Morrie saw that Billy had unquestionably found the pocket at the windup of the second frame, he offered to raise the ante another hundred" (4). In its understated fashion, the narrative shows that wagering involves a skill commensurate with playing the game itself, and as the game goes on, one activity feeds off the other in terms of the nervous energy produced.

At the same time, despite the intense competitiveness of the match, both the formal regulations of the sport and the unspoken rules for a player's behavior remain a central consideration. In a world where the Judeo-Christian morality of the Ten Commandments receives little consideration, the protocols of the game take on paramount importance.

> "You ever throw three hundred anyplace before?" Scotty asked.
> "I ain't thrown it here yet," Billy said.
> So he did it, Martin thought. Scotty's chin trembled as he watched Billy. Scotty, the nervous sportsman. Did saying what he had just said mean that the man lacked all character? Did only relentless winning define his being? Was the fear of losing sufficient cause for him to try to foul another man's luck? Why of course it was, Martin. Of course it was. (9)

For Martin Daugherty and others in the room, the equation is clear: sportsmanship, good or bad, stands out as a characterizing feature in a man's nature.

Without anyone needing to voice such a judgment, everyone in the room knows that Scotty has betrayed himself. The importance that he places on winning does not allow him to recognize the very narrow difference between acceptable and unacceptable behavior. Further, the narrative very neatly uses Scotty's transgression to establish for readers a moral yardstick for larger actions in the novel. Scotty's failure to behave properly under pressure calls attention to the communal expectation that players live according to a code of conduct every bit as sacred as the laws of the church.

Later in the book, Billy Phelan faces a far greater temptation when the McCalls demand that he become an informer. Billy resists pressure to violate his ethical system by spying on a friend, and the McCalls punish him for that loyalty. Subsequently, Martin Daugherty writes a newspaper column about Billy's success at bowling. Though seemingly unconnected, the two incidents operate under similar dispensation. The parallel becomes clear for readers when Martin obliquely outlines the protocols of gaming—strictures that go well beyond the rules of the sport—by a deft description of Billy: "he [Martin] viewed Billy as a strong man, indifferent to luck, a gamester who accepted the rules and played by them, but who also played above them. He wrote of Billy's disdain of money and viewed Billy as a healthy man without need for artifice or mysticism, a serious fellow who put play in its proper place: an adjunct to breathing and eating" (200). From the opening moments of the novel, gaming stands as a consistent yardstick for measuring key elements in the natures of its central characters. Scotty's competitive impulse, overriding the set of standards to which players tacitly abide, emerges as the representative feature of his consciousness. Results of the match, and not how he played it, define his life. Consequently, one can feel no surprise at seeing that losing proves fatal to him. "Scotty doubled up, gasping, burping. He threw his arms around his own chest, wobbled, took a short step, and fell forward, gashing his left cheek on a spittoon. He rolled onto his side, arms still a clutch, eyes squeezing out the agony in his chest" (12). Death by heart attack becomes the punishment for poor sportsmanship, and the fact that no one sees what happens as ironic underscores for readers the serious attention that these men give to every aspect of play.

At the same time, Kennedy's narrative deftly employs uncertainty to disrupt efforts to come to a quick understanding of the characters' actions.

One cannot sustain clear black-and-white judgments about what has happened, even in the tightly defined context of the sporting contest between
Billy and Scotty, and no character holds the moral high ground for any ap-
preciable length of time. Too many factors shape behavior, and good intentions too easily degenerate into pragmatic responses. Immediately after
Scotty's death, for example, Morrie Berman offers his condolences to Charlie Boy McCall.

> "I just want you personally to know I'm sorry. Because I know how
> close you two guys were. I'd a liked him if I could, but Jesus Christ, I don't
> want you sore at me Charlie. You get what I mean?"
> "I get it. I'm not sore at you."
> "I'm glad you say that because sometimes when you fight a guy his
> friends turn into your enemies, even though they got nothin' against you
> themselves. You see what I mean?"
> "I see, and I've got nothing against you, Morris. You're just a punk,
> you've always been a punk, and the fact is I never liked you and like you a
> hell of a lot less than that right now. Good night, Morris." (14)

Morrie Berman's conversation with Charlie Boy illustrates an important aspect of the world that Billy inhabits: it turns on dignity, a trait that Morrie
lacks. He desperately wants to avoid the enmity of a politically well-
connected member of the McCall clan. Charlie Boy understands this, even
in his loathing of Morrie, and indicates that he bears no grudge and signals
that no repercussions will follow: "I'm not sore at you." Unfortunately, Morrie cannot comprehend subtlety, a failing that later features in his undoing,
and so he presses the point. In response, Charlie Boy gives him a scathing
assessment of his position on the social ladder of Albany life that undoes the
reassurances that have preceded it: "you've always been a punk."

This exchange introduces an issue that remains a crucial concern for
men throughout the novel: Where do I stand? Gestures aimed at defining
and maintaining social position shape the behavior of every major character. Assessing the success of these individuals at achieving prominence becomes the imperative interpretive act for every reader.

With the movement of Martin Daugherty to the center of attention, the
narrative presents a second theme that dominates the discourse of the novel
alongside the quest for manly identity: the plight of lost sons. As the later
portions of this novel and *The Flaming Corsage* (Kennedy 1996) make abun-

dantly clear, Daugherty functions as a prototype for members of both groups: he stands both alienated from and devoted to his father, even as he unconsciously acts in a manner that establishes the same sort of relationship with his son.[5] His desire to behave as a proper father motivates Martin's interest in Billy Phelan, and it clarifies what might otherwise be seen as his meandering behavior throughout the novel.

On the morning after Scotty Streck dies, Martin Daugherty awakens worrying about his son's decision to begin training for the priesthood. The boy's intentions are particularly disquieting, for Martin, like many of Kennedy's characters, defines himself as a troubled agnostic. His incertitude over the metaphysical nature of the world deeply disturbs him, and he focuses the resultant anger at the easiest available target: the institutions of the Catholic Church. Consequently, his son's devotion to Catholicism proves a twofold source of agony. Peter Daugherty's faith stands in sharp contrast to his father's absence of belief, and the boy's vocation has taken him at fourteen out of the family home and to a residential seminary. Martin is canny enough to see the implications of his own situation and conjures up the image of Abraham and Isaac as a discomforting illustration of it. It is an allusion made all the more ironic by his lack of commitment to the God to whom he feels he is sacrificing his son.

Immediately following this recollection, the narrative quickly underscores the theme of the contorted relationships of fathers and sons by offering news of another lost son. A telephone call from Chickie Phelan informs Martin that at some point during the previous night someone kidnapped Charlie Boy McCall. To confirm Chickie's tip and gather more information, Martin visits the McCall clan at Patsy McCall's home and gives them his assurance that no story of the kidnapping will appear in his paper, the *Albany Times-Union*. Ostensibly, he is behaving like a newspaper man, but he also assumes an archetypal role that recurs throughout the novel. He is the surrogate father, trying to assist in the recovery of the lost child. (Here and later, the narrative plays with analogies to Christ, the Good Shepherd always in search of lost sheep as well as the Lamb of God and the sacrificial Lamb.)

The visit does more than advance themes of paternity, for it allows Martin also to affirm his communal identity. From the moment that he parks his car opposite the empty lot on Colonie Street, where his parents' home once stood (it was destroyed in a fire that Kennedy describes in detail in *The Flaming Corsage*), he encounters evidence of his past affiliations with the neighborhood as well as contrary signs of his current alienation from the community. He meets the McCalls as childhood friends yet also as men who control the city where he works. He speaks to them of Charlie Boy's kidnapping in a stilted dialogue that does little to hide what he means to say, yet always observes the convention of never saying it directly. In the end, the McCalls reaffirm the connections of a lifetime with the clichéd parochialism that marks them as much as it does Martin: "You're all right, Martin. . . . For a North Ender" (Kennedy 1978, 32).

Martin Daugherty's peregrinations introduce the reader to the cultural geography of Albany, and in the novel's opening sections the narrative rarely allows him to move directly from one location to another without the intervention of a topical digression. After talking to the McCalls, Martin drives downtown, but he does not immediately go to the *Times-Union* newspaper offices. Instead he walks to Spanish George's bar, a dive on the south end of the downtown area. There by chance he runs into Francis Phelan. Francis has been on the bum for twenty-two years, a father who has deserted his family because of his inadvertent role in the death of his infant son Gerald. Francis has returned to Albany only because he wishes to earn some money by voting multiple times in the upcoming local election. Although both men share problematic records as fathers, Francis, the uneducated man of action, seems the antithesis of Martin in all other respects.

Nonetheless, as Martin recalls, a number of events bind them. During the 1901 Albany trolley car strike, Francis threw a stone that killed a scab driver. The incident became the basis of one of Martin's father's more popular plays, *The Car Barns*. There is a closer tie, however, between these men whose homes were once situated next door to one another on Colonie Street. They share intermingled family histories, including the seduction of the teenage Francis by Martin's mother Kristina. Now both stand self-exiled from the old neighborhood.[6]

Although Martin's meeting with Francis illustrates the influence of place on characters' lives, events always return the reader's attention to the centrality of gaming in the novel. When Martin goes to the newspaper office, he yields to an impulse that grows out of a prescient sense alluded to in the previous chapter of the novel. He checks the racing form for horses with derivations of *Charlie* in their names and then makes a bet with Billy Phelan on a three-horse parlay based on that name. That longshot wager—so unlikely as to be capricious—and the consequences of its success become a force that impels action for the rest of the narrative. It calls to mind an equally impetuous gesture Martin made earlier to the McCalls, the promise to keep the news of Charlie Boy's kidnapping out of the papers. Although it goes against the fundamental aims of his profession, Martin warns Freddie Dunsbach of the United Press off the story and gets Emory Jones, his editor, to agree to impose a news blackout. As with his three-horse parlay, instinct and decisiveness—two attributes of any successful player—lead him into the right course of action.

One needs, however, to view such analogies with care, for the narrative will not allow concepts of gaming to become defined in simplistic terms. *Billy Phelan's Greatest Game* makes clear distinctions between those who gamble as an end and those who use it as a means, and the narrative artfully traces the impact of those distinct attitudes. Billy Phelan in particular distinguishes himself as one fully conversant in the gaming culture, but in his case winning or losing has only secondary importance. His real desire rests simply on playing the game.[7] In consequence, instinct and decisiveness create problems for him as easily as they alleviate them.

A narrative flashback illuminates this difficulty. Ostensibly about Billy becoming involved with Angie Velez, it turns on an anecdote that recounts how Billy lost a job at a crap table at a Saratoga gambling club for making a sarcastic remark to Paul Whiteman, the bandleader. Whiteman had provoked Billy by treating him in a dismissive fashion. For Billy, Whiteman's offhanded insult carried a great deal of weight. It denied Billy's status as a player and relegated him instead to the role of a functionary. Because Billy ties his identity to gaming, he could not ignore any slight that questioned that identity. This demeanor marks him as very different from Morrie Berman, a man who shows in his exchange with Charlie Boy a willingness to temper dignity with pragmatism. Time and again in the novel, Billy plays the part of a wise guy, but unlike Morrie he never behaves like a punk.

The news that all three of Martin Daugherty's horses have won their respective races provides evidence of this distinction. In consequence of the bet, Billy owes Martin nearly eight hundred dollars. It is money that Billy does not have, and he spends the afternoon at home mulling over ways of raising it. Again in contrast to Morrie, an ethical code shapes Billy's response to the situation. As he tells Bindy McCall, "I pay my debts" (61). Morrie, on the other hand, allows no set of values to guide his behavior. Thus, after his heavy-handed condolences over the death of Scotty Streck, he compounds the sin of being a bad winner by participating in the kidnapping of Charlie Boy. The narrative, however, does not deal in black and white, and just as it enforces the differences between Billy and Morrie, it shows that they share many of the same flaws.

In pursuit of money, Billy goes downtown to collect a debt, hustle some pool, and get into a poker game. On his first stop, at the Grand Lunch, Billy meets his uncle Chickie, the man who first told Martin Daugherty of Charlie Boy's kidnapping. Billy's exchange with Chickie highlights the animosity Billy feels toward the entire Phelan family because of his sense that they have treated his father badly. In consequence, he behaves like an immature young man with a grudge he can only imperfectly articulate. "I know how he [Francis Phelan] was treated, and how I was treated because of him" (83). At the same time, while in the restaurant, Billy confronts and disarms young Eddie Saunders, an unbalanced boy who is threatening everyone with a knife. Both his rudeness to Chickie Phelan and his courage in dealing with Eddie Saunders seem like reflex acts, done without deep thought or clear purpose. Nonetheless, each gesture demonstrates aspects inherent in his nature.

Lest one assume a connection between the courage Billy has displayed and a nobility of spirit, the narrative is quick to show his predatory nature. From the diner, Billy goes to Louie's pool room, where he hustles an inept player, Harvey Hess—the first step in his efforts to accumulate enough money to pay off Martin Daugherty's improbable bet. The narrative carefully outlines the steps Billy goes through to ensure that he beats Harvey decisively yet still keeps him interested in playing future games. In the process, one comes to see the mixture of pride and loathing that shapes the attitudes of a person who makes money by tricking a man into betting on skills that he does not have: "Billy's impulse was to throw the game, double the bet, clean out Harvey's wallet entirely, take away his savings account, his life insurance, his mortgage money, his piggy bank. But you don't give them that edge even once: I beat Billy Phelan last week. No edge for bums" (91). Although Billy himself does not realize it, the source of his anger comes from a subconscious sense that only marginal differences obtain between Morrie Berman, Harvey Hess, and himself. Throughout the novel, he walks the thin line between being a punk and a bum, and as events show late in the narrative, maintaining his equilibrium will always be a precarious business.

The scene shifts to Becker's, a bar where Martin Daugherty is contemplating the August 1932 photo of Becker's thirtieth anniversary outing, a picnic at Picard's Grove. Once again, the narrative uses a seemingly mundane artifact to illustrate the force exerted by cultural identity on individuals in the novel. This photograph, enlarged and framed by Emil Becker, the bar's original owner, has become a memento mori, for when each individual in the picture dies, he receives a gold star on his chest and a check mark next to his name in a framed list also hanging on the wall. The photo becomes a recurring image throughout the novel as violence claims the lives of many of those mentioned in the narrative. It also provides a neat summary of the Albany milieu in which the work is set. Although the men in the picture now occupy a range of social positions, they share a common working-class origin. Further, they all also associate themselves with Albany's night world. At the same time, diverse and often conflicting aims drive them and provide the source of the action of the novel.

Martin Daugherty has come to Becker's Saloon trying to get information about the kidnapping of Charlie Boy McCall. When Billy Phelan arrives at the bar, he learns that events have involved him in the kidnapping as well. The McCalls have published a coded message to the kidnappers in which they have listed men who would serve as go-betweens for the family's negotiations to free Charlie Boy. Billy finds his name among the group, and he fears that the McCalls see him as some sort of accessory to the crime. Martin complicates Billy's situation by telling him that Patsy McCall suspects that Morrie Berman has some involvement in the kidnapping and that Patsy wants Billy to report on anything that Morrie might say relating to Charlie Boy.

> "Did [Patsy McCall] ask you to snoop around Morrie Berman?"
> "No. He asked me to ask you to do that."
> "Me? He wants me to be some kind of stoolie? What the hell's the matter with you, Martin?"
> "I'm not aware that anything's the matter."
> "I'm not one of the McCalls' political whores."
> "Nobody said you were. I told him you wouldn't like the idea, but I also know you've been friendly with Charlie McCall all your life. Right now, he could be strapped to a bed someplace with a gun at this head. He could even be dead." (105)

Through this exchange, Martin Daugherty does more than simply pass along a message: he gives the young man a lesson on the finer points of the often contradictory ethical system that governs both of them. Billy would like to see things in simple either/or terms: a stoolie or not a stoolie. Martin reminds Billy of a more complex set of relations that—depending on the context—radically changes the way one behaves and how one judges that behavior.

After leaving Billy, Martin wanders over to the offices of the Albany Labor Party (A.L.P.), an ineffectual socialist organization that has sprung out of the conflicting attitudes of disaffection for the local Democrats and admiration for the national party responsible for implementing Roosevelt's New Deal. The McCall machine, which for a few years has tolerated the A.L.P., has recently decided to absorb it by sending hundreds of Democratic Party functionaries to register in the organization. This move has co-opted the party and taken its chairman, Jake Berman (Morrie's father) and other regulars completely by surprise. The scene that confronts Martin illuminates both the political and ethnic realities of Albany life.

As a newspaper reporter, Martin simply wants to get quotable statements from Jake Berman and the others regarding the takeover of their organization by the McCall machine. They respond with understandably bitter invectives, but Kennedy takes their predicable resentment a step further, giving it a form that shows the complexity of the Albany world he has created in his novels. Despite their high-minded political views, when confronted with frustrating, even humiliating defeat, the men at A.L.P. headquarters fall back on the same gutter language favored by those over whom they claim moral superiority. They no longer stand simply as types, admirable paragons of a reformist mentality. Rather, the common human feelings of anger and frustration bring out equally common human responses of separatist hatred. Specifically, the insults hurled at the McCalls and the Democratic machine are filled with sexual, ethnic, and religious slurs that expose the speakers as being as bigoted as those whom they catalog as oppressors. "Fat old Irishmen who loathe us, drunken bums from the gutter, little German hausfraus enrolling with us" (111). "And you can tell the Irish in this town to go fuck a duck" (112). "[P]riests no better than the fascist-dog Catholics who kiss the boots of Franco and Mussolini" (112). The tirade does not expose these men as bad human beings, only as complicated and flawed characters, like the rest of us.

Indeed, Kennedy's descriptions throughout his writing consistently work so well because he does not impose artificial differences on human beings. In his world—as in ours—political liberals labor under the same types of biases and intolerance as political conservatives. Individuals crusading for governmental reform resort to the same low characterizations given by those against whom they rail. This polemic approach punctuates the book, but through deft deflation of its moral authority Kennedy avoids simplistic charges of authorial racism:

> "He's got the luck of the fuckin' Irish," Lemon said.
> "Be careful what you say about the Irish," Footers said. "There's Jews in this game."
> "So what? I'm a Jew."
> "You're not a Jew, Lemon. You're an asshole." (124)

In the end, Kennedy wonderfully conveys the singular impotence of mere invective. In his world, as in the work of writers such as Hemingway, language unsupported by action or by the willingness to take responsibility highlights a degraded nature.

While Martin is receiving abuse from Jake Berman, Billy Phelan is trying to win enough money playing poker to cover his gambling debt. As in every contest between men in the novel (indeed as in every interaction), a very definite though unarticulated ethical standard shapes the action. The opening scene of the game (117–23) features a silent exchange between Billy and Bump Oliver, a card cheat. Billy disapproves of cheating but not for the conventional reason that it breaks the seventh commandment that he learned in religious instruction at Sacred Heart Church (see *Ironweed*, Kennedy 1983a, 148). Rather, cheating cuts off the person who engages in it from people who play games: "Because cheaters, you see, already know how it's going to end, and what the hell good is that?" (117). Billy values his position as part of the gaming community: men who play games with the same commitment that any principled individual makes to his life's work. Bump stands outside that society.

Over a series of hands, Billy makes it clear through glances, gestures, and offhand remarks that he knows that Bump is manipulating the cards. Once Billy makes this point, Bump acknowledges his understanding by quietly folding and leaving the game. No one else seems aware of what has occurred, and Billy bears Bump no malice. He simply does not want to be cheated out of his money.

> Billy saw a cheater caught once: a salesman who played in Corky Ronan's clubroom on Van Woert Street. . . . Joe Dembski reached over and punched the cheater on the side of the neck, and the others were ready to

> move in for their licks, but Corky said never mind that, just take his money
> and he won't come back. . . . Corky's idea was that everybody's got a trade,
> and that's Billy's idea too, now. (117–18)

That "now" stands as the most important word in the quotation. It marks
Billy as an evolving player, one who wants to be part of that world and one
who consequently wishes to master the subtleties of his society. However,
whether the final word indicates that Billy feels that he has finally matured
into this position or that he sees this view as transitional remains for the
reader to decide.

In either case, the game shows the importance that Billy and his world
attach to rules and to the pleasure of the game. Near the end of one of the
hands, while waiting for Billy to bet, one of the players, Lemon Lewis,
shows his cards and claims the pot with a flush. Billy, however, makes a final
bet, forty dollars.

> "Well that's a hell of a how-do-you-do," Lemon said. "I turn my hand
> over and show you I got a four flush."
> "Yes, you did that. And then I bet you forty dollars. You want to play
> five cards open, that's okay by me. But, Lemon, my word to you is still
> four-oh."
> "You're bluffing, Phelan."
> "You could find out." (121)

As everyone waits for Lemon to decide, the narrative offers a glimpse of how
Billy responds to the rising tension of the moment. "[H]e was really feeling
the sweet pressure, and had been, all through the hand: rising, rising. . . . It
was so great he was almost ready to cream. Goddamn, life is fun, ain't it
Billy? Win or lose, you're in the mix" (122). The need for this sort of participation sets Billy apart from cheaters like Bump, and it stands as his central
concern throughout the novel. The need to be "part of the mix" demonstrates an impulse toward community that functions as an essential part of
his nature. In contrast to people like his father, Francis, or the gangster Jack
Diamond, Billy derives his identity from the milieu in which he exists.

Lemon, who lacks Billy's appetite for the game, folds, and moments
later the narrative offers another instance of the consequences of operating
outside the protocols of play. A young boy with a gun bursts into the room
and attempts to rob the gamblers. As he has done already several times this

night, Billy Phelan refuses to be intimidated by threats of violence or to give up money that he feels rightfully belongs to him. In the face of Billy's defiance, the boy does not know how to respond. He is caught off guard by the other players, beaten, and thrown outside. As the boy runs away, Bud Bradt, one of the men who helped to subdue the boy, and Martin Daugherty make final comments on the event.

> "Didn't kick him enough," Bud said. "The son of a bitch can still run. But he'll think twice before he does that again."
> "Or shoot somebody first to make his point."
> "Yeah, there's that." (127)

Martin's comment offers keen insight into the world of gaming that he inhabits. Though not a brutal man himself, Martin, like Marcus Gorman in *Legs*, has a fascination with men who live violent lives. As his comment above demonstrates, however, he has an unblinking ability to confront the full consequences of such violence. On the other hand, Billy sees the situation at a far more simplistic level. He explains his apparent heroism in purely pragmatic terms. He is deeply in debt, trying to win enough to cover gambling loses, so "I just wasn't ready to hand over a night's work to that drippy little bastard" (128).

Of course, a logic and consistency informs Billy's actions. As noted above, he gives allegiance to an unwritten code that governs his behavior. Up to this point in the narration, he has in his own fashion stuck admirably to that code, and as the opening of chapter 8 attests, this adherence has earned for him the respect that is so much a part of the identity he craves: "No man who wore socks in Albany felt better in the nighttime than Billy Phelan, walking with a couple of pals along his own Broadway from Nick's card game to Union Station to get the papers" (131). Later in the novel, when the McCalls have made Billy a persona non grata all over Albany, this ability to feel accepted in the heart of Albany's night district stands out as a crucial need for Billy's psyche.

Billy, Morrie Berman, and Martin Daugherty go off to Becker's for steaks (paid for by the proprietor of the card game, Nick Levine, as a reward for foiling the robbery). Morrie and Billy reminisce about Edward "Honey" Curry and Hubert Maloy, two thugs who specialize in holdups. Both the dialogue and the narrative make clear Billy's position on the fringe of the underworld. He occupies the role of someone who associates with gangsters but who still stands apart from them. He says as much to Martin Daugherty when he first learns that the McCalls have put his name on the go-between list: "I don't belong on that list. That's either connected people or hoodlums. I pay off the ward leader, nickel and dime, and I vote the ticket, that's my connection. And I never handled a gun in my life" (100). Billy's ties to the kidnapping of Charlie Boy, however, go deeper than he suspects, and because the McCalls want to exploit his links to Morrie Berman, whom they see as involved in Charlie Boy's disappearance, they summon Billy to Patsy's house on Colonie Street.

Billy's trip to Colonie Street provides the narrative with the opportunity to digress, to remind readers of the cultural context from which Billy, the Phelans, the McCalls, the Daughertys, and others in the novel have emerged. It also permits the narrative to give readers a sense of the long history of the city of Albany, founded by the Dutch in 1630 as the "vast medieval demesne . . . [of] an Amsterdam pearl merchant named Kiliaen Van Rensselaer, who was also known as the First Patroon, the absentee landlord who bought from five tribes of Indians some seven hundred thousand acres of land" (145). The narrative goes on to chronicle the rise of the Irish in North Albany and Arbor Hill, steadily moving toward and then into the city's nineteenth-century middle class. With this movement came a concurrent development of political power. As the McCalls solidified that power in the early twentieth century, Patsy and his brothers took over the patriarchal role established by the first patroon.

Billy's meeting with the McCalls traces a complex series of conjunctions and divergences. Their backgrounds are so similar that many of the same values naturally inform their lives. At the same time, Billy also feels himself set squarely outside of the world of the McCalls, in part because of his own political naïveté and in part because of his father's desertion of the family in 1916 and the subsequent changes that his branch of the Phelans underwent. (Francis Phelan's departure from Albany marks the culmination of a series of events to which Kennedy refers throughout his Albany novels, but which he examines in detail in the next book in the series, *Ironweed*.)

The confrontation that results from the meeting revolves around loyalties. The McCalls want Billy to keep an eye on Morrie Berman and report to them anything noteworthy that he says. They take their status as political and social leaders of the Irish American community in Albany as analogous to heads of a sept—the ancient Irish clan. They presume that other members of that community will show them unquestioned allegiance. Billy, on the other hand, sees himself as a member of another community—the gamblers and hustlers of the Downtown—and he feels greater loyalty to that group than to the McCalls. The meeting ends with Billy still unsure of how to respond. He instinctively recoils from the idea of spying on Berman, yet he remains acutely aware of the power that the McCalls wield: "All anybody on Broadway needed to hear was that Billy was kinking on Morrie. . . . Who'd trust him after that? Who'd tell him a secret? Who'd lend him a quarter? He wouldn't have a friend on the whole fucking street. It'd be the dead end of Billy's world, all he ever lived for, and the McCalls were asking him to risk that. Asking hell, telling him" (156). As that final sentence makes clear, even as Billy considers what he would lose by cooperation, he is also fully aware that the influence of the McCalls extends beyond him to his whole family and that their enmity could have lasting repercussions. (Patsy Mc-Call has already signaled as much by making reference to Billy's brother-in-law, George Quinn, who is running an unsanctioned bookie operation.)

A scene that immediately follows, this time focusing on male/female relations, reinforces for the reader Billy's sense of the importance of loyalty. His mistress, Angie Velez, tells him that she has recently had an abortion. When Billy becomes upset over her decision to end the life of a child that he sees as his as well as hers, Angie asserts that she has not had an abortion but rather is pregnant. She says that she made up the first story only to test his commitment to having a child. Though Angie claims that she has slept with her husband after learning of her pregnancy (so that she can tell her husband that the child is his), Billy assures her that he will assume responsibility and publicly acknowledge his paternity. Angie then admits that this too was a test of his loyalty and that she is not in fact pregnant. "I needed to know what you felt, Billy" (168). Given Billy's avidity for games, his steadiness in situations characterized by extreme pressure, and his skill at reading the intentions of other players, the exchange with Angie seems forced, but that different tone may well reflect that although Billy truly understands male society, women remain for him enigmatic.

The next chapter offers a contrasting view of male/female relations by representing Martin Daugherty's dealings with women. Billy can sense cunning and read chicanery when someone deploys these tactics in an attempt to mask the facts, but he finds himself stymied when confronted by a situation in which clarity does not lie buried somewhere beneath obfuscation. Martin, on the other hand, has spent his adult life accommodating himself to the prospect of not being able to resolve his world into simple either/or conditions. A brief bout of sleeplessness illustrates this situation by high-lighting a more complex pattern of associations than the ones that torment Billy. Martin thinks about his troubled attitude toward a variety of commit-ments: religious faith, his son, and his fixation with Melissa Spencer, a women who has been his father's mistress. He finds sleep by compartmen-talizing his concerns. He brackets the seemingly irresolveable issues of faith and fatherhood, and determines to exorcize his obsessions with Melissa in a rather methodical fashion. He will go to the local performance of his father's play, *The Flaming Corsage*, to see Melissa as the fictionalized version of his mother Katrina, and then he will find a way to have sexual intercourse with her. Here, too, despite Martin's sophisticated ability to live with ambiguity, there is never a sense of his engaging the complexity of women in any way similar to his involvement with the intricacies of gambling.[8]

The fascination with sport comes across clearly through the narrative, which never strays very far from images of gaming. The last pool match in Daddy Big's round robin takes place on the same night that Martin plans to see *The Flaming Corsage*, and it serves to illuminate yet another protocol of playing. In that final game, the narrative alerts us to a shift in perspective as it highlights Billy Phelan purposely losing to Doc Fay: "Billy is acting. He has just begun to throw his first match" (179). Of course, once Billy has made up his mind to lose the contest, it ceases to be a game, and Billy be-comes an inverted version of Bump Oliver, the card cheat whose behavior had so mystified him the previous night. Though Billy rigs his match to lose rather than to win, both men have given up the pleasure conveyed by the uncertainty of the game for the assurance of knowing its outcome.

In the middle of the contest, the lights go out all over the city, and for once the narrative does not present a full description of the game in progress. Although the narrative calls this disruption a power failure, in fact city workers shut off the electricity at the McCalls' orders. They do not wish people to hear a radio speech by Tom Dewey denouncing the Albany Dem-ocratic political organization.[9] (Ever sensitive to the power of negative opinion, the McCalls have notified all hospitals in advance not to begin any operations unless they have backup power.) Without the illumination that has become a characterizing feature of the twentieth-century city, an animal fear permeates Albany once the city lights go off. "[U]p at Haramanus Bleecker Hall the audience had panicked when the lights went out. People shoved one another and Tip Mooney was knocked down and trampled" (186).

The darkened city intensifies inclinations toward violence in Morrie, Billy, and Martin. They visit a Cuban pimp with two whores.[10] After Morrie has had intercourse with one of the whores, the pimp assures the men that he can testify to her ability to give pleasure because she is his sister. The insinuation of incest outrages Billy. He beats the man, and Morrie joins in, wrecking the pimp's apartment in the process. After calmly witnessing the mayhem, Martin "stood up and opened his fly, then urinated on the pimp's feet" (192).

Complex personal attitudes underlie the motivation for this brutality. For Billy and Morrie, the change in the city's atmosphere plays on instinctual fears. Violence acts as a way of responding to horrors they do not fully comprehend. Martin, who sees fuller implications in the pimp's assertion, responds with a premeditated and calculated act of degradation. The fact that his gesture comes while the pimp lies incapable of defending himself drains the act of any righteousness. Although Martin may feel that he is asserting his moral superiority, he is in fact simply taking advantage of his place in the pecking order.

Having a drink with Martin after this incident, Billy reveals his own sense of the protocols of the game by confessing that he purposely lost the pool match that he played earlier. Because Morrie Berman bet on Billy and would have given Billy a share of the winnings, throwing the contest served as a way of avoiding falling under any further obligation to Morrie. Readers sensitive to Billy's nature will easily comprehend this gesture, for Billy sees himself as a communal animal. He defines himself in part by his relations with others, but he also has a very clear sense of how he wishes those relations to be structured. In dealing with Morrie and the McCalls, Billy finds that he has at best very limited control over how those relationships play out. Ultimately, thinking he is passing along fabricated information and thus not squealing, Billy will tell Bindy McCall that Morrie has intimated that Malloy (possibly one of the kidnappers) is in New Jersey, but he refuses to continue spying on Berman. "I can't do this no more, Bin. I ain't cut out to be a squealer." Bindy's response sums up the stark either/or realities of the McCalls' Albany: "All right, hotshot, you're all by yourself" (198).

The next morning Martin Daugherty visits Melissa Spencer in an episode that parallels Billy's earlier assignation with Angie. The rendezvous provides the occasion for an account of the three-day liaison that Martin had with Melissa in 1928. Although the narrative identifies the earlier event as a watershed in Martin's life, it does not offer a very clear explanation for the ostensibly transformative impact of adultery. Part of the problem, of course, comes from Martin's nature. Like Billy Phelan and so many others portrayed in the novel, Martin sustains a dual role as man-child, and one cannot always accurately measure his behavior by holding it against the standard that one would apply to an adult. Martin's attraction for his father's former mistress certainly makes an implicit commentary on his psychological disposition and, to a degree, on hers, and their approach to sex touches on their level of maturity. For their rendezvous, she has shaved her pubic hair into the shape of a heart, and he has tied a ribbon around his penis. They resemble nothing so much as middle-age children playing at being naughty while also striving for approval from adults.

> Martin sensed the presence of his parents in the room, not as flaming balls of tow this time, but as a happy couple, holding hands and watching him do diddle with Melissa for them, just as he had once done proud piddle for them in his personal pot. Clearly, they saw him as the redeemer of all their misalliances, the conqueror of incoherence, the spirit of synthesis in an anarchic family. Martin, in the consanguineous saddle, was their link with love past and future, a figure of generational communion, the father of a son en route to the priesthood, the functioning father of the senile Edward. More than that he had, here, obviously become his own father. . . . Lost son of a lost father, he was now fatherhood incarnate. (213–14)[11]

Intercourse with Melissa becomes a purgative rather than a developmental experience for Martin.

That afternoon Billy Phelan also undertakes a kind of purgation. Martin tells Billy that his father has been arrested on charges of voting fraud. Billy bails Francis out of jail with a large portion of the stake that he has accumulated to pay his gambling debt and then accompanies Martin and Francis to Lombardo's, an Italian restaurant. Over drinks, Francis learns that Annie, Billy's mother and Francis's wife, has never told anyone that the reason Francis left home in 1916 was that on that day, while holding his youngest child, Gerald, the child slipped through his diaper out of Francis's hands, hit the floor, and died from the fall. Francis has always held himself responsible, and he is touched by the revelation that his wife (who in fact does not believe that the accident was his fault) has revealed his involvement to no one. Billy asks his father for advice about cooperating with the McCalls and is disappointed with the pragmatic advice that he receives. "He thinks it's all right to fink. . . . How could he tell me to rat on a friend?" (226). Like Martin Daugherty, Billy Phelan has been searching for a father, yet when one appears, he is painfully conscious of Francis's inability to fulfill that role.

After Francis has left the restaurant, Martin tells Billy the story (that will be repeated in and form the narrative center of *Ironweed*) about Francis throwing a stone that killed a scab trolley car driver during a strike in 1901. Martin, Patsy McCall, and Chickie Phelan all helped Francis get out of town on that day and then swore an oath (sealed in cat's blood) to keep silent. "We swear by the heart of Bid Finnerty's cat that we won't say what we know about Francis Phelan as long as we live, and that we won't wash this sacrificial blood off our hands until it's time to eat supper" (228). The story explains to a degree Francis's own deficiencies as a father, for he has always preferred absence to presence when dealing with a difficult situation. It also reminds readers of how communal ties in Albany begin early and cross generations.

When Martin returns to the paper, he finds that Patsy McCall wants to meet him. Patsy tells Martin that the kidnappers have picked Morrie Berman as a go-between and that this choice has convinced Patsy of Morrie's involvement in the kidnapping. Patsy calls on Martin to assume the role that Billy Phelan has rejected and to accompany Morrie to New York on the mission to retrieve Charlie Boy. "If he's their man, you're ours. And take care of Charlie when you get to him" (231). With this, Patsy offers Martin a second chance of sorts: serving in the capacity of father surrogate for a not so young man—Charlie Boy—gives Martin the opportunity to move from the man-child role that he has just acted out with Melissa Spencer to the position of full-fledged adult. Patsy and Martin meet Morrie in Washington Park, and the latter two go off to New York to face the kidnappers. The setting recalls for Martin a time in 1921 when he walked there with his father, and the older man used a crimson maple leaf to make the argument that God has a plan for the universe.[12]

While Martin and Morrie make their way to New York, Billy Phelan learns that the McCalls have put out the word that he is not allowed to drink or gamble anywhere in the city. As he walks around Albany, being turned out of one place after another, he feels perhaps the deepest sense of isolation that he has ever encountered. Kennedy sketches these scenes masterfully, managing to capture Billy's pathos without losing the proper perspective for describing how this limited young man would absorb such a blow. Billy is not a deep thinker, nor does he have a sophisticated awareness of the forces that shape his nature. Nonetheless, the sheer force of these cumulative rejections produces in him a poignant sense of his own dependence on a society. From this feeling of alienation, his thoughts turn to his father.

> When Billy's father was gone for a year, his Uncle Chick told him he might never come back and that Billy would pretty soon forget his father and develop all sorts of substitutes, because that was how it went in life. Chick was trying to be kind to Billy with that advice. Chick wasn't as bad as the rest of them. And did Billy develop substitutes for his father? Well, he learned how to gamble. He got to know Broadway. (243)

At this moment of despair, when Broadway is closed to him, Billy turns back to Francis Phelan: "He wanted to see his father and ask him again to come home" (243). Pursuing that idea, he wanders into Spanish George's and finds his father passed out at a table. With him is Helen Archer, a woman who will figure prominently in *Ironweed*. Although the unconscious Francis can offer no material help, his image turns Billy's thoughts back to the family's reaction upon learning that Francis is in Albany. He specifically recollects his mother's plea to Billy and Peg to try to understand their father. "[W]hen a good man dies, it's reason to weep, and [Francis] died that day [that he dropped his infant son Gerald] and we wept and he went away and buried himself and he's dead now, dead and can't be resurrected. So don't hate him and don't worry him, and try to understand that not everything that happens on earth has a reason behind it that we can find in the prayer book" (250). At this stage, Billy cannot resurrect the old Francis, but he can provide a measure of comfort to the one who is before him. As often happens in Kennedy's novels, the father-son role is reversed as Billy gives Helen fifty-seven dollars, all the money he has in his pocket, and leaves.

Billy's gesture is as much an act of defiance as one of generosity. To a large degree, money defines status on the streets of Albany. In divesting himself of money, Billy temporarily steps out of that culture into a world closer to the one that his father inhabits. Walking aimlessly around Broadway, Billy sees Martin Daugherty's story about him in the *Times-Union*. "He turned to Martin's column and read about himself. A gamester who accepts the rules and plays by them, but who also plays above them. Billy doesn't care about money. A healthy man without need for artifice or mysticism"

(252). Although in some ways, Martin's story neatly captures Billy's nature, it outlines a way of life that the young man himself is not capable of recognizing. "What the hell was Martin talking about? Whose rules? And what the hell was that about money? How can anybody not care about money? Who gets along without it? Martin is half crazy, a spooky bird. What is that stuff about mysticism? I still believe in God. I still go to the front" (252). In this moment of confusion, Billy, blackballed by the McCalls and confronted by an alien portrait of himself, cannot fall back on accustomed venues to confirm his sense of self. Instead, he borrows twenty dollars, buys some liquor from a bootlegger, and goes down to the river to drink. Waking up after passing out by the river, Billy goes home to find that the police have visited his house, and his brother-in-law has gone to Troy to lay low until the coast is clear.

In New York, Morrie and Martin get Charlie Boy from the kidnappers. Eight hours later the police arrest Morrie, and the McCalls learn from him that Curry and Malloy were among the others involved. The day after Charlie Boy's return home, Curry is shot dead and Malloy wounded in a gun battle with police in Newark. Kennedy neatly absolves all involved, however, from contributing to the death of Curry, for the narrative lays that death to a last-minute decision to stop in Newark rather than drive to Rhode Island at a late hour. "None of the kidnappers had been in Newark before, during, or after the kidnapping. None of them had any way of knowing that the hangouts of criminals in that city had been under the most intensive surveillance for several days" (271).

The story does not end with Charlie Boy's liberation, for the McCalls still hold a grudge against Billy Phelan for his reluctance to cooperate fully in finding the kidnappers. When Martin Daugherty learns of Billy's ostracization, he appeals directly to Patsy McCall to redress this wrong. Patsy dismisses Martin's request, so Martin, with the help of Damon Runyon, prints a column detailing Billy's aid in supplying information that contributed to finding the kidnappers of Charlie Boy and upbraiding the McCalls for ingratitude. The consequent uproar leads to Billy's reinstatement on Broadway and brings the novel to a conclusion, but the thrust of its narrative has laid the groundwork for a more profound examination of human nature in Kennedy's next novel, *Ironweed*.

The issue of identity has raised troubling concerns throughout the narrative of *Billy Phelan's Greatest Game*. When someone, such as Billy, links his

sense of self completely to his connection with the community, any weak-
ening of the bonds between individual and society will profoundly threaten
the integrity of that individual's nature. *Ironweed* presents someone with an
antithetical approach to defining the self. Francis Phelan has turned his back
on society and all of its institutions, and his quest to establish an identity
based solely on validation from within informs the action of that work.

 CHAPTER FIVE

Ironweed and the Consequences of Resurrection

William Kennedy published *Ironweed* in 1983, and its appearance marked both a creative and a commercial turning point in his literary career.[1] The initial public response to the novel made it an immediate best seller, and literary critics in turn quickly recognized the third book in the Albany cycle as more than simply a popular success. *Ironweed* brought Kennedy a Pulitzer Prize for fiction, which drew attention to earlier writing that heretofore had received little notice. In particular, the notoriety of *Ironweed* inspired a renewed interest in *Legs* and *Billy Phelan's Greatest Game*, making readers aware of the breadth of Kennedy's talent and according both novels long-overdue acclaim. More significantly, from an interpretive point of view, availability of all three works made people cognizant, through readings of the Albany cycle, of the depth and scope of Kennedy's imaginative power.

Nonetheless, although one cannot ignore the substantial creative force of both *Legs* and *Billy Phelan's Greatest Game*, *Ironweed* indisputably stands out as the definitive work in Kennedy's canon to this point. Its plot, centering on a search for spiritual identity, and its characterizations, highlighting the profundity within individuals superficially devoid of all complexity, show him to be much more than a local writer with merely regional appeal. Rather, just as Joyce does in his narrative of turn-of-the-century Dublin in *Ulysses*, Kennedy highlights issues of universal interest brought out by a discourse on particular people and events with his accounts of Depression-era Albany in *Ironweed*. A number of studies illustrate the scope of the novel by taking a look at its classical allusions.[2] Although noting such references is an important interpretive gesture, the broad appeal of *Ironweed*, as I demonstrate in this chapter, comes more directly from its evocation of the pathos in ordi-

nary life. Thus, in its meticulous attention to the details of everyday existence and through its provocative evocation of the general human strengths
and weaknesses embodied in its characters, *Ironweed* legitimizes the cycle of
novels that have grown out of the complex familial and ethnic connections
centered in a small upstate New York city (the second-oldest colonial city in
North America).

Beyond solidifying the fundamental aesthetic elements that vivify the
Albany cycle of Kennedy's writing, however, *Ironweed* also shows the significant creative strides he made as he matured as a writer. The book draws on
the same types of working-class figures and details of urban history characterizing the two previous novels, but it does so with an enhanced awareness
of their potential for development.[3] In its characterization, its plot line, and
its narrative approach, *Ironweed* attests to an intensification of the creative
force already apparent in Kennedy's earlier works. Having read this novel,
one can go back to *Legs* and *Billy Phelan's Greatest Game* with a subtler sense of
their broad purpose. Taken together, they do not so much lay down a prescriptive narrative pattern of subsequent books in the cycle as articulate the
rich cultural background from which the diverse individuals of Kennedy's
novels emerge.

Further, Kennedy's narrative strategy in *Ironweed* significantly augments
the examinations of an individuals' relations with society that characterize
the two preceding Albany novels.[4] Instead of settling for another recapitula-
tion of the modernist/postmodernist struggle for identity within an alienated and alienating culture, the novel foregrounds metaphysics and takes up
the more subjective issue of self-knowledge, and its exploration of a series of
diverse representations of faith—both the specific religious concept and the
more general view of belief—exemplifies the emergence of this new approach. The narrative's contrasting views of Helen Archer and Francis Phelan amply illustrate Kennedy's inclination to engage the intricacies of this
issue, and readers seeking to discern the narrative's meaning from the discourse need both to acknowledge the presence of Catholic dogma and to
avoid any inhibiting categorization that would come from seeing this work
as simply a Catholic novel.

Once again, analogies with Joyce provide a useful means for comprehending Kennedy's achievement. In *Ironweed*, as in Joyce's works, Catholicism occupies part of the imaginative makeup of many of the book's
characters. Likewise, simple faith (though not necessarily belief in Catholic
dogma) also emerges as an important feature of individual identity. Above

all, however, the way that the act of belief, rather than the adherence to a specific doctrine, shapes a character stands as the mystery that Kennedy wishes to engage. This chapter seeks to trace that involvement and to offer the reader strategies for reconciling the diverse elements that this compositional approach produces without blurring their distinctiveness.

Personalized religious associations emerge early in *Ironweed*. Even before the narrative begins, one encounters an epigraph from Dante's *Purgatorio* that combines the impulse for transcendence with an implicit confidence in the power of the intellect: "To course o'er better waters now hoists sail the little bark of my wit, leaving behind her a sea so cruel." Using iconography to build on literary allusion, the novel opens on the outskirts of Albany in Saint Agnes Cemetery on Halloween Day, 1938.[5] These markers and the mordant tone evoked by the subsequent discourse that takes place among the dead in the first chapter make plain for the reader the novel's prominent concern with both the reality of physical demise and the Christian promise of spiritual resurrection.

This concern reflects a more overt regard for metaphysics than anything in Kennedy's previous writing, and stylistic changes complement this thematic shift. With a gesture that reveals a willingness to go beyond the social realism that gives so much strength to the narratives of the two previous novels, Kennedy acknowledges the diverse levels of consciousness permeating the world of his fiction. Further, in a fashion far more overt than the approaches he follows in any previous work, he takes up matters of the soul, with all of the multiplicity that such an oxymoronic phrase implies.

This new emphasis underscores an important artistic shift for Kennedy. The technical brilliance of his previous novels has accounted for much of their allure. Like Hemingway, another novelist with a journalism background, Kennedy beautifully crafts his descriptions in all of his writing so that, no matter how sordid or banal the topic, the reader always finds pleasure in the shape of the discourse. At the same time, the reader can detect a programmatic quality in the narratives of *Legs* and *Billy Phelan's Greatest Game*. Labels readily type Kennedy's previous protagonists: hoodlum for Jack Diamond and wise guy for Billy Phelan. The central character of *Ironweed*, Francis Phelan, however, though quick to identify himself as a bum, emerges as a much more complex figure. Indeed, from its opening chapter, *Ironweed* rejects easy categorizations and instead examines the essence of human nature. In this endeavor, Kennedy plays off his own Catholic background without slipping into orthodox, gnostic, or agnostic dogmatic patterns.

From the first lines onward, the narrative neatly captures the humanity inherent in a combined aura of pain and possibility. Cultural context remains extremely important to the construction of Kennedy's discourse, but in this novel he inverts its pattern for shaping an individual's consciousness. In previous works, places and events have dominated characterization. Jack Diamond, Marcus Gorman, Billy Phelan, and Martin Daugherty form themselves—their essence, their natures, their souls, however one wishes to characterize the elements within them that constitute identity—out of their relation to the society that affirms and to a degree interprets their experiences. In *Ironweed*, events have stripped Francis Phelan, Helen Archer, and the other bums who inhabit the novel of all of the cultural accoutrements that people usually rely on to define themselves.[6] What they have instead is only their own self-perception—often one severely impaired by alcohol abuse and brutal suffering—to define their place in the world. This alienation does not emerge out of an ignorance or a disavowal of the cultural context in which they grew to maturity. Rather, it comes from a painful awareness of their current isolation from the society that has had such a shaping impact on their pasts.

One finds this alienated condition evident in the scene describing Francis Phelan and Rudy Newton doing day work in Saint Agnes Cemetery, and the importance of this structuring feature of the novel justifies a rather close examination of the introductory episode. Francis and Rudy carry on conversations—or more accurately alternate solipsistic monologues that pay little heed to one another—in a discourse permanently fractured by alcohol and the hard lives they have led. Counterpointing their exchange, the dead—including Francis's parents, distant ancestors, and Louis "Daddy Big" Dugal (whose death from choking on his own vomit is chronicled in *Billy Phelan's Greatest Game*)—observe the two men and articulate communal ties that signal to the reader a closer connection and a more lasting influence than Francis himself realizes.

> Francis's mother twitched nervously in her grave as the truck carried him nearer to her; and Francis's father lit his pipe, smiled at his wife's discomfort, and looked out from his own bit of sod to catch a glimpse of how much his son had changed since the train accident. (Kennedy 1983a, 1–2)

.   .   .

> The [Phelan] brothers looked at Francis's clothes, his ragged brown
> twill suit jacket, black baggy pants, and filthy fireman's blue shirt, and felt
> a kinship with him that owed nothing to blood ties. (3)

> . . .

> Daddy Big, trying futilely to memorize anew the fading memories of
> how he used to apply topspin and reverse English to the cue ball, recognized
> Franny Phelan, even though he had not seen him in twenty years. (4–5)

This proximity of the dead, their self-parodic efforts to retain vestiges of the
world that they have left, and their familial interest in Francis highlight a
thematic shift in Kennedy's narrative world. These figures add an ironic perspective to the view of communal society so unreservedly celebrated in *Billy
Phelan's Greatest Game,* and they enforce the idea that the individual and his
heritage have displaced the broader social environment as the preeminent
formative forces in the Albany cycle even if the precise nature of that relationship remains in flux. Although the city's milieu continues to be an important feature of the narrative, attitudes and beliefs exert an equal or in
some cases greater influence on the evolution of characters' identities in this
novel.

Of course, attitudes and beliefs must necessarily appear in context, and
Ironweed skillfully shows how an individual's nature develops out of reactions
to life experiences.[7] With the cemetery acting as a sprawling memento mori,
the narrative turns to considerations of human mortality: Rudy's immanent
death from cancer—"[the doctor] says to me you're gonna die in six months"
(7)—the faithfully departed that surround them, recollections of other
bums who have passed away, and their immediate job of filling in plots
where caskets had settled. As Francis approaches the family burial spot, he
thinks of the death of his own father, Michael Phelan, killed in a railway accident when Francis was a child. At the same time, these images and alternative dialogues of the living and the dead that punctuate the narrative do not
impose a Gothic tone of horror on the discourse. Rather, they offer a subtle
reminder of how an individual's sense of himself depends so profoundly on
the interconnections with the past that remain within his consciousness: experiences live through a memory transmuted by belief.

As Francis stands over the grave of his long-dead infant son, Gerald, he
crystallizes his impressions in a single, poignant phrase: "I remember every-

thing" (18). More than he realizes, he has touched on the central issue of the novel. Characters frequently remember everything, or at least all of the pertinent facts. What distinguishes each individual is the search for the strength to interpret and accept whatever he or she recalls.

In sacramental fashion, a motif that recurs throughout the work, Francis kneels over his son's grave. He articulates the guilt he feels for his part in the boy's death, though he does not yet acknowledge the harm done by his subsequent desertion of the family. The infant Gerald, as integral to the exchange as Francis, assumes the role of a priest, offering absolution on the condition that penance is performed. He "imposed on his father the pressing obligation to perform his final acts of expiation for abandoning the family" (19).

This moment produces only a nebulous resolution, but it unambiguously foregrounds the central concern of *Ironweed*: spiritual rebirth. From the beginning, the novel's discourse asserts the need for a moral system to guide, sustain, and validate the characters. Catholic beliefs, part of the Irish American cultural heritage of the novel, markedly shape the perspectives of many of the characters. At the same time, the narrative avoids privileging a specific, rigid set of rules as the program that would fulfill these requirements. Rather, the action turns around the struggles of Francis Phelan, Helen Archer, and, to a lesser degree, others in the book to discern exactly what personal values will give them the peace and security they so desperately crave.

At the end of the day, Francis and Rudy take a bus back to Albany from the cemetery, and the narrative continues to manifest the evocative power of memory. For Francis, the ride recalls the past—trolleys, the car barns, and the strike in 1901 when he killed a scab with a rock. The bus passes familiar landmarks, and they too bring on memories of his life in the city before he became a hobo: his youth on Colonie Street, his troubled relations with his family, his life as a professional baseball player, and of course his participation in the trolley strike.[8] These elements define for us and for Francis the parameters of his consciousness. In the transient world that he now inhabits, people, events, and even places have an impermanence that robs them of the ability to give definition to an individual's life. Only the past, manifest in memories that retain consistency through repeated recollection, has stability—albeit a subjective stability—and individuals such as Francis come to rely on this stability, even when they feel alienated from their past, as they strive to understand themselves.

Stability, however, does not inevitably produce tranquility. As Francis recalls killing the scab worker, Harold Allen, during the 1901 strike, he sees Allen himself getting on the bus. When he talks with Allen, he recollects another death. While fleeing from Albany on a freight car after the murder of Allen, Francis witnessed the police shooting of a horse thief, Aldo Campione, who was trying to board the same train. Remembering this death evokes a phantom image of Campione getting on the bus. Francis's tolerance for apparitions, however, has fixed ethical limits, and he refuses to greet the man. "I ain't shakin' hands with no dead horse thief" (29).

One might, at this point, feel the inclination to catalog Francis's visions of Allen and Campione as the ramblings of a mind ruined by alcohol and hard living. That view, however, would oversimplify the dynamics of the narrative. Francis may well have fabricated what he is seeing, but these figures nonetheless stand as creations that his imagination evokes to give a referential meaning to the world he perceives himself as inhabiting. In this capacity, his mind functions in much the same fashion as that of any other individual, building associative meanings from the patterns of perception that it experiences. His consciousness differs only in the type of images that it rouses.

After the bus arrives in downtown Albany, Rudy and Francis proceed to the Mission of the Holy Redemption for an evening meal. In a vacant lot outside the building, they come across Sandra—a woman identified as having "been a bum all her life" (31)—lying in a semiconscious drunken stupor. Responding to her condition, Francis offers to bring her some soup. One sees the obvious analogies to the New Testament parable of the Good Samaritan, but the broader implications that complement this gesture assume an interpretive significance extending well beyond the biblical allusion. In the opening sections of the novel, Francis's moody temperament makes his propensity toward violence all too clear. Indeed, up to this point, willfulness, rudeness, and even menace have punctuated his conversations with Rudy and with the apparitions that Francis has encountered. The tender concern he shows for the drunken Sandra stands in stark contrast to this behavior, and it implies a complexity in his nature not heretofore evident.

Antithetically, a pervasive self-righteousness characterizes the atmosphere inside the mission. As Helen Archer waits for Francis, she sits in silent disapproval of the evangelizing methods employed by the Reverend Chester. "She held no hymnal as the others did, but sat with arms folded in defiant resistance to the possibility of redemption by any Methodist like

Chester" (33). Certainly, the revivalist techniques employed here contrast sharply with the Catholic rituals, especially that of the sacrament of confession, that shaped Helen's girlhood, but her resistance reflects more than sectarian truculence. It underscores the profound difference between the system of belief that sustains the Reverend Chester and the values that give meaning to the lives of Francis, Helen, and the other bums.

Reverend Chester's evening service begins with a long sermon on sin and the need for repentance. After emphasizing the darkness and depravity into which humanity has slipped, the preacher then proposes a sort of public penitence, asking the assembly if anyone wishes to come forward: "Will you stand up now? Come to the front, kneel, and we will talk. Do this now and be saved" (35). Others in the mission feel an aversion similar to Helen's, and the invitation meets with passive resistance: "No one moved" (35). The identity of anyone in that room stands in such a fragile relation to the world that none would be able to endure the public scrutiny of his or her soul or the trivializing of his or her offenses called for by Chester's exhortation. Unfortunately, the minister has no real sense of these people and can only respond to their inertia by testily ending the sermon.

In reality, the men and women at the mission do not hold themselves aloof from their transgressions, but the relationship that they feel between their sins and their need for forgiveness emerges as far more intricate than the one outlined by the Reverend Chester's disquisition. Characters such as Helen and Francis judge themselves harshly and will not accept an easy dismissal of the seriousness of their faults. Indeed, in an inverse fashion, their own perceptions of the magnitude of their sins give them a sense of dignity: the weight of their guilt serves as a declaration of their own significance to a world that too readily dismisses them. They desperately wish for absolution, but the mode of forgiveness must take on a solemnity and formality that acknowledges the importance of their transgressions.

Reverend Chester's bullying oratory does not address these conditions because he fails to understand the complexity of the process of reconciliation. Francis and Helen require more than prosaic assurances that they are forgiven. Their absolution can come only through the confirmation of the act of forgiveness by a ritual familiar to and accepted by each. (I discuss later in this chapter how these rituals take place near the end of the novel, giving a form of exculpation to each character.)

With the conclusion of the sermon, the evening meal begins, but Francis, in a role similar to that of a eucharistic minister, postpones eating to bring some soup to Sandra. Before he returns for his own dinner, he stops in a bathroom, "where he washed Sandra's dust and his own stink off his hands" (37). This cleansing marks the first in a series of cleansings in which Francis engages over the course of the novel. (Those wishing to pursue liturgical motifs in *Ironweed* will see in these washings analogies to the ablutions of the priest at mass immediately before the consecration of the Eucharist.) This preoccupation with cleanliness seems an anomaly for a man grown accustomed to grime through twenty-two years of hard living, yet over the course of *Ironweed* this gesture assumes the status of an objective correlative. As the narrative repeatedly affirms, Francis is seeking a less material, more elusive, and certainly more permanent form of purification, but the persistent impulse to clean his body keeps the spiritual quest before us as well.

At dinner, Francis underscores the importance of community for anyone in his situation as he reestablishes contact with Helen. Despite their rambling conversation, the elements that help to form and define their fragile relationship emerge from the topics that they discuss: money, drink and the difficult task of not succumbing to it, and where to sleep that night. After the meal, Francis learns from the Reverend Chester of the possibility of a job with the junk man, Rosskam, and in a gesture of good will the preacher gives Francis a new pair of socks. The quotidian details of domestic life take on a special significance in this context. For these characters, with only a tenuous link to conventional society, each task performed, each obligation met, or even each situation recognized strengthens the association they feel with a world from which they have too long been alienated.

Pee Wee Packer, a reformed bum who now works at the mission, joins Francis and Helen at their table. He tells them about an old drinking buddy, Oscar Reo, a former radio entertainer who after a bout with alcoholism began working as a singing bartender at the Gilded Cage. Helen, who was also an entertainer at one time, recognizes Oscar's name, and the three of them decide to go to the Gilded Cage to visit him. Despite the emphasis on music, alcohol and alcoholism remain the recurring features in this series of associations. By way of illustrating how alcohol overturns even the simplest arrangements, the narrative recounts the expulsion of one of the bums, Little Red, from this mission for coming into the building drunk for the third time.

On the way to the Gilded Cage, Helen, Francis, Rudy, and Pee Wee check on Sandra, still lying in the lot next door and wanting nothing other than drink. Although we may accept as necessary the Reverend Chester's sternness with Little Red, the sight of Sandra prostrate in the weeds naturally gives us pause. She has been treated according to the criteria that sent Little Red away, but, when we see that her weakened condition puts her perilously close to death, we cannot ignore the need for mercy tempering justice. As in several other instances in the novel when organized religion seems sadly lacking in humanity, the Reverend Chester's moral system, which decrees that Sandra must remain in the dirt outside the mission, proves to be fundamentally flawed.

At the bar, Francis and Pee Wee renew their acquaintance with Oscar. The music evokes more memories, and, as Helen reminisces, Francis's fractured recollections set up a dialectic that suggests either that drink has completely corroded his memory or that Helen allows imagination a free hand in the way she hears a reconstruction of her past. Helen is coaxed into performing two songs, and the extent of her power to reconfigure events by filtering them through a creative perception comes home to readers in an account that contrasts her idealized view of the reception to her songs with a more detached assessment of the crowd's reaction:

> Thunderous applause! And the elegant people are standing for Helen, when last did that happen? More, more, more, they yell, and she is crying so desperately now for happiness, or is it for loss, that it makes Francis and Pee Wee cry too. And even though people are calling for more, more, more, Helen steps delicately back down the three platform steps and walks proudly over to Francis with her head in the air and her face impossibly wet, and she kisses him on the cheek so all will know that this is the man she was talking about in case you didn't notice when we came in together.
>
> .   .   .
>
> Some odd-looking people were applauding politely, but others were staring at her with sullen faces. If they're sullen, then obviously they didn't think much of your renditions, Helen. Helen steps delicately back down the three steps, comes over to Francis, and keeps her head erect as he leans over and pecks her cheek. (57–58)

After the group leaves the Gilded Cage, the need for illusions to meliorate one's perception of the world becomes all too clear when the narrative underscores the perilousness of life on the streets with a material demonstration well in keeping with All Saints' Eve. Rudy goes off to find a place to flop, but Pee Wee, Francis, and Helen stop in the vacant lot to check on Sandra. The narrative does not specify who initiates this action, but given all that Francis has already done, the gesture seems part of his ongoing concern. Unfortunately, they find that Sandra died sometime during the evening and that animals have already begun to chew on her still warm body. While Francis and Pee Wee attend to the corpse, a group of children in Halloween costumes accost Helen and steal her handbag. Helen is as much distressed by the loss of a rosary that she has carried for twenty years—another memento of a carefully reconstructed and preserved past— as she is by the theft of fifteen dollars hidden in the lining of her purse. Pee Wee promises to take care of Sandra's body, and Francis and Helen set off to find a place to sleep for the night.

While walking around the city, Francis tells Helen of his visit earlier in the day to Gerald's grave. As if to enforce the concept of how the past haunts characters in the novel, throughout this conversation Francis sees the figure of Aldo Campione, the dead horse thief, following them. By this point, the apparition surprises neither Francis nor the reader. Characters from his past appear with predictable regularity as he moves about Albany. Indeed, to the degree that these ghosts reflect both Francis's historical past and the consciousness that has evolved out of that past, they stand as mediators between harsh experience and the insights that one derives from those events.

Eventually, Francis and Helen arrive at the apartment of Clara and Jack, a couple living in a partitioned section of a former mansion once owned by one of the city's turn-of-the-century lumber barons. The flat, with a tawdry decor matching its diminished expectations, attests to Clara and Jack's peripheral existence, their lives proving only minimally better than those of people existing out on the street. Reflecting the shared insecurities of their marginal status, the conversation between the two couples veers between tired familiarity and open hostility. In this fashion, the self-doubts and the alienation that plague each character come to the foreground. Indeed, isolation remains a dominant feature of the work, for although the narrative introduces any number of people who inhabit the same world that Francis and Helen do, these figures do not constitute a society in the way that the hoodlums of *Legs* or the gamblers of *Billy Phelan's Greatest Game* do. Although they face the same ordeals, suffer the same afflictions, and seek the same solace, no communal spirit or common bond gives them a sense of solidarity.

After a bickering exchange with Clara, Francis retires to the bathroom. He again washes himself, asks Jack for clean underwear pants, and also requests the loan of a razor. (As with the hand washing at the mission, these ablutions figure in a series of tentative steps toward material and spiritual purification that will culminate in the bath and change of clothing Francis gets when he later visits the house where his wife and adult children live.) This effort at cleansing brings to Francis's mind some of the guilt he still carries, and as a result he sees apparitions of Aldo Campione and Rowdy Dick Doolan, a bum whom Francis killed in a 1930 struggle under a bridge in Chicago, ostensibly over a pair of shoes that Francis was wearing at the time.

The narrative takes an interesting turn at this point, for, slipping into Free Indirect Discourse, it gives a description of that fight from Rowdy Dick's detached perspective. As the reader learns through this account, the confrontation really took place because Rowdy Dick envied the fact that Francis, who had been talking about his baseball experiences, was "gifted not only with so much pleasurable history but also with a gift of gab that could mesmerize a quintet of bums around a fire under a bridge" (73–74). Although Francis succeeds in cracking Rowdy Dick's skull, the hands that have caused him so much anxiety take a beating. He loses "in the process two thirds of a right index finger and an estimated one eighth of an inch of flesh from the approximate center of his nose" (74). After the fight, Free Indirect Discourse again enters the narrative, this time to give readers a clearer sense of Francis's feelings in the aftermath of the brutal encounter. His immediate impulse is kinetic:

> Francis began to run, and in so doing, reconstituted a condition that was as pleasurable to his being as it was natural: the running of bases after the crack of the bat, the running from accusation, the running from the calumny of men and women, the running from family, from bondage, from destitution of spirit through ritualistic straightenings, the running, finally in a quest for pure flight as a fulfilling mannerism of the spirit. (75)

The lyrical description of the complexity of Francis Phelan's consciousness reminds us of his belligerent, and one might even say defensive, declaration of his own courage, curiously set in the third person, in an earlier conversation on the way to the cemetery, when Rudy had said nothing impugning that courage: "Francis is no coward. He'll fight anybody" (10). Throughout the novel, when time after time Francis seems on the brink of violence with very little provocation, one does well to remember both of these passages. Francis is a man for whom flight has become an instinctive response informed by a complex array of psychological needs that he does not understand. At the same time, he has both a tremendous capacity to endure physical pain and a heightened sensitivity to spiritual trauma. In consequence, he must repeatedly demonstrate to himself and others that cowardice is not what provokes his running. More often than not, his willingness to confront physical danger stems from an effort to compensate for his fragile emotional state.

When Francis returns from the bathroom, the animosity between the two couples continues to bubble just beneath the surface. The level of tension in the air reflects an exhausted lechery that finds the pleasure of sex more related to the ego than to the libido. It is also exacerbated by the clash of finely drawn distinctions of class. The presence of Francis and Helen suggests to Jack and Clara an affinity to their own lives that they do not wish to acknowledge. Their seedy flat stands as a testament of respectability, yet their acquaintance with two people on the bum calls that assertion into question. Ultimately this connection leads Jack and Clara to tell Francis and Helen that they cannot spend the night at the apartment.

After leaving the flat, Francis and Helen drift into rather pointless bickering. Ostensibly, they are trying to decide what to do with themselves for the evening, but the narrative's reference to Francis's inclination toward flight—"[o]n the street, Francis felt the urge to run" (82)—suggests broader unresolved issues as the source of conflict. Without being able to articulate the cause, Francis once again finds himself confronted by a situation that he cannot control and feels the familiar impulse to flee. At this point, he does not recognize that condition, but the narrative is already giving attentive readers a sense of its dominance in the novel.

For the short term, both Francis and Helen realize that she lacks the strength to spend another night outdoors, so Francis takes her to a derelict car occupied by Finny, its putative owner, and Little Red, the bum whom Reverend Chester had thrown out of the mission earlier in the evening. Both Francis and Helen know that she will have to perform sexual favors to stay the night in the wreck of an automobile, for sexual continence has become a luxury unavailable to those on the street. Neither acknowledges this prospect to the other, for the bleak sexual economics of life on the streets has become simply one more hardship to endure. Indeed, after leaving Helen with Finny, Francis thinks about the consequences of that decision with an acceptance that borders on indifference.

In Finny's car Helen would probably be pulling off Finny, or taking him in
her mouth. . . . [Francis] knew, though [Helen] had never told him, that
she once had to fuck two strangers to be able to sleep in peace. Francis accepted this cuckoldry as readily as he accepted the onus of pulling the
blanket off Clara and penetrating whatever dimensions of reek necessary
to gain access to a bed. Fornication was standard survival currency everywhere, was it not? (89)

Francis himself goes off to sleep in an old barn in North Albany near the
home he left twenty-two years earlier: "Seventy-five feet from this spot,
Gerald Phelan died on the 26th of April 1916" (89). Thus, a certain circular-
ity informs the day for Francis. After thinking of running away from Helen
(and arguably in fact doing so by leaving her in Finny's car), he sleeps in
proximity to the spot where the event that precipitated his more prolonged
Odyssey took place, an incident he memorialized that morning through his
colloquy at Saint Agnes Cemetery.

The next day, Francis begins his work with Rosskam, the junk man. The
ride around Albany on the junk wagon reverses the pattern of Francis's
adulthood peregrinations by traversing neighborhoods of his childhood.
Rosskam spends the day retrieving the detritus of the North End of the city,
and the job takes on a metaphoric significance for Francis. With plenty of
time for thought stimulated by familiar landmarks and their associations
with his past, Francis's initial recollections reflect the immediacy of his environment: he wonders if Helen has followed her plan to attend mass on All
Saints' Day. He thinks of his son Billy and of the events related in *Billy
Phelan's Greatest Game*. Rosskam is himself preoccupied, for despite his sev-
enty-one years he is still on the alert for sexual opportunity: "Women. They
ask for it. You go to a house, you get offers" (94). When Francis happens to
see Rosskam taking advantage of one such offer, it turns his mind to sex. He
thinks first of early lovemaking with Helen and then of the sexual history of
his parents: "Because he was the firstborn, Francis's room was next to theirs,
and so he had heard their nocturnal rumblings for years; and he well knew
how she perennially resisted her husband. . . . For she hated the fact that
people even knew that she had committed intercourse in order to have children, a chagrin that was endlessly satisfying to Francis all his life" (98). In a
fashion that remains refreshingly non-Freudian, the narrative lays out the
sexual territory of Francis's early life without forcing it into a predictable,
claustrophobic scenario. A later novel, *Very Old Bones* (Kennedy 1992), will

make evident the significance of the elder Phelans' ruptured sex life, and the passage above nicely anticipates that exposition. Indeed, it stands as one of the many proleptic gestures that punctuate the Albany cycle and gives evidence of Kennedy's masterful control of the metanarrative.

Eventually, these experiences bring back for Francis a series of recollections relating to his initial sexual encounter with Katrina, Martin Daugherty's mother, during the time when, as a seventeen year old, Francis did handyman work for the family. First, however, readers get a quick revelation of how ties to the Phelans still exert a powerful hold on him. As a woman beckons Rosskam to pick up some junk, Francis refuses to help. "I don't want her to see me. Mrs. Dillon. Her husband's a railroad man. I know them all my life. My family [his brother and sisters] lives in that house over there. I was born up the street. I don't want people on this block to see me looking like a bum" (Kennedy 1983a, 100). For a man who has shown callous disregard for his dignity throughout the narrative, this sensitivity offers an illuminating insight into the impact that place and family can still exercise on him.

The proximity of his parents' home and of the lot where the Daugherty house stood before it burned down returns Francis's thoughts to the past, and while waiting for Rosskam he dwells on his seduction by Katrina Daugherty. Because the act culminated only after a long, careful process in which Katrina methodically made her intentions known to Francis, it became a shaping incident both in his life and, as will be made clear in *The Flaming Corsage* (Kennedy 1996), in Katrina's as well. The narrative in *Ironweed* gives a disjointed yet detailed account of those events in a way that both mimics Francis's imperfect memory and shows the lasting impression of the experience. By emphasizing need rather than desire, the description of Francis's seduction eschews eroticism and instead features sexuality as a means to fill a void.

> Francis embraced Katrina and shot into her the impeccable blood of his first love, and she yielded up . . . a word: clemency. And the word swelled like the mercy of his swollen member as it rose to offer her the enduring, erubescent gift of retributive sin. And then this woman interposed herself in his life, hiding herself in the deepest center of the flames, smiling at him with all the lewd beauty of her dreams; and she awakened in him the urge for a love of his own, a love that belonged to no other man, a love he would never have to share with any man, or boy, like himself. (Kennedy 1983a, 115–16)

Although the description is sufficiently graphic for anyone to picture the scene, the narrative allows readers to judge for themselves the motivations and morality behind both characters' actions.

During that same day, Helen too has let reminiscences dominate her thoughts, but the difference between her actions and Francis's lies in her knowledge that she is preparing for her immanent death. Early in the morning, she leaves Finny's car, having paid for her stay by allowing Finny to spend some time exploring "her only between the thighs, trying mightily to ejaculate" (119). Her first act is to celebrate All Saints' Day, a holy day of obligation for Catholics, by going to Mass at Saint Anthony's Church. (In Catholic tradition, St. Anthony is popularly invoked by individuals seeking lost property. The irony here is less overt than if the church were named St. Jude's, for the patron of lost causes.)

During the Mass, Helen considers a series of abandonments, all tinged by sex and sexuality, that trace the sense of isolation so central to the formation of her identity. First she assesses the significance of Francis's leaving her sexually vulnerable in Finny's car—a gesture that she does not claim to understand fully—as the act that finally ruptures their relationship. From carnality, she turns to consequences and, looking at one of the altar boys, imagines what the child whom she miscarried would have been like. This association brings up thoughts of her own experiences as a daughter. She recalls her mother's vindictive treatment of her while pampering her brother, a muted but nonetheless insistent theme of sexual competitiveness. Linked to this memory, she recollects the suicide of her father, Brian Archer, whose death ended her music studies at Vassar. In a fairly predictable fashion, Helen had sought to replace both her father and her career by going to work in a piano store, where she became the mistress of the owner, Arthur, until he left her for another woman. When she found out that her mother had diverted half of her father's estate away from her and to her brother Patrick, she left for New York City. (Patrick was not aware of the theft and felt no concern for his mother. In consequence, he responded to Helen's departure by putting their mother, who had become an invalid previously cared for by Helen, into a nursing home.)

After leaving St. Anthony's Church, Helen spends the morning wandering from the Waldorf Cafeteria to the Pruyn Library and finally to a music store, where, caught by its beauty and with no sense of irony, she steals a phonograph recording of Beethoven's *Ode to Joy*. (The fact that Helen has no way of listening to the record once she leaves the store only compounds the irony of the gesture.) She then checks into Palombo's Hotel, using the money that she had hidden in her bra and had feared Finny would find during his fumbling attempts at sexual congress. Helen knows that she is about to succumb to the tumor in her stomach, so she spends time reviewing, without rancor or sentimentality, events of decades past. She remembers life in New York City and traces her gradual shift from singer to bum. These memories are all punctuated by recollections of sexual activity and by speculations about its effect on her soul.

> In her nakedness on that continuing Tuesday and Thursday and unchanging Friday, Helen now sees the spoiled seed of a woman's barren dream: a seed that germinates and grows into a shapeless, windblown weed blossom of no value to anything, even its own species, for it produces no seed of its own; a mutation that grows only into the lovely day like all other wild things, and then withers, and perishes, and falls, and vanishes. (126)

Dogma and desire stand at the material and spiritual extremes of Helen's nature. All that she remembers serves to define her, yet its significance remains unclear. In a fashion paralleling Francis's efforts, but with a more overt acknowledgment of the impact of religious belief, Helen struggles to interpret that definition in light of her idiosyncratic sense of her Catholic faith.

Francis, in the meantime, is still traveling around the city on the junk wagon and continues to remember his past. Now, however, he focuses on recalling the way that violence has shaped his life. The stench from a warehouse fire on lower Broadway recalls for him the burning sheets tossed over the electric lines to trap a scab-driven trolley during the strike of the 1901. This memory in turn conjures up a vision of Fiddler Quain, who had ignited the sheets with Francis and then had his skull split by a soldier's rifle butt after Francis threw a stone that killed a scab worker. When Fiddler died twelve years later, his sister made Francis feel responsible for the death. Now Fiddler's spirit gives Francis a hint as to how he might obtain absolution: "It's those traitorous hands of yours you'll have to forgive" (142).

In a neatly understated fashion, the narrative uses the remark to draw attention to a central aspect of Francis's guilt. Throughout his adult life, Francis has avoided accountability for his behavior by making his hands—a key feature in his skill as a ball player—the disembodied source of his troubles. His hands threw the rock at the scab. His hands caused him to drop Gerald. His hands are culpable for the lives of men he has killed while on the bum. Nonetheless, Fiddler's synecdochical advice points Francis toward the real task that faces him: he must forgive himself. It would mean taking responsibility, though, and he is not yet prepared to do that, as intimated in his unsatisfactory conversation with Rosskam about his hands:

> "I got the idea that my hands do things on their own, you know what I mean?"
> "Not yet," said Rosskam.
> "They don't need me. They do what they goddamn please." (143)[9]

Here Francis still seeks disassociation rather than forgiveness, yet the fact slowly emerges that even with this effort he cannot sustain the avoidance of responsibility. He needs absolution, but to get it he must accept his role in the events that give him so much pain. The novel reaches a turning point when he begins to struggle to find someone who can assist him toward that forgiveness.

This course of action remains difficult for Francis, and in a way that might seem evasive he slips back into recollections of his professional baseball career and events from his life as a bum. In fact, he dwells on incidents of violence as if trying to understand how they shaped his life. During these reveries, Harold Allen, the scab whom Francis killed, appears, and he and Francis discuss that act. Harold interrogates Francis to determine his motives for throwing the stone, and Francis's truculent answers evoke the manner of a disgruntled teenager rather than that of a fifty-eight-year-old man. This conversation does, however, show him—in the process of reconsidering the events in his life from which he has fled and of trying to comprehend the forces in his nature that lead him to leave—that to which he feels most strongly attached.

The ride through his family's neighborhood heightens the pull of community and finally spurs Francis to action. When he decides to leave the wagon, he must threaten to fight Rosskam—another potential act of violence—in order to receive his salary. This time, however, a recourse to confrontation represents a significant change of behavior. Instead of reflecting his efforts to flee from his recollections, it demonstrates his determination to face them. He has decided to return at least temporarily to his family. It is an important gesture on his part, for it represents a movement toward reconciliation and an acceptance of responsibility, two conditions he has spent a lifetime avoiding.

Francis, understandably, does not wish to arrive on the doorstep as an obvious supplicant, so he buys a turkey and brings it to the house where his wife Annie and his son Billy live with his daughter Peg, her husband George Quinn, and their son Danny. Although Billy had told him, when they met a few days earlier (an incident recorded in *Billy Phelan's Greatest Game*), that there was no need to bring something when coming to visit, arriving with the turkey obviously means a great deal to Francis. It clearly alludes to the role of breadwinner that he forsook many years ago, and it also serves as an unvoiced acknowledgment that he cannot simply appear on the threshold but must offer something by way of propitiation.

Annie Phelan greets her husband with affection but understandable reserve. To offset the effect of Francis's earlier recollections of Katrina and to help readers understand the bond that still exists between Annie and Francis, the narrative recounts their courtship through Free Indirect Discourse. Here, understanding emerges as the dominant emotion, in contrast to the passion that characterized the affair with Katrina. A domestic scene in the present counterpoints this chronicle of Annie and Francis's early love. Annie prepares the turkey for dinner, passing the time talking of the family. Francis in turn takes the opportunity to tell Annie about his conversation with Gerald. Reintroducing his dead son into their world and acknowledging his sense of guilt stands as another stage through which he must pass in his movement toward reconciliation.

An alternative opportunity for the employment of memory arises when Danny, Peg's ten-year-old son, comes home from school and begins to get acquainted with his grandfather. Simultaneously, Billy awakens from an afternoon nap, and husband, wife, son, and grandson go to the attic to look through a trunk full of Francis's baseball memorabilia. In the trunk, Francis finds neatly stored his clothes of twenty-two years ago. They represent memories of a better time, an alternative to the painful recollections that have dogged him throughout the narrative.

The reintegration progresses through definite stages, and Francis undergoes his final ablution. After a bath and shave, he dresses in apparel from a previous life and goes downstairs in an entrance described in a breathless, paragraph-long sentence.

> Francis, the 1916 dude, came down the stairs in bow tie, white-on-white-shirt, black laceless oxfords with a spit shine on them, the gray herringbone with lapels twenty-two years too narrow, with black silk socks and

white silk boxer shorts, with his skin free of dirt everywhere, his hair
washed twice, his fingernails cleaned, his leftover teeth brushed and the
toothbrush washed with soap and dried and rehung, with no whiskers
anymore, none, and his hair combed and rubbed with a dab of Vaseline so
it'd stay in place, with a spring in his gait and a smile on his face; this Francis dude came down those stairs, yes, and stunned his family with his res-
urrectible good looks and stylish potential, and took their stares as
applause. (172)

The change in clothing gives material evidence of Francis's desire to turn
back the clock, to return to the world he left when he ran away for the last
time in 1916. This transition, of course, like his shoes without laces, remains
incomplete. Nonetheless, it marks another necessary stage in his process of
recuperating the identity he abandoned twenty-two years ago. As he goes
through old newspaper clippings of his baseball achievements, apparitions
begin to fill the backyard. Although the narrative never fully explains their
presence, they seem to relate to Francis's struggle to relocate himself. They
are the past from which he is trying to break free: "You're all dead, and if you
ain't, you oughta be. I'm the one is livin'. I'm the one puts you on the map"
(177). When Peg comes home, she is initially hostile to her father, but he
wins her over with a docility and sentimentality (evinced in the form of a
letter from Peg that he has saved for twenty-eight years) that he has displayed only infrequently in the novel. Despite the good feeling surrounding
this reunion, however, Francis does not yet feel that he can permanently return to the family.

Consequently, he leaves the house after the turkey dinner, making no
immediate plans to come back, but with a sense that he will be welcome
there in the future. Initially, he seems to be resuming the hobo life he has
followed for twenty-two years. Francis finds Rudy in an abandoned house
and, because the police have been raiding these places, convinces him to
leave. On a hunch, the two stop at Palombo's Hotel, where Francis learns
that Helen has taken a room. They then buy some wine and whiskey and go
to a flop house. Francis's belligerence at the flop house starkly contrasts with
the meekness that characterized his demeanor during his visit with his family. The setting of course has changed, but the narrative also underscores the
role of alcohol: "Francis began to drink for the first time in a week" (192).[10]

Through this scene, one sees both the contrast between the two lives
open to Francis and the steps he needs to take to regain what he has lost. By

relating the brutal and violent Francis Phelan to alcohol, the narrative makes more believable the transition that will come about at the end of the novel. Leaving the environment of hobo jungles becomes simply a matter of giving up drinking, or at least a matter of forgoing drinking as a way of numbing reality. When Francis does this, he can return to the family home. Before he can do so, however, he has to reach the stage where he no longer needs to numb his senses to blunt the pain of life.

At the flop house, Francis meets Moose Baker, another hobo, and Old Shoes Gilligan, a former bum who now claims to be living a respectable life. Francis sits drinking with them and reminiscing in a scene analogous to the gathering in Jack and Clara's apartment and completely different from the domestic one that took place earlier in the evening at the family home. As in the scene with Jack and Clara, tension pervades the conversation. For Francis, amiability suddenly gives way to anger, and the sense of security and tranquility that characterized his family visit is nowhere evident. Presently, Finny and Little Red come into the flop house, and Francis, by now a bit drunk and probably resentful of what Finny did with Helen the previous night, gets into an argument with them. Finny is too drunk himself to respond, but Little Red does and receives a brutal beating from Francis for his trouble. After the fight, Rudy and Francis leave the flophouse with Old Shoes.

The three men drive in Old Shoes's car to a hobo jungle. There they meet other bums, finish drinking the liquor that they have, and engage in a desultory, vaguely hostile exchange. Again, this scene starkly inverts the tone of the exchange between Francis and his family earlier in the day. Although unvoiced sympathy and mutual understanding characterized the scene in the Phelan household, the conversation in the hobo jungle remains devoid of any comprehension or acceptance. In fact, when Francis expresses his sense of reconciliation with the scab that he killed in 1901, a momentous change for him, it meets with a cautious indifference:

> "I forgive the son of a bitch," Francis said.
>
> "Who's that?" Old Shoes asked. Rudy lay all but blotto across the backseat, holding the whiskey and wine bottles upright on his chest with both tops open in violation of Old Shoes' dictum that they stay closed, and not spilling a drop of either.
>
> "Guy I killed. Guy named Allen."
>
> "You killed a guy?"

"More'n one."

"Accidental, was it?"

"No. I tried to get that one guy, Allen. He was takin' my job."

"That's a good reason."

"Maybe, maybe not. Maybe he was just doin' what he had to do."

"Baloney," Old Shoes said. "That's what everybody does, good, bad, and lousy. Burglars, murderers."

And Francis fell quiet, sinking into yet another truth requiring handling. (207–8)

Unlike Annie Phelan, Old Shoes has no real interest in assuaging Francis's psychic wounds. He seeks to distance himself from Francis's confession of murder, using generalizations in an attempt to depersonalize what has been said rather than confronting the implications of the disclosure.

Conversations in the hobo jungle replicate those at the flop house. Alcohol lubricates the exchanges. Solipsistic recollections dominate, and an aura of hostility lurks just beneath the surface. Francis continues to demonstrate a moody, embittered nature. He shares a turkey sandwich with Michigan Mac, and then when he hears of a couple with a baby needing food, he rudely takes back the sandwich and gives it to the young family. Again, the narrative gives intimations of Francis's fundamental decency, but it also shows how life on the road has led him to adopt a gruff, even brutal veneer.

In the midst of this scene—in the novel's violent climax—men from the American Legion raid the camp. They beat anyone whom they encounter and burn the shanties. On a broad level, their intolerance presages an end to the life Francis has lived for the past two decades. The immediate aim of the Legionaries, with no thought of any further consequences, is to drive away the unfortunate men and women inhabiting the hobo jungle. When one of the attackers hits Rudy with a baseball bat, Francis takes the bat from the man, strikes him with it, and kills him. (Just as Francis's first murder, killing a scab by throwing a rock, ironically mimics his skill as a baseball player, so does his last act of violence.) In the past when he killed a man, his immediate impulse was toward flight. Now, however, in a reflection of the change already taking place in him, he demonstrates a greater concern for another by taking Rudy to a hospital.

Rudy dies in the hospital, and when Francis returns to Palombo's, he finds that Helen has also died. From this point until the final pages of the novel, the narrative shifts to the subjunctive mood, perhaps as a way of underscoring Francis's sense of being disconnected from reality. This account describes the low point in his spiritual life, his dark night of the soul that will end with a moment of revelation.

> Francis would remember then that when great souls were being extinguished, the forces of darkness walked abroad in the world, filling it with lightning and strife and fire. And he would realize that he should pray for the safety of Helen's soul, since that was the only way he could now help her. But because his vision of the next world was not of the court of heaven where the legion of souls in grace venerate the Holy Worm, but rather of a foul mist above a hole in the ground where the earth itself purges away the stench of life's rot, Francis saw a question burning brightly in the air: How should this man pray? (223)

The tone of Francis's thoughts, more Calvinistic than Catholic, evokes a bleak and joyless view of eternity. Francis, however, without realizing it, has already affirmed his spirituality in his care for the dying Rudy and has articulated his own prayer in his grieving for Helen.

Although salvation is closer than Francis realizes, at this point habit takes hold, and he succumbs to the familiar impulse to flee when confronted by trouble. He hops a freight out of town, fearing that the police will be seeking him for the death of the Legionnaire. While riding on a Delaware and Hudson railcar, he sees an apparition of Strawberry Bill, a long-dead bum. Bill assures Francis that the police are not pursuing him and suggests that, rather than run away, Francis hide out in Albany. Although this vision hardly stands as analogous to Saul on the road to Damascus, nonetheless for Francis an epiphany-like quality suffuses the experience.

The novel abruptly shifts to a conversation between Annie and Francis in the Phelan attic. Francis has taken up residence there, living the peaceful life of a man avoiding the law and enjoying a kind of reconciliation with his family. This scene stands as the perfect ending for a novel whose epigraph comes from the *Purgatorio*. For Francis, salvation is in sight, if not in his grasp. He has been through a cleansing experience, and, if he has not yet achieved perfect contrition, he certainly has demonstrated attrition. His rebirth will come in an understated fashion, told parenthetically in *Very Old Bones*, but the obliqueness of that account serves only to underscore Kennedy's determination to avoid proselytizing.

Part Three

Maturity

 CHAPTER SIX

The Consequences of Time in *Quinn's Book*

Through the narratives of the first three novels in the Albany cycle (*Legs, Billy Phelan's Greatest Game*, and *Ironweed*) Kennedy establishes a compelling social milieu for his writing: an early-twentieth-century, working-class, ethnic world that mimics without fully replicating the dominant attitudes of contemporary American society. This construction, despite its prescriptive qualities, creates an unmistakable resonance with the diverse experiences of any number of readers because of Kennedy's imaginative skill in evoking a universal quality in the daily rhythms of his fictional, lower-middle-class, Irish American community of Albany. Although the protocols of this world may stand at variance with those of the reader's world, the combination of a deft ability for descriptive detail and a clear sense of the humanity of his creations vivify every event and make every locale seem familiar. This configuration allows his subtle characterizations of flawed, and in some cases quite stupid though nonetheless complicated, individuals to convey to readers the variety of life within relatively narrow economic, social, and chronological boundaries.

Kennedy's next novel undertakes a very different creative project, one clearly intended to broaden the scope of the Albany cycle. Like its predecessors, *Quinn's Book* shows clear thematic affinities to the characters and events of the works that preceded it. Nonetheless, its setting in the nineteenth century and its narrative task of sketching the events that lay the foundation for the world that emerges in his other novels require Kennedy to create a cultural context far different from any in his earlier writings. Broadly considered, *Quinn's Book* meets those challenges, and even when aspects of its narrative do not match previous imaginative achievements, it marks an important transitional phase in the Albany sequence.

The differences in the constitution of *Quinn's Book* from that of any of Kennedy's previous writings also compel readers to turn to interpretive paradigms distinct from approaches they successfully applied to earlier works. In previous chapters of this study, I have posited analogies between the social environment that Kennedy has created and Joyce's Dublin: lower middle class, economically deprived, and defined by religious affiliations often more communal than theological. For *Quinn's Book*, readers may find more useful comparisons in parallels between the Albany of its narrative and the Yoknapatawpha County of William Faulkner's novels. Juxtaposing the two, readers will see striking similarities in the breadth of characterization, the claustrophobic clannishness, the complex interconnected relations between a range of characters, the generational memories that nurse long grievances and a punctilious sense of honor, and the consequent vicious internecine squabbles. The same difficulties that challenged Faulkner as he attempted to sketch a chronicle spanning one hundred years of Mississippi history also face Kennedy as he limns the features of nineteenth-century Albany. Seeing this grand design as implicit in *Quinn's Book* allows readers to acknowledge areas in the work that are not completely successful while remaining aware of all that the book does achieve.

As with Faulkner's depictions of the Compson and the Snopes clans, *Quinn's Book* reflects Kennedy's emerging ambition to sustain a multivolume and multigenerational account of Albany life beyond the perspective of a few interrelated, Irish American families. In this novel, however, efforts to lay the foundation of a full-blown, complex social history encounter difficulties not evident in attempts to work within a more limited cultural context. Just as the Studs Lonigan trilogy did for James T. Farrell, the first three Albany books establish Kennedy's voice in describing a particular ethnic, economic, and historic milieu. When he endeavors to evoke a broader community—influenced by a range of economic classes, nationalities, and cultural codes, the transition to a new voice proves extremely challenging for both author and readers.

Kennedy's first collection of essays—*O Albany!*—attests to his detailed knowledge of the rich historic import of the city, and he brings to *Quinn's Book* a reporter's determination to ensure the accuracy of his nineteenth-century descriptions. At the same time, he adopts an approach to the Albany of 1848 to 1864 that is markedly different from his descriptions of the Depression-era city, shifting his focus from evocation of the details of everyday life to a panoramic delineation of an era. One sees in the three preceding novels the intimate awareness of the ordinary incidents and objects shaping the lives of the citizens of twentieth-century Albany in the period between the two world wars. In *Quinn's Book*, one finds no analogous representation in its delineation of mid-nineteenth-century life. Rather, momentous historical events—a city flood, labor conflicts, Civil War battles, the New York draft riots—and wrenching personal traumas—disease, mutilation, kidnapping, murder—propel the narrative forward.

At the same time, fathoming the discursive aims of this book remains crucial for comprehending what Kennedy is attempting to do throughout the Albany saga. The wide-ranging narrative of *Quinn's Book* establishes a picture of the inchoate modern city—a sense of the seventeenth-, eighteenth-, and nineteenth-century worlds—from which the twentieth-century environment emerged. Later augmented by *The Flaming Corsage* (Kennedy 1996), it traces the salient features of Albany's cultural legacy: the recklessness of a frontier town; the paradoxical provinciality of a multiethnic society; and the ongoing tension between financial, political, and social influence. (I discuss *The Flaming Corsage* in detail in chapter 8. Suffice it to say for now, however, that this more recent book remedies any flaws one might choose to critique in *Quinn's Book*.)

Understanding these associations between the microcosmic and the macrocosmic societies of Albany becomes increasingly important as one progresses through Kennedy's narrative cycle. The construction of the past—both by Kennedy's characters and by his readers—evolves into a dominant component of the narrative development. His discourse ties the history of individuals and of their families to the heritage of the city and the region. Indeed, for both *Very Old Bones* (Kennedy 1992) and *The Flaming Corsage*, comprehending accounts of the rise and fall of a number of families depends heavily on a knowledge of the events of nineteenth-century Albany. Further, the rich tradition of the city continually reminds readers that they derive various meanings from selected perceptions of complexly related events. To assess the validity of any and all possible interpretations, it becomes necessary to understand the context from which they spring. *Quinn's Book* goes a long way toward establishing that context by outlining important intersecting alliances and long-standing feuds.

Despite its sweeping regard for events relating to mid-nineteenth-century Albany, *Quinn's Book* also seeks to understand the essence of those fundamental human relationships that animate its action. Thus, in a manner that hearkens back to *Legs* and *Billy Phelan's Greatest Game*, the narrative focuses attention on a single character, Daniel Quinn, a young orphan whose family had recently emigrated from Ireland but subsequently perished in a cholera epidemic. Announcing its concern for momentous events, the novel opens "on a late December day in 1849" (Kennedy 1988, 5) with the fifteen-year-old Daniel describing a fatal attempted crossing of an ice-clogged Hudson River. On that day, the great courtesan, Magdalena Colón—or La Última, as she is also called—has determined to travel by boat from Albany to Greenbush (current-day Rennsalier) and has taken out an ad in the *Albany Chronicle* affirming her willingness to pay one hundred dollars to any boatman willing to ferry her, her maid, and her young niece to the other side of the river. The gesture nicely sums up Magdalena's character: self-dramatizing, reckless, and extravagant. It also announces Kennedy's thematic shift from the personal ruminations that dominate the discourse of *Ironweed* back to the publicly driven narrative structure of earlier novels. *Quinn's Book*, however, gives even greater emphasis to the repercussions of significant events, for rather than shaping the consciousnesses of characters, as in *Legs* and in *Billy Phelan's Greatest Game*, these incidents provide the driving force for plot development.

This is not to say that individuals have a diminished importance in *Quinn's Book*. Rather, the narrative simply pays more attention to what they do than to what they think. In keeping with this approach, sex or violence or both stand at the center of nearly every occasion of public interest in the novel. It is this particular confluence that causes a large crowd to gather along the docks to watch the spectacle of La Última's attempted crossing. When the skiff capsizes, John the Brawn McGee, the boatman who employs the young Quinn, jumps into action as a scavenger, hauling both Magdalena's trunk and her seemingly dead body into the boat. Meanwhile, Daniel in his turn rescues Maud Fallon, Magdalena's niece and the only apparent survivor of the mishap.

The drownings mark only the first in a series of catastrophes that set the novel's course of action. In quick succession, the bridge connecting the Great Albany Pier to the shore collapses under the weight of the crowd of onlookers. A large ice floe temporarily dams the river, and the resulting buildup of water sends a tidal wave across the Great Pier and onto the quay. The chaos of the flood is complicated by fires that break out across the city, ultimately burning "600 buildings" and leaving "5,000 people without lodging" (37).

John the Brawn, by his response to this disaster, lays down the paradigm for effectively coping with the chaotic environment of the novel: success comes through clear and decisive action in which the individual operates beyond the conventional restrictions of society but without going so far as to become a renegade. John the Brawn, for example, would never attack Magdalena and rob her of her possessions, but as a scavenger he does not hesitate to profit from her misfortune.

These opening episodes present a thematic pattern that the narrative reiterates throughout the course of the novel. Urban living, with its inordinately dense concentration of ill-controlled, economically exploited workers, inevitably creates pressures that can be relieved only by explosive events, such as natural disasters, class warfare, mindless rioting, or reckless bacchanal. As *Quinn's Book* explores the early stages of the integration of the Irish—both individually and as an ethnic group—into the larger American community, it chronicles at nearly every point the violence that punctuates that integration. Although Daniel Quinn later refers to perils of the western frontier visited by Lyman Fitzgibbon and Emmett Daugherty, the narrative repeatedly enforces the idea that the greatest dangers lie in the settled towns. As *Quinn's Book* traces the roots of the urban environment from which the Daughertys, the Phelans, the Quinns, and all the other denizens of twentieth-century Albany have evolved, the overall brutality of the city helps one understand the coarseness of their individual lives.

John the Brawn decides to take Maud and her dead aunt to the home of Hillegond Staats, and during the trip to the Staats mansion Daniel expresses his growing infatuation for Maud with a kiss on the young girl's cheek. This act stands as an ironic counterpoint to the bite wound on Magdalena's face, inflicted on the inert body that John the Brawn pulled from the river by an Albany woman who resented La Última's power over men. In its own way, each gesture attests to the power of sexuality to exert a formative impact on the way lives unfold. Thematic and symbolic representations of sexual appetites and sexual practices, which have always been regular if not dominant features in Kennedy's fiction going back to *The Ink Truck* and *Legs*, gain new interpretive significance in *Quinn's Book*. Its discourse centers attention on the way that carnality both defines an individual's self-conception and struggles against it. Further, the narrative forwards the assumption that these appetites do not simply delimit individuals, but also set up conditions that will shape family lines for generations.

Quinn's Book also strives to identify an overriding order in the lives of individuals, but it does not admit to anyone's ability to take control of his or her life. "You can't avoid your fate, you goose," Maud tells Daniel. "That's why they call it your fate" (17). She goes on to tell him about destiny. " 'It's you who have the first right to my life,' she told me, 'for it was you who kept me from sliding to the bottom of the river' " (19). This dual perspective counterbalances the volitional thrust of preceding events: an overriding, if undiscerned, plan circumscribes the lives of many of the characters in the novel, and by a single action one character can become inextricably bound to another. Maud's pronouncement also introduces what becomes another thematic concern: superstition and mysticism as metaphysical alternatives to religion.

The arrival at Hillegond's house gives the narrative an opportunity to go into a fairly detailed account of the ancestry of the Staats family and of the Dutch influence on Albany from the seventeenth century onward. The Staats link is an important one, not only in this book but in *The Flaming Corsage*, where Katrina Daugherty has ties to this family. In *Quinn's Book*, the rise of the Dutch Staats family from obscurity to wealth serves as a model for subsequent Irish settlers. The head of the clan, Wouter Staats, came to America in the seventeenth century and "gained renown as a trader by perfecting counterfeit wampum" (22). From there, through a series of practical marriages, audacious business enterprises, and a measure of luck, the family has become by Hillegond's time both wealthy and respected. Over the next few generations, as noted in other books in the Albany cycle, this same pattern will repeat itself among some of the Irish in a twentieth-century Albany dominated by families such as the McCalls and the Daughertys. The Phelans—no less inclined to questionable business practices but less pragmatic in their alliances and less canny in their dealings—will trace the opposite trajectory.

The geneologic account of the Staats family is followed immediately by an admittedly farfetched demonstration of the validity of one of the novel's themes: the power of sexuality. Magdalena is laid out in the *Dood Kamer*, "the room set aside in substantial homes of the old Dutch to accommodate death" (21). As everyone else is getting settled in the house, John the Brawn begins a necrophilic assault on what is presumed to be Magdalena's corpse. Hillegond, watching this assault, becomes so aroused that she falls into a groaning swoon. When John hears this response, he obligingly turns his amorous attentions to Hillegond. As he brings Hillegond to a climax, Magdalena regains consciousness, prompting John the Brawn to return to her for yet another encounter. This rather fantastic sexual ballet has been witnessed in its entirety by Daniel and Maud, who react with a mixture of bemused naïveté and jaded sophistication.

> "He is a low beast, and they are both fools for a man. Would you want to do that to me?"
> "I think so," I said, though I had not considered it in such an individualized context.
> "I'm not at that stage yet," said Maud.
> "I guess I am," I said.
> "It seems to be very affecting, what happens to one."
> "That's what I've heard."
> "I should have thought you'd have already tested it."
> "I've not had the opportunity," I said.
> "When I am ready to do it," Maud said, "I shall seek you out."
> "I look forward to that," I said. (31)

Grotesque as the scene is, it offers a valuable gloss on the novel's thematic construction. Sensual drives are so strong that they can overcome any inhibition or prohibition, and sexual gratification absolves all transgressions that may surround the act. (The fact that what is depicted can be seen as little more that sexual assault, at the very least on Magdalena and arguably on Hillegond as well, passes surprisingly without comment.) Further, sex stands as a vital activity in more than just the conventional sense: it does not merely create life; it also sustains the lives of the participants. The salubrious aspect of intercourse is a concept obliquely woven into many of Kennedy's novels, but nowhere is it introduced with greater bluntness. "Magdalena Colón was resuscitated by love, the same commodity used by the Christ to effect a similar end" (33). Thus, a description that at first might seem only a baroque and blasphemous flight of fancy in fact establishes early on the efforts of the narrative to transform sensuality into a metaphysical, even religious experience.

The appearance of Will Canaday, the founder and editor of the *Albany Chronicle* offers another example of the narrative's tendency to collapse the literal and the symbolic.[1] Canaday announces that an escaped prisoner, a Swede overcome with despair by the ill-treatment he has received in this strange new country, has hanged himself over the tomb of Amos Staats. Joshua, a captured runaway slave, remains handcuffed to the dead Swede. He is quickly freed from the manacles and is secreted in a basement where three other escaped slaves are hiding. The house is one stop on the Underground Railroad, and the gesture that brings Joshua back to life reflects the powerful force of spiritual love—a general concern for humanity—that counterpoints the admittedly more spectacular force of John the Brawn's carnal energy.

A final examination of images of death occurs in a passage that insistently threatens to slip from pathos to bathos. The narrative describes the damage done when Will breaks the slab covering the tomb of Amos Staats as he cuts down the dead Swede. With the remains now exposed, the group has no choice but to bring the marble coffin into the house. Very briefly, the household views the nearly perfectly preserved remains of Amos, but this short exposure to the open air causes the corpse to crumble into dust. While this transpires, Maud and Daniel kiss over the coffin. With yet another variation on images of eros and thanatos, the narrative contrasts the fate of the loveless and the loved, but here the desiccated remains leave no doubt as to the message. It is not, as Magdalena with willful ignorance assumes, that love can overcome death but rather that love powerfully affirms the transitory vitality of the living. For the remainder of the novel, it is clear that the individuals who demonstrate the greatest engagement with life are those most taken by love—whether sensual, emotional, or spiritual.

Will Canaday now takes Daniel under his wing, giving him a tutoring of sorts that serves as an apprenticeship to the newspaper business. In a tour that provides the opportunity for lengthy narrative exposition, Will brings Daniel into the city of Albany, ravaged first by the cholera epidemic that killed all of Daniel's family, then by the flooding Hudson, and finally by the Great Fire, which came as a direct consequence of the flooding. Amidst the ruins, Daniel finds a pig about to devour a dead infant and chases the animal away. Once again *Quinn's Book* offers an overtly literal insight into an individual through his response to death. Earlier, John the Brawn took what seemed a necrophilic advantage of Magdalena's presumed death, and throughout the novel he is equated with swine. Here Daniel refuses to allow a swine to treat a dead infant as a slab of meat (what John was doing earlier) and is praised for his humanity. The association admittedly functions at a crude level, and it certainly lacks full elaboration. It does, however, reflect Kennedy's initial efforts to work out the intense savagery that surrounds human desire, a construction he displays more effectively in his descriptions of Malachi McIlhenny in *Very Old Bones*.

In another of the melodramatic scenes that have begun to accumulate in the narrative, Hillegond's son, Dirck Staats, who is writing a book composed in a form of cipher, is abducted, and a thug steals a portion of Dirck's manuscript. Unfortunately, the passage describing Dirck's kidnapping moves directly away from Kennedy's creative strengths: dialogue and characterization. If the action in this episode and in the subsequent one at the Staats mansion seems stilted, it reflects the creative problems with which Kennedy struggles throughout this novel. He is attempting to write a sweeping chronicle that will establish the basis for events that inform the rest of his saga, but the structure of this novel does not permit a leisurely accumulation of the kinds of everyday incidents that give so much power to the narratives of *Legs*, *Billy Phelan's Greatest Game*, and *Ironweed*. Instead, circumstances change with a rapidity that seems almost forced.

On the one hand, these rapid shifts in the situations confronting characters may seem a flaw in exposition. On the other hand, they aptly capture the emotional atmosphere of the novel. They reflect the tumultuous uncertainty that many feel for the world around them and underscore a bafflement with life summed up in the final pages of *Quinn's Book*: " 'If you lose it's fate,' Joshua said. 'If you win, it's a trick.' Quinn would dwell on this, and perceived that he himself had changed, that he was forever isolated into the minority, a paddynigger and an obsessive fool whose disgust was greater than its object, who was trying to justify in this world what was justifiable only in another cosmic sphere" (288). Like his central character, Kennedy works throughout this novel to convey and perhaps comprehend that condition.

The difficulty of such a task becomes evident in the haphazard and at times arbitrary development of the action. For example, when Daniel returns to Hillegond's mansion with the news of Dirck's abduction, Magdalena abruptly decides that they cannot remain there during Hillegond's troubles. She, Maud, John the Brawn, and Daniel set off by canal boat for Utica, but during the first night John the Brawn has Daniel put off the boat and left on the towpath at the edge of the canal.

During the walk back to Albany, Daniel composes a telepathic letter to Maud that in fact serves as a review of all of the major events of his family's history culminating in their deaths. (In subsequent novels—*Very Old Bones* and *The Flaming Corsage*—Kennedy will show a much more skillful sense of how to convey such information. Here, it comes rolling out like so many facts that the author needs to get out of the way so that he can continue the narrative proper.) Like the previous recollection of the Staats family history, this account illuminates the cultural milieu for readers unfamiliar with the

ethnic foundations of Albany. Just as the Staats family serves as the prototype for the Dutch, the oldest immigrant group in the city, the story of the
Quinns offers a representative view of the experiences of the most recent
faction, the Irish.

Arriving back in Albany, Daniel returns to his deserted family home to
spend the night and to recover a birdcage that his mother had bid him hide.
The next day, he is awakened by Peaches and Outa Plum, two young thugs
who demand to know what he has gotten from the house. Daniel tricks
them into taking a broken shovel, and after they have left, he discovers a
metal platter hidden in the bottom of the birdcage. (This platter, whose material value is never fully explained to Daniel, reappears throughout the narrative and, through the ambiguity surrounding its worth, becomes the
objective correlative for the unease that troubles him for the rest of the
book.)

At the Staats mansion, Will and Daniel find that Hillegond is engaging
in a seance, which has suggested that Dirck is being held at the Plum farm.
Though patently ridiculous in any of its narrative representations, such instances of mysticism inform the action of the novel on various levels. Perhaps, after the overt Catholicism of *Ironweed*, some might see this shift to
mysticism as reflecting a move toward metaphysical pluralism. I think more
likely it shows what happens in a world in which characters operate without
benefit of the support afforded by ethnic traditions. Whatever their background—Dutch, English, Irish—the principle characters of *Quinn's Book* do
not live within the cultures of their own national groups, so they are unable
to draw on the spiritual traditions meant to sustain individuals existing
within each of those societies.

In what at first seems like a digressive aside, the narrative records Will
Canaday's visit to the Plum farm to recover the broken shovel taken earlier
from Daniel. A brief account of the background of the Plum family emphasizes the aura of degradation that has consistently plagued it.[2] Taken with
the previous chronicles of the Staats and the Quinns, the story of the Plums
reflects a third ethnic option for coping with life in the New World.
Kennedy is not so much interested here in arguing for the preference of one
approach over the other, for readers will make that choice on their own.
Rather, he seeks to lay out the alternatives that face settlers as they reconstruct society in this new land.

Understanding the mores of the Albany community, however, proves
to be a complex process even for those seemingly acclimated to it. Will

Canaday learns this when he has a sample of Dirck's cipher analyzed by "a scholar at Columbia College in Manhattan. The scholar saw instantly that the designs came from more than one language: ancient Teutonic runes and Hebrew and Arabic characters forming most of the consonants, and signs of the zodiac serving as vowels" (88). The manuscript proves to be a hyperbolic excoriation of the Society, a secret group eponymously named that strives to control "commerce, finance, politics, industry, and invention, and that as a way of preserving power over what they consider lesser beings, they are, in seriate accumulation, as guilty of fratricide as was Cain, as guilty of ritual murder as are the disciples of Kali, as devout in their myriad hatreds as any demon from the caverns of hell" (89). The turmoil that results from publication of the manuscript significantly overturns the power that the Society has wielded unchecked for years, yet Kennedy never satisfactorily integrates the incident and its consequences into the larger narrative.

Thus, another abrupt shift in the action again reinforces a reader's sense of the disjointed structure of the work, as if Kennedy is trying to accommodate too much action in too little time. Nonetheless, although *Quinn's Book* admittedly lacks the sure pacing of his other books, this condition becomes less damning if one sees the role of the novel as laying a foundation for the rest of the Albany cycle. Kennedy's perspective of the nineteenth-century world makes readers aware of how both momentous and quotidian events can shape the course of lives over several generations. Through diverse and seemingly unrelated incidents, readers come to see the causes of apparently random attitudes and obscure allegiances that emerge decades later.

Daniel is still very concerned about locating Dirck Staats, and eventually he stumbles into a barn on the Plum farm, where he finds Dirck ready to succumb to the effects of a severe beating and a severed tongue. While Dirck is recovering, Daniel learns that labor trouble at Lyman Fitzgibbon's foundry has led to the murder of an Irish immigrant. A number of men have been replaced by lower-wage workers, and the ensuing ill-will has stirred up both the Irish and the nativist communities in Albany. This latest development, coming fast upon the events surrounding Dirck's abduction and Will's battle with the Society, seem to suggest that the novel aims at affirming Thomas Hobbes's view of life as "solitary, poor, nasty, brutish, and short." Indeed, one might too easily see the pessimism of the seventeenth-century English philosopher as a ready gloss for Kennedy's descriptions of nineteenth-century America. However, the discourse of *Quinn's Book* does not so easily give in to this sort of despair, and in fact the narrative seems to struggle to present a picture that might overturn the views expressed by the author of *Leviathan*.

Wandering around Albany, Daniel witnesses the brutal clash of the rival gangs of immigrant Irish and native Yankee workers. Rather than confirming the depravity in human nature, however, the horror of this confrontation shocks people to moderation. It underscores the view that one must retain one's humanity by struggling against these brutish impulses. On the day after the battle, with a combination of largess and threats, Lyman Fitzgibbon brings an end to the hostilities. What remains elusive, however, is any sort of explanation. With a neat synopsis of the events of the first half of the novel, Daniel conveys the uneasiness he feels over the ambiguities of life's experiences:

> Only an intuition persisted that one day I might find the grand signifi-
> cance of this oracular object [the platter that had been hidden in the bird
> cage], as well as how it related to Joey Ryan and his slungshot, to the bum-
> blebees in Maud's script, to the bleeding wrist of Joshua the fugitive slave,
> and to the exploding soldier's melancholy dust. The message emerging
> from my febrile imagination during these tumultuous days was a single
> word: "linkage"; and from the moment I was able to read that word I be-
> came a man compelled to fuse disparate elements of this life, however im-
> probable the joining, this done in a quest to impose meaning on things
> whose very existence I could not always verify. (129–30)

Although readers may debate the success of Daniel's subsequent efforts, they cannot deny that the impulse to impose unity on the diverse experiences of life dominates the remaining discourse of the novel.

Calm descends on Albany, and Daniel determines to go to Saratoga Springs to find Maud. Here, as previously, a penchant for tying together messy domestic details makes the action seem a bit too pat: Hillegond buys him several suits of clothing, and Dirck gives him a sizeable sum of money. In consequence, Daniel sets off considerably more secure financially than he was when the novel began. Meanwhile, the narrative switches to accounts of Magdalena's theatrical career since leaving Albany. Though Maud is gaining a reputation as a performer, Magdalena has fallen into a torpor. She has moved with Maud and John McGee to the mansion of Obadiah Griswold on the shores of Saratoga Lake, hoping that proximity to the lake will help her recover her passion. Daniel goes to the mansion and struggles to understand how this ménage is functioning.

Thus begins the final phase of the novel—and the one most difficult to accept—as Kennedy attempts to construct a discourse that blends spirituality and sensuality. One can see the narrative's intention to present a logical thematic development beyond *Ironweed,* but for it to carry off such an effort requires characters far more complex than John the Brawn, Magdalena, Daniel, and Maud. John is little more than a brute with no feelings other than fundamental physical drives. Magdalena is simply an aging coquette whose sophistication does not go beyond a thumbnail rule for the amount of cleavage a woman should show. Daniel's nature seems incapable of progressing past solipsism and bad manners. And Maud is so shallow as to be nearly invisible. These characters heighten by comparison one's sense of Kennedy's achievements in all of his other works.

Secondary characters are even less suited to meeting these increased narrative demands. They show no range and indeed behave with an artificiality that makes them marionettes. Coincidence and good luck advance the action with unbelievable regularity. For example, in an effort to experience some form of physical contact with Magdalena, Obadiah takes them all to the weekly ball held at the Union Hotel. At the hotel, John the Brawn becomes involved in a fight with the prize-fighting champion Michael Hennessey. Each knocks the other down, and then they go off for a drink, marking the beginning of a new career for John the Brawn.[3] At the ball, Daniel dances with both Maud and Magdalena, and then the narrative gives a brief account of Maud's life to this point. The details are sufficiently banal as to make the attraction Daniel feels for her all the more baffling.

Over the next few days, Maud realizes that relations with Daniel are becoming more serious, and she determines that she must come to some idea of what to do. She bakes a "dumb" cake, a confection that a gypsy taught her to prepare and one that supposedly will reveal to her the identity of the man whom she will marry. When Daniel asks her what she has learned from baking the dumb cake, she makes no reply but instead presses him first to shave. Daniel complies and then goes to the verandah to wait for her. After some time, Obadiah tells him that Maud has disappeared and that he, Daniel, must leave.

If the scene seems unsatisfactory, it reflects the difficulties that run through the narrative whenever individuals delve into metaphysics without benefit of spirituality. As characters throughout Kennedy's earlier novels demonstrate, the search for one's identity remains fruitless if one concentrates only on materiality. (This idea is most clearly illustrated perhaps in *Billy Phelan's Greatest Game*, when Martin Daugherty's newspaper column shows a side of Billy that the young man himself, caught up in the material world, does not understand.) Materialists fill *Quinn's Book*, and they repeatedly prove their imperfection as human beings.

The narrative now jumps forward fourteen years to the summer of 1864 and reveals radical material changes in the lives of the individuals within this neatly delineated social order. Daniel has established his reputation as a newspaper writer and is currently enjoying a measure of notoriety gained as a war correspondent who has traveled with the Union army. He returns to Albany to find that six months earlier someone had strangled Hillegond in her bed. Dirck, unwilling to stay in the unhappy house, has sold the Staat mansion to Lyman Fitzgibbon and has moved to Sweden with a singer whom he has recently married. The rapidity of such changes suggest an impatience with the composition process that one does not usually find in Kennedy's writing.

As with so much of the exposition in this novel, this recitation of the changes that have taken place in the lives of the principal characters comes in the rapid-fire manner of a narrative eager to disburden itself. After hearing of Hillegond's death, Daniel encounters Gordon Fitzgibbon, son of Lyman Fitzgibbon, who peremptorily announces his plans to marry Maud. Later, Daniel kisses and fondles Maud in her bedroom, and readers are offered yet another recitation of events that have transpired: Maud presents in broad outline an account of her sexual experiences and gives Daniel a letter that attempts to explain her actions. Still later, Daniel meets Will Canaday, who brings him up-to-date on Albany newspaper life. All this fills the gaps in major portions of the narrative, but the rapidity of the way events are recounted has made the whole process seemed forced and mechanical.

Tension at this stage in the novel builds in an ad hoc fashion; again it appears as if the narrative feels the burden of resolving too much in too little space. Events transpire without proper motivation and certainly without the careful preparation that stands as the hallmark of Kennedy's other fiction. For example, at the Army Relief Bazaar, Phoebe, Gordon's cousin, subtly disparages Maud, and Daniel comes to Maud's defense by crudely insulting Phoebe. Though it hardly seems likely that Gordon would have let the remarks pass, the narrative rushes on to take up Maud's poetry reading, a performance greeted by "stout applause" (221). When one compares this scene with Helen Archer's singing in *Ironweed*, it seems disappointingly heavy-handed. It is as if Kennedy does not wish to invest the space necessary for a gradual unfolding of characterizations. Instead, he uses fairly blatant devices to signal which trait will dominate the one-dimensional personality of each particular character.

When Daniel ends the evening by acceding to requests that he talk of the reality of war, he does so with brutal frankness and sums up his accounts with the story of the execution of Peaches Plum for desertion. The anecdotes, tinged as they are with melodrama, ring false at several points, and even worse they seem to support a self-righteousness in Daniel that the narrative does not give any indication of challenging. By this point, the discourse has lost its tension and direction. Instead, it devotes all of its energy simply to wrapping up any of the unresolved details introduced in the first portion of the novel.

Other elements in *Quinn's Book* contribute to a growing impression that for Kennedy the work has become little more than an exercise, a series of literary gymnopaedie. The form of the narrative on pages 228–29, for instance—a stilted conversation between Daniel and Will Cannady that circles around an inquiry into the meaning and direction of life—has a coyness and artificiality evident to even the most cursory reading. At the same time, the brittleness of the style precludes the engagement that one has with similar formal experiments in the works of Joyce.

To solve the mystery surrounding Hillegond's death, Will and Daniel go to the Staats mansion and there encounter Maud and Joseph Moran, a singer who had become Hillegond's last paramour. Together they discuss Hillegond's murder and then go to the bedroom where she was killed. Upon entering, they see that two owls have taken up residence in the room. Maud then goes into a sort of trance and describes the murder. Moran is implicated, but of course there is no way to prove his guilt in court. To obviate this difficulty, the two owls attack and kill him.

The narrative shifts again as Daniel offers an account of John the Brawn's rise to prosperity and a sort of respectability. After knocking down Michael Hennessey, John became a prize-fighter. His success as a boxer enabled him to reestablish himself as a saloon keeper as well. An epic victory over Arthur (Yankee) Barker, known as the Pet of Poughkeepsie and the True American, allowed John the Brawn to retire from the ring. He next became involved in Manhattan Democratic politics by assuming the leadership of a gang of thugs. He did his job so well that he earned the right to run gambling houses without police interference. There he employed Joshua, the former slave who in the meantime has continued to help runaway slaves escape pursuit.

As the novel comes to a close, the narrative returns to August 1864 and the inaugural race at John the Brawn's Saratoga Springs track, though recollections about Joshua punctuate the discourse. Gordon and Daniel's rivalry for Maud takes the form of petty bickering and has an embarrassingly adolescent tone. Kennedy, although very good at describing street-corner male interactions, can sometimes stumble, as evident here, when he tries to capture the flow of dialogue in other classes and between men and women.

Outlandish behavior now dominates the story, and the narrative relies too heavily on a form of free association to bring together the diverse elements of the plot. At the racetrack, for example, a Negro woman who enters into the bidding for a betting pool puts Daniel in mind of Joshua, which leads the narrative to a desultory and far-fetched claim that Joshua is the son of Cinque, the leader of the slave revolt on the Amistad (269). Daniel's recollections go on, tracing Joshua's gambling career in New York as well as his efforts with the Underground Railroad. On the racecourse, one of the horses, owned by Abner Swett, is discovered to have been dyed to disguise its true identity and thus to raise the stakes. Meanwhile, a pair of Negroes dressed in imitation of Magdalena and Maud ride onto the track. They circle the course in mocking evocation of the two women and then ride off. Of course, everyone laughs, and Magdalena is mortified. The second heat of the Griswold stakes is run, and Maud's horse wins, although it breaks its leg just after it crosses the finish line and must be destroyed.

The death of Maud's horse turns Daniel's mind once again back to Joshua. Daniel describes in detail the New York draft riots of the preceding summer. The account culminates in a painful description of Joshua's murder at the hands of a frenzied Irish mob. Despite the clear and logical links for all of the transitions between past and present, the facts rattle across the pages in a hurried fashion that makes the recital seem perfunctory.

That evening, a party at Obadiah's mansion serves as a mock wake for Magdalena, but a forced and brittle tone dominates the atmosphere. Behavior is stilted and characters behave more like caricatures. The bickering between Daniel and Gordon continues. During the dancing, Maud tears off Phoebe's clothes as retribution for Phoebe's arranging the mocking imitations of Maud and Magdalena at the racecourse. Amazingly, nothing is made of the incident, and the party simply continues. After more bickering with Gordon, Daniel takes Maud into the house and, in possibly the most joyless representation of sexual foreplay that appears anywhere in Kennedy's fiction, the novel ends as they are about to have intercourse.

As my comments throughout the chapter make clear, I do not see *Quinn's Book* as a work able to stand on its own merits outside the Albany cycle, and indeed it strikes me as fundamentally flawed in several ways. At the same time, the book occupies an important contextual place in Kennedy's canon. It provides the historical background for any number of works to follow. With that background, Kennedy establishes the communal identity of the city that contextualizes his novels. He also experiments with temporal displacement, a technique that appears to a much better effect in *Very Old Bones*. Finally, he has had the opportunity to test his own limits. This is not to say that subsequent works are diminished in their scope, but rather to assert that in them Kennedy shows a certainty of where his artistic strengths lie.

CHAPTER SEVEN

The Centering of *Very Old Bones*

Although Kennedy anchors *Very Old Bones* in the 1950s, like all of the books in his Albany cycle, the narrative of this work moves back and forth in time. This oscillation does not so much fragment its discourse as extend an invitation to readers to complete the book's meaning by uniting its nonsequential chronologic segments. Although that task presents some obvious challenges, it is made easier for those familiar with the Kennedy canon by his decision to return to the by now familiar history of the Phelan family, unfolding across the first half of the twentieth century. This reversion to topics in which the author finds himself most conversant ensures that none of the flaws in *Quinn's Book*, noted in the previous chapter, recur. Instead, the discourse shows a wonderful balance in its pacing and exposition, and it reflects the continuing technical evolution of Kennedy's abilities.

Indeed, *Very Old Bones* exudes the aura of quiet assurance that one finds throughout Kennedy's writing. Its similarities to earlier works affirm his ongoing interest in the thematic concerns that by now stand as characterizing features of his canon. As in *Billy Phelan's Greatest Game* and *Ironweed*, Kennedy wishes to examine how the personalities of ancestors and the events of several preceding generations continue to influence the nature and the behavior of any individual. The search for a system of belief, religious or secular, that animates *Ironweed* remains a subject of ongoing investigation. Although the representations of sex stand as important aspects of Kennedy's fiction going back to *The Ink Truck* and *Legs*, its role in *Very Old Bones* becomes more complex, emerging as a force that defines one's self-conception even as it struggles against the boundaries that such an image imposes. And the issue of loyalty—familial, sexual, communal—reasserts itself here in a series of problematic situations. At the same time, stylistic changes set *Very Old Bones* apart and overtly evince the evolution of Kennedy's artistic abilities and his aesthetic expectations. By this point in his writing, the ambiguities imbedded in his narratives underscore his growing confidence both in his approach to his craft and in his readers' ability to respond to it.

In keeping with this attitude, the narrative structure of *Very Old Bones* invites the reader to begin the interpretive process well before the first chapter. A paragraph-long epigraph from Plato's *Republic* speaks of showing consideration toward a person experiencing the perceptual bewilderment that occurs after moving from light to dark or from dark to light. This passage offers a caveat to readers who might otherwise draw conclusions too quickly or interpret a character's nature too harshly, and it signals concerns important to the structure of *Very Old Bones*: the way a shifting environment poses inevitable impediments to comprehension and the necessity to overcome or at least to accommodate the challenges posed by those impediments.

Immediately following the epigraph, a genealogy of the Phelan family further plays on the concept of ambiguity. Although it ostensibly clarifies the complex relations that act as a framework for the work, its proleptic quality in fact raises as many questions as it answers. The mundane mixes with the portentous in undifferentiated fashion. One learns, for example, the full given name—Anna—of Francis Phelan's wife. The family tree alerts readers to the subplot of Molly Phelan's brief marriage to Walter Mangan and to the fact that Billy Phelan will actually marry Agnes Dempsey, a proposition that remains unresolved over the course of this novel. On the other hand, Daniel Quinn's putative marriage to "[a] Cuban girl" (Kennedy 1992, 260) remains unrecorded in the genealogy and so becomes a matter of speculation that may be cleared up only in subsequent volumes.[1]

Daniel's place on the genealogy itself calls attention to an interesting question. He bears the same name as that of the central character of *Quinn's Book,* and he is the son of Margaret (née Phelan) and George Quinn. He was born nearly eighty years after his namesake fell in love with Maud Fallon during the rescue of those involved in Magdalena Colón's ill-fated attempt to cross the Hudson in midwinter and sixty-four years after the assignation between Maud and Daniel that ends *Quinn's Book.* Nonetheless, the parentage of Daniel's father, George Quinn (b. 1887), remains tantalizingly vague. Was he born in the waning years of Daniel and Maud's life together, if in fact they remained a couple? Was he the child of a later marriage? Is he the grandchild of Maud and Daniel with another generation sandwiched between them?[2]

The range of information presented, suggested, and withheld in this 145-year genealogy turns readers back to the epigraph from Plato. The family tree insinuates a relationship between perception and understanding that is more oblique than direct. And, paradoxically, the increased knowledge afforded by the chart leaves readers less sure how best to comprehend the events that unfold in the novel.

Like the genealogy, the narrative structure of *Very Old Bones* seems neatly contained, but in fact it tends toward digressions and hiatuses that complicate the reader's understanding as well as any explication of that structure. The discourse opens and closes on July 26, 1958. Although the time period examined on that day encompasses ten hours in contrast to the eighteen-plus hours of Joyce's June 16–17, 1904, once again the reader cannot ignore the narrative's echoes of *Ulysses*, especially in the way that Kennedy, like Joyce before him, uses the ostensibly quotidian incidents of a single day to evoke events covering several generations in the family considered in his novel.[3] In fact, as with *Ulysses*, it remains unclear whether the reader should see this account simply as a record of an ordinary day in the lives of the novel's central characters—with the same sort of multiyear references and recollections that might accrue in anyone's mind on any day—or rather as a very unique moment in the histories of the various individuals who appear throughout the work.

The opening of the novel, set in the old Phelan family home on Colonie Street, functions like an operatic overture, preparing us for what will follow yet not preempting the complexities of a full exposition.[4] Orson Purcell, the illegitimate son of Peter Phelan, starts his account of the events of the day beginning with his awakening at around 5:00 A.M. The discourse, however, quickly expands beyond a single day to sketch an outline of the family history, spanning the late nineteenth and early twentieth centuries and introducing the important events and motifs that dominate the narrative. This account is notable for two reasons: it lays out in a straightforward fashion most of the salient facts and familial relations that one needs to know in order to understand the action of the novel, and it shows—albeit retrospectively—how one can comprehend the significance of this information only by seeing it within the complex context that informs the lives of the characters.

In this circular fashion, the narrative, from the initial page onward, evolves out of Orson's seemingly omniscient first-person voice. This perspective may at times produce some transitions that appear forced. Nonetheless, with the continuing use of Free Indirect Discourse, Kennedy manages to sustain with great credibility Orson's perspective through most of the narrative. Further, this technique clearly signals the importance of Orson as the dominant consciousness of the novel. He emerges as the one whose impressions the reader will either accept or reinterpret, but always as the one with whom the reader must contend.[5]

By way of further classification, Orson identifies this account as a "memoir," something that he had started writing five years before the novel's opening, during his recovery from a mental breakdown. In their current state, however, these recollections do not stand as a strict factual account. Rather, they "began as a work of memory, passed through stages of fantasy, and emerged, I hope, as an act of the imagination" (8). They serve a therapeutic purpose, enabling Orson to revisit and reconcile himself with the shaping features of his family's history. The transitional nature of this composition process warns readers against simply accepting these statements and instead suggests strategies for interpreting what Orson has already fictionalized.

Thus, what begins as Orson's perfunctory explanation of how father and son came to live in the Phelan family home quickly gives way to the exploration of an issue that shapes the action of the entire book: sexuality as it informs identity throughout his family's history. This examination goes beyond a survey of hormonal urges from generation to generation. As previous books in the Albany cycle have demonstrated, for the Phelans, sex has a self-referential quality. It creates an intimacy with another that in turn produces insights into the self. Thus, just as *Ironweed* charts the search for identity through spiritual connections, *Very Old Bones* examines the same sort of quest through physical bonds.[6]

This digression on sexual mores both gives readers a revealing sense of Orson's world view—more naïve than he realizes—and hints at the complexity of the Phelan family sexual history. He first alludes to his father's ambiguous relationship to him, one that turns on the question of paternity. He mentions his "all-but-frigid" grandmother, Kathryn, without really understanding the cause. And he takes a patronizing tone toward Tommy, his uncle the "holy moron," whose interest in women led him to buy underwear for a number of female acquaintances who may or may not have reciprocated such gifts with favors of their own. This brief survey of the stunted sensuality of earlier generations lays out a framework for understanding the complexities of the Phelan family and, when fully revealed, serves as a cautionary tale for readers who too quickly impose simplistic interpretations on the actions of ostensibly straightforward characters.

Sexuality exercises a greater and more diverse impact on Orson's life than he initially realizes, for it has an inextricable link to his conceptions of family ties and ultimately to his self-awareness, creating a layered texture that heightens multiplicity. Orson outlines his childhood as shaped by a triad: Peter Phelan, his natural father; Claire Purcell, his mother; and Manfredo the Magnificent, the magician for whom his mother works and whom Peter claims to suspect is Orson's real father. Perversely, over the course of Orson's childhood the magician's technical skills seem to have a greater impact on Orson's immediate development than do the creative talents of his artist father. From Manfredo, Orson learns how to manipulate cards, and later in college he realizes that such a skill allows him to win money at poker. "I was light-years beyond them all in handling both the deck and myself" (10). Like so many of Orson's self-descriptions, this statement is both perfectly accurate and incredibly naïve, for although it attests to his mastery of the little portion of the world that he inhabits, it fails to acknowledge the complexities that exist beyond that sheltered environment. Despite his family's Bohemian lifestyle, their experience of the world is far more limited than Orson realizes.

Orson's parochial sense of the world becomes evident when, while stationed in Germany during his army service in the early 1950s, he meets Giselle Marais. At this point, the narrative links between sex, cheating the system, and money becomes quite clear, though Orson's imperfect grasp of the connections becomes evident only later. When he urges Giselle to dump the army captain whom she is seeing, she asks bluntly, "Can you take me to Paris for a weekend as he does?" (13). Because Orson must answer no, he quickly decides to use his secret ability to cheat at cards to finance his efforts to possess her. Although he does not realize it, this juxtaposition of sex and fraud sets the paradigm for his long-term relations with Giselle. Whether love ever exists between them remains an issue for the reader to resolve. Nonetheless, as the narrative repeatedly demonstrates at crisis points in their relationship, materialism always becomes a measurement of the strength of the bonds between them.

The opening chapter ends by conjuring up two recollections that summarize Orson's troubled sense of self. Hearing his father move around the house reminds him of an argument that he witnessed decades earlier between Peter and Claire, both naked, that concluded with Peter accusing Claire of having an affair with Manfredo the Magnificent. The implied doubts about paternity are later reinforced when Orson catches his mother and Manfredo copulating. From the time he was a young child, this blurred sense of origin has served as a source of anger and distress for Orson: hating Peter for not acknowledging paternity and hating Manfredo for making the situation so unclear.

The novel continues its exploration of the relation between art and life in the second chapter, beginning with a paragraph-long definition that assigns to the artist the role of intermediary similar to that which Orson assumes as narrator. It asserts that Peter "could never have painted his *Malachi Suite*, that remarkable body of paintings and sketches that made him famous, without having projected himself into the lives of the people who had lived and died so absurdly, so tragically, in the days before his birth" (20). In an extension of this view, full of unconscious irony and with a nod toward Keats's "negative capability," Orson then goes on to explain how, while sustaining his first-person narrative, he can nevertheless describe the events in the Quinn household occurring at the same time as those in the Phelan family home. "And so I invoke Keats, without any claim to art of my own, both to drain myself of myself, and to project myself into realms of the family where I had no credentials for being, but am there even so; for I do know the people in this memoir, know where and how they lived, or live still" (21). Although admittedly this explanation of how a third-person omniscient narration can be integrated into a first-person account suffers from a certain clumsiness, the act stands as a rather minor transgression in literary history.[7] Readers must indulge an even greater suspension of disbelief, for instance, to accept the change in the portrait and the perpetual youth of Wilde's central character in *The Picture of Dorian Gray*, yet without such acceptance most of the pleasure of the work disappears.

As becomes clear later in *Very Old Bones*, the domestic situation in the Quinn household replicates the fractured familial relationships of the preceding generations and reflects in microcosm the erosion of the world that characterized the previous novels in the Albany cycle. Annie Phelan is slipping into senility and in consequence acts as both a dominating and a detached presence in the family. Agnes Dempsey, Billy's girlfriend, lives in the house ostensibly to care for Annie, but she is really waiting for Billy to agree to marriage. Billy Phelan himself, now fifty-one, is still awkwardly attempting to lead the life of the young man detailed in *Billy Phelan's Greatest Game* while only partially acknowledging the demise of the Broadway and the lifestyle that defined his world twenty years ago. (The cast on Billy's ankle, which was broken in a car accident, neatly reflects this fractured world.)

George and Peg Quinn represent the only marriage in the house. When Annie Phelan barges into their bedroom as they are having sex, their interrupted intercourse serves as emblematic of the contingent nature of their union. After Annie has barged in on them, George tries to go back to sleep, while Peg, frustrated over not having achieved an orgasm, turns her mind from George to the young attorney Roger Dailey. "He has a way about him, and funny too. Smart and funny and so young. It's so silly" (24). Peg at fifty-nine is a quarter century older than Roger, but her fascination with his flirtatious demeanor betrays the inherent shallowness of her character. Being impetuous, brazen, and attractive might be perfectly acceptable traits for an unmarried girl of twenty, but they seem ridiculous characteristics for a woman approaching sixty with a husband and a grown son. Like her brother, Billy, Peg embodies the sentiments of the book's epigraph. Her perceptions have not yet adjusted in the move from light to dark or dark to light. She remains in a state of arrested development, still seeing things as she did in the years when she was a young girl. Despite the maturing experiences of her life, she cannot yet give up the role of brash young girl.

The conversation at the breakfast table elaborates the image of a fractured family characterized by disagreements and grievances. George Quinn does not want to own a home, although Peg does. Billy Phelan does not want to get married, although Agnes does. Annie Phelan now perceives the flecks of pepper that season her eggs as bugs. When Orson shows up, he becomes a sounding board on which all characters attempt to amplify their grievances. Billy gripes to him about the lack of action on Broadway; George grumbles that he cannot afford to buy a house; and Agnes complains that she wants to get married. With the exceptions of Agnes and Orson, everyone rejects the responsibilities of being an adult.

Family stands as a vexed concept for almost everyone in the novel, and as Orson sums up his affinities with Billy, he articulates the problematic feature of blood ties. "[Billy] and I are first cousins, sons of most peculiar brothers, I the unacknowledged bastard of Peter Phelan, Billy the abandoned son of Francis Phelan, both fathers flawed to the soul, both in their errant ways worth as much as most martyrs" (33). He defines his status in and his relations with the family in terms of absence and missed connections rather than in terms of sustained bonds. The psychic damage done by those lacunae soon emerges as a dominant concern in *Very Old Bones*.

When Billy and Orson leave to go on a tour of the fast-disappearing landmarks of the Albany that flourished between World War I and World War II, the environment outside the house seems as unstable as that existing within it. They begin with a visit to the doctor's office, where Billy learns that the cast on his leg cannot yet be removed. Next they go to the filtration plant, where workers who are tearing it down to make way for a new super-highway have found some very old bones, a misleading reference to the title. The real significance of the find lies in Billy's recollections of Iron Joe Farrell, his grandfather, who used to run the plant, and Tommy, his uncle, who worked there as a sweeper.[8] Billy calls each relation by his first name, giving neither of them the title that would identify his familial relationship—grandfather, uncle. (Likewise, in *Billy Phelan's Greatest Game* and in *Ironweed*, neither Billy nor Peg call Francis *father.*) Within the Phelan family, individuals are rarely identified by their position in the family, and one cannot help but wonder to what degree this habit reflects the clan's very tenuous grasp on familial ties.

Throughout the novel, characters find the outdoors too open and un-predictable to feel secure, so from the construction site Billy and Orson go for a drink in the more confined and familiar environs of a saloon owned by Sport Schindler. It perfectly captures the aura of the bars that are havens for the men who appear in *Legs*, *Billy Phelan's Greatest Game*, and *Ironweed*. "The place had a pressed-tin ceiling, a long mahogany bar with brass rail, shuffle-board, dart board, and years of venerable grime on the walls" (34). In truth, however, as the narrative notes, "Schindler's was a historic monument" (34), standing only as a remnant of a way of life long past its heyday. The defin-ing images of an earlier age have fallen into neglect. Places such as Becker's Saloon, scene of much of the action in *Billy Phelan's Greatest Game*, "had changed hands in the early fifties, and after that nobody paid any attention to the photographic mural behind the bar, mural of two hundred and two shirt-sleeved men at a 1932 clambake" (37). Even a shooting that occurs while Billy and Orson are having their drink fails to revive the wide-open image of the Albany of the 1930s. Buffalo Johnny Rizzo tries to murder Morty Pappas, already on crutches with a broken leg that was the result of Rizzo's earlier attempt on his life. The scheme goes awry when Billy uses his cane to knock the gun from Johnny Rizzo's hand. This act hearkens back to

Billy's facing down the knife-wielding kid in *Billy Phelan's Greatest Game* and forward to Edward Daugherty's subduing Matty Lookup in *The Flaming Corsage,* but in its description the incident has a slapstick quality that leaves one more amused than shocked by the violence. Bathos has replaced pathos on Broadway.

The narrative once again moves from one enclosed environment to another as Orson takes Billy back to the Phelan house. There Orson demonstrates his ability to manipulate cards, a skill that he had used with some success in Germany to raise money to spend on Giselle. However, unlike many of the characters in *Billy Phelan's Greatest Game,* Orson sees gambling as a means to an end. He does not, and perhaps cannot, respond to the pure pleasure of playing. As he explains his motivations for gambling to Billy, Orson may sense the disparity in their attitudes, for he tries to redefine his compulsion for money as less a means of securing the materialistic Giselle and more a matter of giving each of them a measure of freedom: "I vowed not to become a prisoner. I vowed not to let Giselle become one. I vowed I would have money enough for us to live idyllic lives of love and freedom. I vowed to keep her with me now and tomorrow; always now, always tomorrow" (49). Ironically, the first vow is reversed, and the second comes true only when Giselle escapes from Orson.

This declaration introduces a major narrative shift: a long account of Orson's previous behavior. Orson's statement also gives readers a very clear sense of his conflicted nature, emphasizing the limitations of his self-awareness, at least during his time in the service. As we learn from Orson's recollection, to take Giselle to Venice for their honeymoon Orson becomes involved in currency deals with a man eponymously named Meister Geld. From the start of this adventure, the narrative signals how little awareness Orson has to the world he has entered. He makes an elaborate attempt to disguise his identity so that he can enter the bar where Meister Geld can be found and is immediately asked to leave when the bartender recognizes him as an American. A whore leads him to Meister Geld, and the conversation with the gangster that follows shows Orson awed like a schoolboy without any real sense of the seriousness of the commitment that he is making. (Even the older Orson remains unenlightened, for he remarks in an editorial aside: "The danger was minimal" [57].) His work moving currency gets him enough money to take Giselle to Venice, but, despite his assumptions of invulnerability, he is immediately arrested by the military police on his return to Germany.

Orson now finds himself more alienated than at any other time in his life, and his gradual realization of that condition ultimately leads to a complete breakdown. He escapes from military custody and goes on a tour of the city's criminal haunts in search of Meister Geld. He is incapable of independent action at this time, however, and he quickly calls on Giselle for help. While retrieving him from Fritz's Garden of Eden Club, where he is entertaining the locals with his bizarre behavior, Giselle takes a number of photographs that will launch her own professional career. Orson is headed in the opposite direction. He has had a breakdown in the bar, and he is subsequently put in the care of a psychiatrist, Dr. Tannen, whose account to Giselle of Orson's condition provides a chilling summary of Orson's life to date:

> He is living in the very real world of his second self, where there is always an answer to every riddle. He believes he is . . . an unwanted child. He was seriously neglected by mother and father, though he exudes love for them both. He is so insecure that he requires a façade to reduce his anxieties to manageable size; and so every waking moment is an exercise in mendacity, including self-delusion. He has found no career direction, and has completed nothing of significance to himself. . . . He sees nothing worth doing, including completing the last contorted sentence of his unfinished book, which now ends on a high note of suspense with a comma. (72)[9]

In the meantime, Giselle meets with unqualified success. *Paris Match* magazine has printed her photos and has given her an assignment in Berlin. Alienated and unable to cope with the European milieu, Orson leaves to go back to New York to live with his father, wondering if Giselle and his cousin Daniel Quinn—the family he leaves behind—are having an affair.

This undercurrent of uncertainty growing out of blurred sexual connections recurs throughout Orson's recollection and serves as an important characterizing feature of the novel. Presumptions of betrayal, real or imagined, cloud many of the sexual relations chronicled in *Very Old Bones*. Consequently, more often than not intercourse ends up undermining rather than cementing relationships. Except in the case of Molly Phelan and Walter Mangan, intimacy rarely produces emotional resolution. The act that should attest to the commitment of two people to one another becomes instead a way of underscoring their isolation.

At the same time, as the narrative persistently reminds us, characters are extremely dependent on one another. (Even the aggressively independent

Billy and Peg both need to be driven around on the day the novel takes place.) The only allegiances that provide genuine and continual props are familial, yet most of the characters have a blurred sense of self that makes it difficult to sustain those bonds. Confidence in family backing relies on a measure of trust, and Orson exemplifies the difficulties in making such a commitment. Many other Phelans, however, remain equally unsure of their status and consequently uncertain of the support they will receive.

Heightening this sense of rupture, Orson's narrative begins to focus on the fragmentation of the family. Recollections of the death of Kathryn Phelan on December 9, 1934, provide in turn an occasion for offering an account of Peter Phelan's decision in 1913 to leave the family home in Albany and go to New York City. The move is a consequence of a fight with his mother and his sister Sarah over the morality of the Daugherty family. When Edward Daugherty's *The Flaming Corsage*, a play that has scandalized Albany, closes after two days (Kennedy 1996, 82), Kathryn and Sarah Phelan use its failure as an occasion to renew their condemnation of the Daughertys.[10] Peter objects in language as violent and abusive as that employed by the two women. He leaves home while a thunderstorm rages, and the next day he takes a train to New York City. As his brother Francis has done and will do again, Peter flees the site of a confrontation. In his case, the cause is sex and not violence, but like the trauma that in 1916 drives Francis out of town for twenty-two years, the conflict is rooted within the family. In New York, Peter's prolonged affair with Claire Purcell results in the birth out of wedlock of Orson in 1924. However, because Peter suspects that Rico Luca, a.k.a. Manfredo the Magnificent, may be the real father, Orson is born without benefit of any man acknowledging paternity. Orson begins his life without clearly defined family ties, and for his first thirty-four years he bears the scars of that absence. Somewhat perversely, much of his suffering relates directly to efforts to deny his need for the support afforded by a family.

A solid family structure, of course, does not inevitably lead to peace and tranquility. As one can see from Orson's own accounts, much of the Phelans' suffering comes directly from individuals seeking to deny the need for the family to adapt to a world inexorably reforming around them. Events surrounding the death of Kathryn Phelan in 1934 sharply illustrate these conflicting forces. During the funeral, Sarah endeavors to preserve the old order by assuming her mother's matriarchal role and customary black dress, but the presence of Orson, whom Peter has brought to the ceremony, unmistakably announces the inevitability of change. Orson's ambiguous status precludes his calling any of his relatives by such designations as *aunt* or *uncle*, even if the Phelans felt sufficient kinship to use such labels. Someone needs to articulate his status within the family, yet they all understand their own roles too imperfectly to be able to extrapolate to define a place for him. Indeed, although Orson seems to be the one most obviously in search of a family, most of the characters in the novel find themselves struggling to understand what it means (both in terms of ties and responsibilities) to be part of a family.

The search for understanding and the acknowledgment of change do not move forward unopposed, and Peter has several struggles of will with Sarah centering on these issues. The real clash, however, begins with the unexpected appearance of their brother, Francis, for the funeral, and it shows the limits of Peter's ability to reconfigure the Phelans' world. As Francis sits down for a meal in the kitchen, Peter remembers an evening thirty-six years earlier. It marks the first open confrontation within the Phelan family over the Daugherty household, and it demonstrates, though perhaps recognizably so only in retrospect, how sexual trauma has profoundly weakened ties within the family. Three days before this clash, both Peter and Sarah had seen Katrina Daugherty and Francis having sexual intercourse. When Sarah finally alludes to this incident, it provokes Kathryn to knock Francis backward into the china closet. Sex exerts a powerful, even violent force on each person involved, and each behaves in a manner justified by what he or she knows. At this point in the narrative, Francis's mother and sister seem little more than repressed, vindictive harridans. Because Kathryn Phelan has kept secret the scandal of her brother Malachi McIlhenny's murder of his wife, it is not possible for the others to know or understand the source for the abiding aversion she feels.

When Francis returns for Kathryn's funeral in 1934, everyone but Sarah welcomes him. Sarah, however, brushing aside general objections, demands that he leave the house. Like her mother's outburst three and a half decades earlier, her animosity goes unexplained at this point in the narrative, and readers can only put it down to spite. By the end of the novel, however, when the narrative reveals the details of the tragedy perpetrated by Malachi McIlhenny and the extent of Sarah's knowledge of that tragedy, her reasons become more apparent. She sees something perverted in the McIlhenny blood, and she fears that perversion being passed from generation to generation. In Sarah's view, sex is the source of transmission, and abstinence becomes the only solution. Francis, however, appears as a force of blind sexuality whose appetites cannot be curbed as the appetites of others in the family—Chick, Molly, and Tommy—apparently have been. What shocks Sarah is Francis's insinuation that she too carries the very perversion that she so dreads. Only he and she are old enough to remember the horrific events, and he deftly evokes them for her without making them explicit for the others: " 'You know, you turned out just right, Sarah,' Francis said. 'Just like I knew you would. You ain't got a speck o' the real goods in you. You ain't got one little bit of Papa. You got it all from the other side of the family, all from that Malachi crowd. You're somebody they oughta cut up and figure out, 'cause you ain't hardly human, Sarah' " (Kennedy 1992, 115). The exchange evinces a bitterness in Francis rarely evident in *Ironweed*. It strikes directly at Sarah's hidden fears that she too is capable of such depravity, and it underscores the profound alienation that Francis feels toward his sister and mother.

Like the confrontation thirty-six years earlier, Francis's charge only provokes the bitter response that was doubtless intended. Faced with Sarah's belligerence, Francis ignores the will of the majority and slips off. The narrative makes no judgment, but it seems clear that he leaves because he places demands on acceptance that brook no exception. His own skin is rather thin, perhaps because of a lingering guilt over his son Gerald's death, so like Sarah he has a secret that exerts powerful control over his behavior.

Orson and Peter, trying to find Francis, end up at the railroad yards. There they see him apparently contemplating suicide by stepping in front of an oncoming freight train. Orson senses what he is about to do and runs toward him. Francis steps back from the tracks and angrily accuses both Peter and Orson of being voyeurs. It is of course the same crime that Peter had committed when he watched Francis and Katrina Daugherty, leading to the terrible confrontation between Francis and his mother. In this case, however, we see Kennedy's deft sense of narrative balance when that voyeuristic impulse redresses the balance by saving Francis's life.

Peter's intervention also has a reciprocal benefit. Voyeurism again gives him artistic insights that he could not attain through his own actions. (In an interesting side note, a quarter century later the 1950s residents of Colonie Street look voyeuristically at Peter painting as he moves back and forth in the second-floor room that has become his studio by that point.) He uses the inspiration of Francis's attempted suicide as a goad to produce "six canvases and many sketches . . . during the years 1936–1939" (131). These works, called the *Itinerant* series, mark a profound stage in Peter's artistic development.[11] At the same time, they reveal the limits of his inspiration, for the completion of the series marks the beginning of a nearly twenty-year fallow period.

The narrative abruptly shifts to Orson's account of his life in the months immediately after his return from Germany in 1953. Having nowhere else to go, he has lived uneasily in New York City with his father. During this time, he meets his mother for a drink at the Biltmore Hotel to discuss his paternity, a topic that still haunts him.[12] As becomes evident through the conversation with his mother, Orson seeks only the answer to a deceptively simply question: Who am I? For the remainder of the novel, he seeks to resolve his question by gaining an unambiguous affirmation of affiliation with the Phelan family.

When Orson learns that Giselle, who has been working in Europe, will be coming to New York, he attempts to force a familial commitment by telling Peter that he is bringing Giselle home. Peter, unwilling either to acknowledge formal ties or to deny any connection, leaves it ambiguous whether he accepts Giselle as a daughter-in-law and by extension Orson as a son.

> "She might not stay, but I want to bring her here."
> "Bring her, bring her," Peter said. "I'd like to see the look of anybody who'd marry you."
> Peter smiled. I examined the smile to evaluate its meaning. Was it a real smile? It looked like a real smile. I decided to return it with a smile of my own.
> Son?
> Dad? (146)

The unvoiced dialogue of the final two lines masterfully conveys the ambivalence that still inhibits the behavior of both men.

In fact, no one involved seems willing to trust all to an unqualified commitment. Orson reveals that "[i]t had been my plan to use the one hundred dollars my mother gave me to pay for a weekend at the Biltmore with Giselle" (150), so the question of staying with Peter, although still valid, is a bit less straightforward than it at first seems. Giselle has herself been busy setting up contingencies. She has avoided dependence on Orson and insinuated a measure of sexual independence by arranging to stay in the vacant apartment of an editor at *Life* magazine whom she met in France. When she and Orson arrive at the man's Westside flat, Giselle explains the connection by then telling Orson that *Life* has offered her a job. As the narrative clearly demonstrates, they make love both as a means of communication and as a way to establish a transitory alternative to familial stability. In fact, the act only underscores Orson's realization that they will soon separate.

Orson next goes to visit his editor, Walter Pettijohn, at a major commercial press that also likes to publish authors with a literary appeal.[13] Pettijohn, acting very much the father figure, tells Orson that his book manuscript is brilliant but that no one else at the press will support this opinion. Like Peter earlier in this episode, Pettijohn gives Orson ambiguous affirmation that will not allow him to form a clear sense of their relationship. The only direction the editor can offer is to encourage Orson to continue editing the memoirs of Meriweather Macbeth, a man for whom Orson has only contempt and whose memoirs, though without literary merit, are maddeningly saleable.

In response, Orson behaves like the rebellious child. He goes back to the flat lent to Giselle, steals the apartment owner's checkbook and business cards, and leaves a message for Giselle to meet him at the Plaza Hotel. With these acts, he begins his self-destructive response to all that displeases him in the world. He registers at the Plaza, buys a new suit, and furnishes the hotel room with the luxuries that he knows Giselle loves. This orgy of materialism dramatizes the way he thinks he would behave had his novel been accepted, had Peter acknowledged paternity, had the world been perfect. It also underscores the commodification of his relationship with Giselle.

When Giselle arrives at the Plaza, the conversation becomes increasingly surreal, indicating the breakdown that Orson is beginning to experience. They retire to the room he has rented and before engaging in intercourse attempt in a desultory fashion to determine what makes Giselle "at this moment . . . the most fucksome woman on the planet" (171). As with their previous lovemaking, their sexual activity does not establish commitment but underscores their inability or unwillingness to communicate beyond physical connection.

As a way of dramatizing his current preference for public display over private intimacy, Orson continues the evening by taking Giselle to a strip club. Although his motives are probably not clear even to himself, he seems to wish to emphasize the grotesque.[14] When he introduces Giselle to Brenda the stripper, the narrative draws a parallel between the two women by playing on the idea of photography (178). In a pattern of behavior that parallels the events leading up to his first breakdown, and with the stripper and Giselle as audience, Orson undertakes a rambling monologue similar to a conversation he had with a stranger in the Oak Bar and to his performance in Germany at Fritz's Garden of Eden Club. On the point of blacking out, he finally declares himself an eschatophile and an eschatophiliac, a lover of extremes and an extremist. In fact, he is saying, perhaps without realizing it, that he has reached the end of his rope and feels his sense of self slipping away. All this serves to establish that Orson has propelled himself into his second mental breakdown.

The penultimate section of the novel begins with a hint of why the Phelan family has become dysfunctional. "In the early spring of 1953, and with blinding illumination on through the fall of 1954, Peter Phelan came to perceive this: that individuals, families or societies that willfully suppress their history will face a season of reckoning, one certain to arrive obliquely, in a dark place, and at a hostile hour, with consequences for the innocent as well as for the conspirators" (189). After devoting the first three parts of *Very Old Bones* to these consequences, the remainder of the novel offers in highly deliberate fashion the specific details that show the how, why, and wherefore of this suppression in the Phelan family.

Because the narrative follows this epiphany with an account of Peter's return to Albany from New York to live in the old family home, the reader has a reinforced sense of the importance of communal roots, no matter how conflicted individual family members' feelings have become. The narrative takes up a series of family conflicts, centering on Sarah's inflexible Puritanism, that precede Peter's return. In 1954, Chick Phelan is being pressured to make a decision about marriage by Evelyn Hurley, a woman with whom he had been keeping company for seventeen years. Because of Evelyn's status as a widow and Chick's as a former seminarian, Sarah feels that the marriage would be sacrilegious. While Chick and Sarah bicker over the issue, the police bring home Tommy for interfering with a woman. (He has used a stick to lift her skirt, imitating a scene from a Charlie Chaplin film that he had seen thirty years earlier.)

Before describing Sarah's reaction to this event, the narrative digresses from this story to describe a photo of Molly, holding a cedar waxwing in her hands, taken by Giselle later in September 1954. It has significance because of Molly's expression of pathos. "Molly had been declining into melancholia before the photo was taken, the onset of decline dating back to the day Tommy was arrested for imitating Charlie Chaplin" (196). The creature can evoke such profound feeling in Molly because it is this bird, now stuffed, that began her romance with Walter Mangan. Like so many of the memories in the novel, very old bones serve as a reminder of deep sexual or familial trauma.

Molly's despondency has come about as a direct response to her sister Sarah's violent fanaticism. Shocked by Tommy's precociousness with the neighbor woman, Sarah decides that he must be punished. She beats him as she has done before, but this time with such fury that she "damaged Tommy's spine so severely that he could not walk" (199). The ferociousness of the attack sends Molly into her depression and causes Chick to make the decision to marry Evelyn and move to Miami. Molly too leaves the house, taking Tommy with her to the Grand View Lake House, a vacation spot that the Phelans have patronized for sixty years, in the hope that she might overcome the depression that engulfs her. Sarah's pathological abhorrence of all things sexual finally breaks up that generation of the family after years of adherence to a claustrophobic routine.

At the hotel, Molly finds Orson recuperating from his second breakdown, and they have a chance to define their own relationship. Before they do so, however, the narrative highlights a "colloquy" that takes place between Molly and Giselle. Although their exchange seems little different from other portions of the narrative, highlighting it underscores its significance. Giselle relates the degrading details surrounding Orson's crack-up, and she tries to justify her manipulation of Orson. Molly tells of her courtship by Walter Mangan, of their sexual relations, of their marriage, of their separation because of Sarah's illness, of Walter's death, and of his burial. Though neither says so directly, each speaker seems to try to instruct the other on how a woman should behave toward the man she loves. They both, in effect, use the discussion to justify past behavior. At the close of this exchange, Giselle takes the picture of Molly holding the cedar waxwing, since stuffed, that first brought her and Walter together. Giselle has been having difficulty getting the right pose until Orson calls out, evoking in Molly an enigmatic expression. Like so many casual, unselfconscious gestures in the novel, Molly's response is fraught with meaning, and Giselle jealously realizes that Orson loves Molly.

Orson then gives his account of his second breakdown through a narrative that ultimately traces his journey of integration with the Phelan family, ushered in by his drunken flight from all ties. After Giselle and Peter rescue him from alcohol poisoning, Giselle takes him to Albany. However, as she did after his first breakdown, she again leaves to pursue her career. Molly assumes the job of nursing him and decides that his recovery will be accelerated if he goes to work at Grand View Lake House, earning his keep by doing odd jobs.[15]

Sexuality always stands as an important feature in Kennedy's narratives. Characters who combine sexuality with strong family ties—and there are precious few who can do that—stand as particularly well-balanced individuals. At the hotel, Orson and Molly acknowledge a strong attraction, speak of love for each other, and tacitly agree not to act on their urges. Molly goes on, in a discourse punctuated by passages from Anna Livia Plurabelle's closing monologue in *Finnegans Wake*, to describe lovingly the sexual encounters that she had with Walter as they were courting. The allusions nicely counterpoint the bittersweet element in Molly's disquisition, for, in the process of talking about herself, she also comments on the sexual repression within her family. Finally, she talks about the stillborn child that she had and then buried in the basement of the family house.

Just as Orson must work out his feelings toward paternity (like Stephen Dedalus in *Ulysses*), Molly must also declare her maternity by taking full responsibility for the child in the basement. Within a year of Molly's revelations to Orson, Sarah dies, and before the wake Molly has Orson dig up her dead child's remains—more very old bones. She seeks to fulfill her duty as a mother by ensuring that her baby will lie in consecrated grounds, so she hides its body in the coffin with her sister. The dignity that Kennedy gives to the ritual of Catholic burial and to its importance for Molly says a great deal about the spirituality that permeates his own writing. More to the point, the peace that the gesture brings to Molly underscores the interdependence of sexual, familial, and spiritual obligations.

As the book moves toward a conclusion, it narrows and clarifies the reader's interpretive task. In a fashion analogous to what will be made graphically explicit in *The Flaming Corsage*, this novel raises the issue of whether psychologically scarring events can alleviate responsibility for a lifetime of aberrant behavior. Sarah's death accelerates the narrative's movement toward climax, for it brings to light the scandal that took place in 1887, shortly before Peter was born. Newspaper clippings saved by Sarah detail how Malachi McIlhenny, who was Kathryn Phelan's brother, murdered his wife Lizzie. The event itself is emblematic of Kennedy's approach to representations of the human psyche. The narrative leaves it to the reader to determine whether the bitterness, ignorance, and superstition that cloud

Malachi's life in any way mitigate such brutality. As with Jack Diamond and other violent characters in the Albany cycle, Kennedy refuses to offer unimpeachable evidence as to the source of evil, and one hesitates uneasily between seeing it in the world or in the individual.

The ambiguity functions as an important aspect of what occurs, for it helps us understand the bewilderment and fear that Kathryn Phelan must have felt. Because she cannot fully explain her brother's behavior, she must set up elaborate defenses within her own family to prevent its recurrence. Documents chronicling that deed lead Peter to undertake a series of paintings, the *Malachi Suite,* that parallels the *Itinerant* studies he did in the late 1930s. As with the latter paintings inspired by Francis on the railroad tracks, this record of sexuality and violence becomes Peter's way of purging his own feelings of alienation from the family structure. (Peter makes evident the significance that he attaches to the artwork when he uses the *Malachi Suite* paintings as a backdrop for the climactic family meeting that he has arranged.)

The novel's final section opens with representations of familiar problems and recollections of insufficient responses to them. A synopsis of the final years of Francis Phelan's life presents his efforts at reintegration into the family. Kennedy leaves it to the reader to decide whether they are simply futile gestures or acts of profound contrition. As people arrive at the family house, the sexual tension increases. The news that Giselle is pregnant provokes in Orson an unvoiced ambivalence similar to what Peter must have felt after the conception of Orson. Molly enters flirting with both Billy and Orson. Peg brags about the proposition that Roger Dailey has earlier made to her and announces that Danny Quinn seems about to marry a Cuban girl. (Orson cannot help wondering if this news shocks Giselle.) Even at this late stage, sexuality has not been integrated into the family structure, but rather it continues to exert a jarring, disruptive impact.

The narrative rapidly moves to a climax as Peter has his will read. He does not wish to wait for his death to share his estate with his family, for he seeks to alleviate "the collective evil to which so many members of this family have been heir, heiress, or victim" by "the easing of the financial woe that periodically besets us all" (262). Among other things, his gesture gives Peg the money she needs for a down payment on a house, and it acknowledges Orson as his son. (In this case, Peter proprietorially finally gives Orson the title "our son" though Orson's mother is not there to witness the event.)

After chronicling Peter's efforts to efface the impact of evil, the narrative goes back to a final account of the event that produced so much of it: the violent death of Lizzie McIlhenny. The account attests to Kathryn Phelan's vain efforts to stop her brother, and the brutality of the scene mitigates most readers' judgments of both Kathryn and Sarah's harsh behavior resulting from their consequent sexual frigidity. The final painting that Peter shows the family is entitled "*The Protector*, a portrait of Kathryn Phelan smothering the flames on Lizzie's clothing, her own maternity dress aflame at one corner" (271). It demonstrates Peter's forgiveness, and by extension the family's, of Kathryn, Sarah, and all of the flawed Phelans, including themselves.

The final pages consist of a series of revelations, like Molly's story of the secret bootlegger's legacy that she inherited years previously. (Because the narrative has so carefully prepared readers for such a contingency by showing Molly's inner strength, her ability to keep secrets, and her empathy, the revelation has none of the deus ex machina aura that clouds so many similar revelations in *Quinn's Book*.) These pages also detail efforts at reconciliation—notably Billy's and Orson's—within the family in general. There is a final word on Malachi's brief life after his crime, and then the novel ends with a description that makes it clear that with the ambivalence surrounding all the characters' lives, no happy ending is guaranteed.

Nonetheless, in *Very Old Bones* Kennedy has unmistakably declared what he feels necessary for a stable family structure. The elements of sexuality and spirituality are present in his novels from as early as *Legs*. In this work, however, Kennedy takes the discourse to a more sophisticated, more mature level. He explores the need for communal empathy—analogous to that of individual understanding examined in *Ironweed*—and introduces the concept that even the most stereotypical of characters has a complexity in his or her nature that requires very close attention before anyone can begin to understand that individual. As with the works of Joyce, the writer whom Kennedy so deeply admires, the humanism that permeates this book transcends sentimentality and instead establishes the author as a powerful observer of communal interaction.

 CHAPTER EIGHT

The Cyclical Impulse of *The Flaming Corsage*

As noted in chapter 6 of this study, *Quinn's Book* may raise questions regarding Kennedy's ability to write in eras other than *le temp entre les deux guerres* featured in the first three Albany novels. However, *Very Old Bones*, with its confident evocation of the 1950s, reiterates Kennedy's talent as a skillful narrator with a sharp ear for dialogue and a sure sense of characterization. Further, it establishes beyond doubt his capacity to represent in a convincing fashion periods and locations other than those featured in *Legs*, *Billy Phelan's Greatest Game*, and *Ironweed*. Nonetheless, for any readers still skeptical of Kennedy's command of broad historical periods, *The Flaming Corsage* affirms his adeptness at vivifying the last decades of the nineteenth century and the first few years of the twentieth century.

Each successive novel in the Albany cycle has foregrounded elements that attest to Kennedy's growing virtuosity as a writer, and *The Flaming Corsage* in its turn provides ample evidence of the thematic diversity of his work. In exploring the lives of the Daugherty clan, this novel asserts the potential of a family other than the Phelans to provide a narrative axis for subsequent Albany stories. Additionally, it offers revealing elaborations of the events introduced in the recollections of Martin Daugherty in *Billy Phelan's Greatest Game* and in those of Francis Phelan in *Ironweed*. It also shifts the topical perspective from that of previous novels by moving the emphasis to individuals from the fin-de-siècle generation. This gesture in turn gives a much stronger sense of the complex personalities and the frustrated lives of the novel's central characters, Edward and Katrina Daugherty.

Familiar thematic concerns recur to punctuate the discourse of *The Flam-*

ing Corsage as it continues the accretive pattern of narrative development that has marked Kennedy's books since *Billy Phelan's Greatest Game*. Just as the conclusion of *Very Old Bones* provides information that can mitigate our response to Kathryn and Sarah Phelan's repressive behavior, the discourse of *The Flaming Corsage* greatly enhances our understanding of Edward and Katrina Daugherty's conduct. By the end of the novel, we have a sense of their conflicted consciousnesses that extends far beyond the characterizations in *Billy Phelan's Greatest Game* and *Ironweed*. Although selfishness remains a prominent aspect of Edward's identity, a measure of sensitivity now emerges in his nature. A series of tragic events cannot fail to leave their mark on Katrina's consciousness, but in *The Flaming Corsage* we see a willfulness bordering on mania as a compelling aspect of her personality from a very early age. These revelations present a degree of complexity informing the motives of the characters that makes them vastly more interesting than suggested in previous novels.

Kennedy also uses the structure of *The Flaming Corsage* to expand on a stylistic approach, introduced in *Very Old Bones*, that adopts a much more flexible chronologic scheme than any found in the previous novels. *Very Old Bones* breaks up the conventional, linear pattern of narrative development and consequently succeeds in illuminating elements in the lives of individuals in the Phelan clan that show them as much deeper characters than readers might initially assume. Though it opens on July 26, 1958, the narrative ranges in a rather leisurely and somewhat disjointed fashion back and forth across seventy-five years of family history. Nonetheless, *Very Old Bones* maintains its continuity by the use of topical references, well known at least for those who have read other Albany novels, that allow a reader to adjust fairly easily to the periodic oscillation.

A progressive movement away from linear development gives an episodic quality to successive segments of the discourse in *The Flaming Corsage* and throws into relief features delineating individual figures. The reader sees in the nonsequential episodes of the novel intense reflections on human identity. At the same time, these passages operate without the contextualizing framework that usually provides interpretive support to a reader's sense of a particular character. (Think, for example, of how the meticulous development of the idiosyncratic world of Dickens's Victorian London provides us with an environment against which to measure Mr. Micawber's eccentricities.) In consequence, as figures appear in chapter after chapter outside the conventional temporal progression of narrative, readers focus all attention on aspects of identity as the only means to form a unified impression of the discourse.

This decontextualization represents an impressive expansion of the disrupted chronology employed in *Very Old Bones*. By way of contrast, *The Flaming Corsage* introduces briefer narrative segments, with shifts from one period to another coming much more abruptly. This episodic approach conveys the narrative's ability to introduce complex polymorphic development in compact descriptions. Such changes testify to the author's technical polish and to his confidence in the reader's capacity to respond to his multilayered discourse.

The book's epigraph—made up of two short passages taken from Gilbert and Sullivan's *The Mikado*—provides an early and useful example of a key creative feature, the inclination to play on antinomies, that enables Kennedy to pack so many interpretive possibilities into a relatively brief passage. In the selection quoted, first Yum-Yum laments the fact that she will be put to death as a consequence of marrying Nanki-Poo. Then Yum-Yum and Nanki-Poo elaborate on the dilemma of being genuinely in love yet knowing that " 'Tis death to marry you!" In *The Mikado*, of course, the gruesome fate that threatens the lovers loses much of its menace because the comic context of the Gilbert and Sullivan operetta offers the formulaic promise of a contrived happy ending. In *The Flaming Corsage*, the bathos and pathos commingled in the epigraph introduce conflicting protocols for the narrative that follows. Specifically, one wonders, given the comic opera allusion, if a reader should assume that, as often as not, banality rather than dignity will inform the catastrophes of the novel.

Just as an unconventional style makes new interpretive demands on readers, a self-conscious thematic multiplicity challenges them to avoid assumptions. Horrific events, like those detailed in the opening chapter of *The Flaming Corsage*, seem to invite one to give the novel the classification of tragedy, yet, as with the epigraph, context insistently generates resistance to conventional readings. The description of a brutal murder-suicide in a Manhattan hotel, the Millerton House, in 1908 introduces the major themes—violence, promiscuity, deception, and misprision—that will dominate subsequent action. More significantly, however, it presents the shaping incident of the novel in language that insinuates ambiguity into a putatively straightforward account. The conflicting reports of Giles Fitzroy's last words before killing his wife Felicity preview the way a range of often contradictory descriptions surround key events throughout *The Flaming Corsage*. Further, in the chapter's final lines, a heavy-handed play on words underscores the tawdriness and the ambiguity of what has transpired in this incident. It describes the naked, adulterous Felicity as Giles's "exposed wife" (Kennedy 1996, 2) and leaves the reader wondering what to make of the conflated representation of her physical disposition and public shame.

Immediately after this episode, the narrative turns to an account of events set in 1885, a time twenty-three years previous to the hotel killings, and establishes parallel patterns of achronicity and venality that figure so prominently in the discourse. The second chapter introduces Edward Daugherty and Thomas Maginn as two young men with complimentary literary ambitions and a shared, coarse sensuality that dominates their immediate consciousnesses. They are visiting a bordello, where Maginn is recognized as a frequent patron.[1] Familiarity, however, does not translate into acceptance, another theme reiterated throughout the novel. The whores quite obviously prefer Edward's patronage, and Maginn immediately evinces a competitiveness that, periodically reinforced by Edward's dismissiveness, stands as an undercurrent throughout the narrative.[2]

In the world of the novel, however, status and disapprobation emerge as conflicting forces driving nearly every character, no matter what his or her position on the social scale. Thus, in the layered society of late-nineteenth-century Albany, Edward finds himself as vulnerable to scorn as Maginn. When later that evening Edward encounters the beautiful and privileged Katrina Taylor dining with her mother and father at the Kenmore Hotel, Katrina's parents can barely conceal their disdain for him. The antipathy they feel echoes, in a heightened form, Edward's condescension toward Maginn, an early sign of the pattern of narrative oscillation—familiar from other Kennedy writings—that permeates the novel: a tendency to link apparently antipathetic figures by tracing similarities that shape their lives.

Further chronologic fluctuation, however, disrupts easy generalizations about the social framework of the novel. A retrospective glance at events in 1840, for instance, recounts how Emmett Daugherty saved the life of Lyman Fitzgibbon. The gratitude of Fitzgibbon shaped the lives of two generations of Daughertys when he underwrote the education of Emmett's son. This benevolence established a relationship that explains how the working-class Edward might come to know Lyman's granddaughter, Katrina Taylor, and feel the confidence to tell her of his plans "to pursue you with a fervid Irish passion, unlike anything you've ever imagined" (20). Edward's febrile dic-

tion expresses the same sort of lightning-bolt desire that Francis Phelan recalls feeling for Annie Farrell in *Ironweed,* that Daniel Quinn undergoes for
Maud Fallon in *Quinn's Book,* and that Molly Phelan experiences for Walter
Mangan in *Very Old Bones.* The analogues are telling, for in each case the figure affected assumes that mere passion will prove sufficient to ensure happi-
ness. Events in *The Flaming Corsage* instead demonstrate the catastrophic
results of reliance on such a feeling alone.

Even as the narrative announces the commencement of Edward's intense courtship, it goes to great lengths to warn against a sentimental reading, reminding us how class differences—apparent throughout the Albany
novels—enforce the hopelessness of ambitions to effect any accommodation between the world of the Taylors and that of the Daughertys. In a neat
reversal of expectations, for example, the narrative traces Edward's abrupt
realization that an alliance with the Taylor family means a break with life-
long friends, not because they feel that he is marrying above his class but
rather because they hold the world inhabited by the Taylors in contempt.
While visiting a saloon owned by Black Jack McCall to ask him to be best
man at his wedding, Edward is caught in the middle of a brawl between
Maginn and a drunken lout named Matty Lookup, who has taken exception
to a perceived ethnic slur. Edward ends the melee by throwing a pot of hot
bean soup into Matty's face.[3] In thanking Edward for his help, Maginn
drains his remarks of any real gratitude by gratuitously emphasizing class
distinctions. "Quick thinking, old man. I myself might've reached for a bottle to club him with, but I'd've never gone for the soup. A genteel weapon.
Your prospective in-laws would doubtless approve the choice" (28).

The heavy-handed sarcasm of the remark not only reflects Maginn's
envy, but also makes Edward realize the class prejudices among his own
people. "Edward could not now ask Jack to be his best man. A great fellow,
Jack. A generous man if ever there was one. . . . But he doesn't approve of
Katrina. Everybody's generosity ends somewhere" (29). Taken no further,
the issue of social position would settle into a lampoon of sectarian snob-
bishness, but Kennedy explores the matter by deftly accentuating the ambiguities of Edward's own status: working-class ethnic by birth and upper-class
nativist by education.

A subsequent visit to the Taylor household presents the obligatory view
of Katrina's parents as stuffy and prejudiced, but it also foregrounds Edward
as a young man with the subtle insecurities that come from finding himself
between two cultures and unable to assimilate into either. As Edward waits

in the library of the Taylors' home, every book in the room confirms his
sense of their anti-Irish prejudices; this leads him into "conjuring his own
seventeenth-century forebears," who through Cromwellian confiscations of
their estates were "reduced to lowly cottiers tilling the land of others"
(32–33). He then goes on to trace the Daugherty family's immigration to
Albany and its subsequent economic and social recovery "to heights where
you [he tells himself] can court the modern get of an ancient devil" (34). Edward quickly chastises himself for "demonizing my love . . . to make her the
equal of what her parents think I am" (34), but he does not fully comprehend
the direction of his own thoughts. Though clothed in references that seem
to decry the English persecution of the Irish, on close inspection his grievances take a very individualized form with his concern focused not on Irish
suffering in general but on the way events have shaped his own status in the
community. Christian Michener has rightly summed up a driving force of
the novel as "Edward's dream of becoming a representative upper-class Irishman" (Michener 1998, 247). What emerges as the tragic aspect of this desire
is not so much Edward's failure to achieve it in the end but his failure to see
how circumscribed such an ambition is.

When he finally does confront the Taylors, his rapid-fire announce-
ment of his intention to marry their daughter—in a speech mired in shaky
logic and delivered in an offensive tone—never rises above the facile and
serves to corroborate the biases that these people hold. (Katrina later confirms this impression, telling Edward that "her mother thought him 'a rude
social climber' and was furious at his suggestion that her family had committed violence against the Irish; and her father, baffled by Edward's 'babbling
about atrocity and slavery,' wondered, 'What world is that overeducated
maniac living in?' " [Kennedy 1996, 50].) Indeed, the inherent flaws in
Edward's speech, despite the time he has had to prepare it, suggest to the
reader that a rhetorical sleight of hand remains the only argument Edward
can offer for the acceptance of his proposal.[4] Although the couple does not
yet realize it, the pronounced differences of their backgrounds in fact preclude any sustained union between them other than a physical one.

Along these lines, the next episode offers a glimpse of the amalgamation of calculation, sensuality, recklessness, and cruelty that makes up
Katrina's character. In meeting Edward at the Albany Rural Cemetery, she
torments another suitor, Giles Fitzroy, who has brought her to the assignation; offends the sensibilities of her ancestors by proposing to Edward that
they engage in intercourse in the graveyard; and takes control of the sensual

life of their marriage by dictating, in chilling clinical jargon that under-scores her emphasis on biological rather than emotional issues, where and when sexual activity will occur. "It's nineteen days since my time. I now have nine days when I cannot conceive. It's an ideal moment for the estrus to strike, and strike it has" (Kennedy 1996, 47). Both Edward and Katrina see this act as a pledge of their love, though each interprets that pledge differ-ently. Indeed, as the narrative later makes clear, the experience has contra-dictory implications that ultimately blight their marriage.

Even at this point in the novel, however, the attentive reader will begin to detect signs that, despite the commitment implicit in their intimacy, Ed-ward and Katrina still do not understand the profound contradictions that plague their proposed union. The narrative demonstrates their continuing naïveté in an account of a meeting with Edward's parents analogous to his visit to the Taylor house. Just as Edward's tirade on social equanimity stunned the Taylors, Katrina's declaration of her intention to convert to Catholicism renders the Daughertys speechless. And, as with Edward's dis-quisition before the Taylors, the young couple seem to take silence for con-sent, but unperceived complications persist.

Specifically, several issues arise out of this exchange that, because they remain unresolved and even unacknowledged, presage significant difficul-ties for their marriage. Some years previously, Edward's uncle, a union or-ganizer, had been brutally beaten and left permanently injured by men employed by Jacob Taylor. This incident set up a Montague and Capulet-like feud, so that any association with the Taylors shows a deficiency in Edward's family loyalty. It begs the question of how, if he does not demon-strate a clear sense of his obligations to his family, his marriage will survive. Further, neither Katrina nor Edward seems to understand religion as any-thing other than a social institution. They see it as a public acknowledg-ment of adherence to certain rituals that distinguish but do not mark the individual. To their detriment, they do not grasp the need for ethical com-mitment to some structure of belief whatever its basis, nor do they under-stand the broad communal repercussions set off by a public affirmation of a commitment to a particular religion. Characters can survive quite well in the world of Kennedy's novels without either an ethical commitment or a sense of communal affiliation, but whoever operates without both is court-ing destruction.

Of course, in *The Flaming Corsage* this deficiency rarely results in an abrupt shift in fortune. Rather, the narrative builds with meticulous care the interrelated conditions that precipitate disaster. This accumulation of forces often occurs through the most ridiculously grotesque gestures, such as Fintan (Clubber) Dooley's report of a practical joke in which he and Culbert (Cully) Watson put the head of a bull on the porch of Dr. Giles Fitzroy in 1908. At this point in the narrative, the incident seems to reflect merely the coarse humor of a certain level of society, with only its date, one day before the murder-suicide described in the opening chapter, hinting at more ominous implications. Clubber's account nonetheless serves to enforce the reader's sense that anarchy and violence continually lurk at the margins of this society, posing a constant threat to those who cannot avail themselves of communal protection.

The next episode, jumping forward to nine years after Edward's courtship of Katrina, shows how quickly danger can move from the periphery of ordinary life into the center of the action. The understated irony of the chapter's title, "Dinner at the Delavan Is Interrupted, December 30, 1894," chillingly alludes to the impending tragedy of the hotel fire and graphically underscores the omnipresent threat of chaos overwhelming order.[5] Although the violence of the blaze dominates the reader's sense of the immediate action, an undercurrent of profound emotional discord counterpoints events. Edward has enraged the Taylors by writing a play, *The Baron of Ten Broeck Street*, with a central character based on Jacob Taylor. To counteract this affront, Edward has arranged a conciliatory supper with his in-laws to announce that he is withdrawing the play from production. He aims to placate Katrina, who has begun to show signs of regret over leaving behind her family home and the world of her childhood, and to indicate resentment of Edward "for luring her away from her maidenly joys with his eloquent tongue, his hot love" (68). Edward has already attempted to address this resentment by building "a scaled-down replica of the Taylors' Gothic Revival town house . . . to assuage her loss of the resplendencies she had left behind" (68). The irony of this description subtly insinuates itself through the architecture—a style simultaneously derivative and pompous. Like "the candelabra . . . once owned by the Bonaparte family" (39) and now a Taylor family treasure, the house of Edward's in-laws, with its expensive and borrowed pedigree, validating itself with relics from another arriviste clan, betrays its occupants as parvenu.

Edward's concern draws the reader's attention to an instability in his marriage and to the growing influence of erratic elements within his wife's consciousness. The truly unbalanced behavior that emerges in Katrina's seduction of Francis Phelan will not take place for four more years. Nonetheless, one can already note that, without the anchors of family and moral belief, her willful, ungoverned nature is dangerously adrift.

The calamitous events of the evening alluded to in the chapter title, however, interrupt a close examination of Katrina at this point. When a fire breaks out in the hotel, Edward keeps his head and saves his wife, his father-in-law, and another woman abandoned by her husband. Unfortunately, the physical courage he displays does not prevent his wife from blaming him for the suffering that the fire inflicts on her family. Its traumatizing effect goes well beyond the physical injury she herself endures when a blazing stick ignites her dress and the corsage she is wearing (creating the image that provides the novel with its title). In fact, the tragedy of the fire deals with the Taylors in a cruelly ironic fashion. Katrina's sister Adelaide survives a jump from the top-floor window ledge of the hotel only to die seven days later from a ruptured spleen. Firemen rescue Adelaide's husband, Archie Van Slyke, but the shock of the event turns him into an ineffectual alcoholic. Jacob Taylor escapes the burning building, but two months later dies of a heart attack. Katrina takes an immoderate interest in all of the suffering and, like others in her family, feels a need to fix blame: "Katrina was not the one to articulate the accusation, but she came to believe what her mother had said first: Edward killed Adelaide and Jacob" (81).

Just as the conflagration at the Delavan House underscores Edward's isolation from the world in which Katrina's family exists, the death of his father eight and one-half years later, in 1902, shows his wife's tenuous understanding of the environment from which he emerged. Further, it suggests how mania and bitterness have warped her. Katrina, feeling more compassion for Emmett than for her husband, visits her dying father-in-law, but holds herself aloof from the Daughertys' working-class world.

This alienation becomes apparent from the moment she sets foot in the house and meets Annie Phelan, Francis's wife, who as a former neighbor has come to offer her condolences. Katrina finds herself unable to treat the woman as either a subordinate or an equal. "I can't call her Annie. Mrs. Phelan? No" (83). She solves the problem by speaking without using either name. This seemingly trivial exchange reminds readers of the impact of class distinctions on concepts of identity. Katrina Daugherty does not face Annie Phelan as a social equal or even as a kind of rival, the wife of a former lover. Rather, she relegates the woman to the position of nonentity, refusing to grant her any status whatever.

This conflicted view of Annie Phelan remains unvoiced, and the dynamics of the struggle within Katrina are subtle enough to elude perception. Subsequent events, however, throw her own dubious social position into relief. At Emmett's request, she goes to find a priest to administer the last rites and to buy ale for a final drink. Her exchange with Father Loonan shows that she does not have a clear sense of what liberties her position allows her. When she attempts to patronize him, Father Loonan refuses to grant her that privilege and delivers the sort of rebuke reserved for shallow creatures who require correction but no explanation: "Don't get flibbertigibbet on me" (86). When she enters a saloon to buy ale, her imperious manners cannot overcome prohibitions against serving unaccompanied women. She receives a dispensation only after invoking Emmett's name.

Near the conclusion of the episode, after Father Loonan has anointed Emmett, Katrina proposes that they drink a final toast to him. Although her gesture seems to spring from genuine emotion, her tone and language prove more embarrassing than moving: "All praise to Emmett Daugherty. . . . All praise to a great man, I say. The truly great men are the poet, the priest, and the soldier, and Emmett Daugherty is a soldier of the righteous wars" (94). Katrina has dismissed her poet husband at the chapter's opening; she has tried unsuccessfully to patronize the parish priest in its middle; and in praising the "soldier of the righteous wars" she seems to forget that her father is responsible for crippling that soldier's brother. Although her comments are not yet the ravings of a lunatic, she shows how profoundly self-delusion grips her even when striking a noble pose.

In harsh succession to the scene of Emmett's death, the narrative flashes forward to a newspaper story announcing the lynching of Cully Watson, a year and a half after he participated in the bull's head practical joke. The story recounts Watson's being returned to New Orleans in the custody of two detectives when armed men kidnapped him. A short time later, police discovered Cully's body hanging from a telegraph pole in front of a Bourbon Street hotel where he had raped and tried to kill a woman ten days earlier. The details of Cully's New Orleans crime (95) proleptically mirror Edward's recollection of Felicity Fitzroy's account of Cully's assault on her (129). Nonetheless, when arrested, Cully attempts to bargain with police by giving a lengthy account of his version of the events leading up to the Fitzroy killings at the Millerton House eighteen months earlier. Both the violence and the achronicity may seem jarring here, but in flashing forward to Cully's death, the narrative alerts readers to the long-term significance of the upcoming description of the seemingly senseless mayhem occurring in 1906 at an annual outing on the Hudson River sponsored by a number of Albany social organizations.

Like the account of the fire at the Delavan House, "A Picnic on the Barge, June 17, 1906" gives a graphic description of unexpected violence that impels a number of characters toward courses of action that will lead to profound unhappiness. Unlike at the Delavan fire, however, Katrina is not present at the picnic, and her reasons, recounted by Edward, make it clear that she has given up any illusions about fitting into the world that her husband inhabits. "[S]he said she couldn't abide all that family sweetness, all those dowdy biddies, all the rowdiness. So she stayed home. Avoiding the class struggle" (98). Katrina's expectations are accurate on all counts, but that precision only heightens our awareness of her alienation. Giles Fitzroy, coming from the same background as Katrina, avoids such isolation by using practical jokes as a way to negotiate class differences. In a bitterly ironic twist, however, the fireman's wife joke that he initiates here, which turns on the false promise of an adulterous liaison and a feigned murder, presages real adultery and the actual killings at the Millerton House.

Edward himself endures his own measure of alienation, using an aura of familiarity to mask his sense of inhabiting neither the world of his parents nor that of his in-laws. A chance encounter with Francis Phelan, paralleling the earlier meeting between Katrina and Annie Phelan, reflects this strained condition. Edward behaves in a cordial if slightly distant manner toward the young man. Nonetheless, his unvoiced response to Francis's well-intentioned comments contrasts Edward's own bitter accommodation to events with the disarming naïveté of a man still too young to realize that all acts have consequences. " 'If the Daughertys ever need anything. I'm there.' Edward nodded and thought: I'll pass the word to Katrina" (103). A further irony charges this already conflicted situation. Despite his bitterness over his wife's infidelity with Francis, Edward does not hesitate to form his art by drawing vicariously on the working-class world of the young man's experiences. He has already used Francis's killing of a scab during the trolley strike of 1901 as the basis for the play *The Car Barns*, and he will later weave Francis's affair with Katrina into the play *The Flaming Corsage*, whose production concludes this novel.

Unvoiced animosity gives way to real violence when a gang of thugs led by Cully Watson starts a fight over beer. With a catastrophic rapidity that reminds readers that even the most established social groups have a tenuous hold on order, the thugs beat two policemen, take the officers' guns, and escape during the ensuing brawl to the Rensselaer shore in a lifeboat rowed by Maginn. Unlike the battle twenty-one years earlier in Black Jack McCall's saloon, Maginn switches sides in search of a story and perhaps excitement. Although the narrative seems to treat the matter as a momentary lapse, it in fact marks Maginn's shift to the fringes of society. It is a gesture that mimics Edward's effort to reposition himself among the social groups of Albany, with only the direction varying—down instead of up. In both cases, the move proves ultimately disastrous.

A seemingly ancillary episode immediately following the fight on the barge sets in motion the chain of events that will culminate tragically two years later in a New York City hotel room. Giles Fitzroy, Jimmy Cadden, and Edward Daugherty make a fool of Maginn, who is taken in by the fireman's wife joke. Like any false effort at conviviality, the hoax produces alienation rather than congeniality. The humiliation "generated a predictable withdrawal in Maginn, but also in Edward, whose guilt was such that he stopped work on his new play" (113). What the perpetrators of the joke fail to recognize, in a lapse common to characters in *The Flaming Corsage*, is that any such action will provoke an equal and opposite reaction.

One year after the barge picnic, a Fourth of July gathering at the Daugherty house reveals the corrosive effect life has had on a number of principal figures in the novel. All of the characters, with the exception of the ingenuous Giles, now operate under dissolute protocols very different from those suggested by their public personae. Katrina presides in a drawing room filled with mementoes meant to evoke the hotel fire, "her chamber of venerated memory, her sumptuous crypt of exhausted life" (115). As she looks on with jaded indifference, Edward choreographs a dinner that will allow him to begin an affair with Melissa Spencer. The young actress in turn wishes to cultivate Edward because of his reputation as a playwright. Felicity Fitzroy has assumed the dual role of public prude and private coquette. And Maginn struggles through bravado to suppress a sense of sexual insecurity brought on by the fireman's wife joke.

When the narrative finally takes up the events surrounding the violent incident that opens the novel, the contrasting descriptions are now charged with the reader's evolving sense of the various characters' conflicted attitudes. In the first account of these events, Edward transmits Felicity's description of Cully Watson robbing and raping her and then dressing her in the cloak and mask that she is later wearing when Giles shoots her. When

Cully is later arrested, he offers a radically different version, asserting that he had consensual sexual relations with Felicity and insinuating a lesbian relationship between Felicity and Melissa. He claims to have had no part in the murders. "When I heard about them I didn't blame the Doc. His wife was no good. But she was a pretty good fuck" (132). That bit of coarse bravado leaves the reader, like Edward, "sifting what happened" (132).

Intertwined themes of sexual desire and emotional betrayal haunt Edward and compel him to seek the truth about the killings in New York. The bullet from Giles's pistol penetrated his left chest but missed his heart. The injury is analogous to the burning stick that injured Katrina, and, like Katrina's wound, it exerts significance as a psychological rather than a physical scar. Clarification becomes a means of expiation, and toward that end Edward turns to Melissa, who offers yet another conflicted account of events surrounding the murder, making it clear that she feels no impulse to reexamine those events.[6] Although this attitude does not necessarily reflect guilt, it does underscore her genuine disinterest in anything but the moment, anything but physical gratification. Edward ends his interview by complimenting her ability as an actress and casting doubt on her story. "You make it quite credible. . . . I don't doubt any part of your story. But I'm absolutely certain you're a virtuoso liar" (142).

By this point in the novel, the narrative adopts an accelerated pace that mirrors the hectic, fragmented condition of Edward and Katrina's disintegrating lives. When Edward returns home after speaking with Melissa, he finds that Katrina has left on his desk two volumes of the diary that she keeps, one for the year 1894 and one for 1908. Vivian Valvano Lynch (1999) has commented very perceptively on Katrina's possible motivations for offering these intimate insights. Although for my readings these motivations remain of subsidiary importance, I agree with Lynch that Katrina's actions, nonetheless, enhance the interpretive complexity of the novel.

In the 1894 diary, Katrina has marked a passage for April 19. It details a series of seemingly unconnected impressions: recollections of her mother's selling jewelry to cover her father's financial losses in the panic of 1893; mention of her father's mistress, Madame Baldwin; a description of an antisuffrage meeting that her mother chaired; and an account of Giles Fitzroy's declaration of his love. Despite the episodic nature of these anecdotes, they offer evidence of the madness growing in Katrina's mind well before the hotel fire:

I have no desire for Giles, but the idea of a lover is taking hold. It has
everything to do with resisting my age, for I will be thirty soon. I know
how vain and foolish this is, but it is no less real for that. Also, I must punish Edward for despoiling me. I sought it, yes, but he did it, as he should
have, or I would not have married him. But I cannot forgive him. He does
not yet understand the craft of dying. I wonder, shall I be truly beautiful all
my life? (145)

This irreconcilable condition that Katrina constructs in her diary underscores her mental and emotional turmoil and mitigates any harsh attitude
the reader might have regarding Edward's treatment of his wife based solely
on impressions gathered from the narrative of *Billy Phelan's Greatest Game* and
Ironweed.

The second entry is dated October 17, 1908, the day that Giles murders his wife and kills himself. It gives an account of a visit from Giles in
which he shows Katrina a poem, put in his mailbox at the same time that the
bull's head appeared on his porch, that implicates Felicity, Edward, and
Melissa in a ménage à trois. Katrina's response is the sort of non sequitur
that now characterizes her life. She disrobes for Giles and tells him not to
touch her. "He stared at me and we didn't speak, but I felt glorious, basking
in the light of my dear friend's wan smile. . . . I had banished his frenzy"
(146). The passage ends without further comment, leaving the reader to interpret how this stark solipsism offers a chilling glimpse of the disturbed
features of Katrina's mind.

In counterpoint to these emotions, Edward very deliberately continues
his efforts to reconstruct both the events and the causes of the tragedy at the
Millerton House. He goes to see Clubber Dooley to pursue Maginn's connection in the matter. In the process, he convinces Clubber that the bull's
head joke in fact precipitated Giles's trip to New York and the murder of his
wife. As a result of Edward's revelations, Clubber twice tries to kill himself
and is consequently committed to a mental institution. The narrative's dispassionate report of Clubber's end provides a relentless account of the ram-
ifications of violence, even on those ignorantly involved in its perpetration.
The sense of the importance of community that has run as an undercurrent
through the novel is thus reinforced, for awareness of one's social group
heightens one's sense of the repercussion of acts.

By this point in the novel, the narrative has focused on Katrina to embody an individual's fragile grasp on sanity and the vulnerability of anyone who moves through the world unsupported by community or individual belief. Though both she and Edward have prided themselves on having a knowledge of the world that produces a superior understanding of it, the discourse reiterates the unreliability of what each knows. As Katrina prepares to leave her house on what will be the last day of her life, a disturbing exchange with Maginn *seems* to take place in her parlor. Maginn offers lurid new information about Edward, Melissa, and Felicity, and he urges Katrina to commit adultery with him as an act of revenge. The conversation abruptly ceases, and later in the narrative (171) it becomes clear that Katrina has been remembering an exchange that took place earlier. The seamless integration of the incident into the narrative at this point, however, forces the reader to ask how Katrina herself perceived it and what distinction, if any, she now makes between the material and the imaginative world.

As the narrative continues to trace Katrina's movements, it shows that her actions do not simply underscore an increasingly eccentric behavior. They reflect certain dominant themes of *The Flaming Corsage*, specifically the unavoidable and far-reaching consequences that inevitably grow out of any deliberate act and the inability of an individual to exist without communal support. Seemingly on a whim, Katrina has her photograph taken after she leaves the house. In the picture, she assumes a self-advertising, even slightly flirtatious pose.

> The billowy V-neck of her dress was adjustable by hidden buttons, two of which she undid, allowing the neck to open to the edges of her shoulders. The separation of her breasts then became visible, but she concealed most of that with the sunflower, whose stem she snapped to shorten it, then tucked the stem inside her bodice. In her mirror image she had become different, new yet again. And, for the first time, the top of her white, oval scar from the Delavan was visible to the world, above the edge of her dress. (159)

This picture of a forty-seven-year-old coquette becomes Katrina's unwitting valediction and establishes her self-image as the paragon for female allure. "With the making of this picture MacDonald would elevate himself, for a time, to the status of master photographer of eastern American beauty" (160). The irony of this legacy, which would not have been lost on her had she lived, is that it derives its charm from revealing so much in her nature that she has spent a lifetime time concealing.

During this day, Katrina also visits her brother-in-law, Archie Van Slyke, at the State National Bank. Her errand ostensibly aims at tidying papers that have accumulated in a safety deposit box, but their inventory serves to adumbrate the decline of her family: jewelry, "what remained of the Taylor fortune"; birth certificates, endowments, deeds, all documents relating to wealth no longer held and individuals no longer alive; all seven volumes of her diary; and several of Edward's play manuscripts, one "Katrina cherished . . . for its compassion and insight—into her, of course—she the enduring heroine of all of Edward's works" (163). As Vivian Valvano Lynch has noted, Katrina here preserves her own version of her life (Lynch 1999, 231–32). In the midst of this familial nostalgia, however, Katrina reinforces her sense of isolation from those around her. With an imperiousness seen as early as her drive to the cemetery with Giles Fitzroy in 1885 and with a remarkable lack of connection to other people, she lectures Archie on his inability to cope with life.

> "Thank you so much, Archie. I must go up to the Hall now and see a bit of the dress rehearsal of Edward's play."
>
> "Yes, I saw a notice in the paper."
>
> "I believe he's written the tragedy of our lives. And do stop drinking, Archie. You're such a good man without it."
>
> "You should learn to mind your own business, Katrina."
>
> "Yes, I suppose I should. But I have so very little business to mind."
> (Kennedy 1996, 164–65)

The flippancy of those last lines enhances rather than diminishes their impact. Like her stunning last photograph, this final pronouncement on her life carries the full weight of an accurate representation strengthened by its heedless disregard for audience. What Katrina does not acknowledge is that she has "so very little business to mind" because she has, in a premeditated fashion, cut herself off from the communities represented in the keepsakes so carefully preserved in her safety deposit box.

In the final and most revealing scene before Katrina returns home, she makes good her intention to visits Harmanus Bleecker Hall to watch a rehearsal of *The Flaming Corsage*. The scene that she views features an exchange between the two women who represent her and Melissa. Marina (Katrina) talks of how Mangan (Maginn) conceived the plot to expose her husband and his lover, Clarissa (Melissa). As the two women spar back and forth, readers of the novel have for the first time a delineation of Edward's own view of his infidelity.

> You linked yourself to my husband when he was a rising star, and now, after you've risen on his back, you want to destroy what remains of his life as a fallen star. . . . You began as a frivolous soubrette, full of intrigue, and in short order you've risen to become a sublime slut. Do your sluttish things, as you must, but don't speak to me of love. . . . Love is vertical. You are relentlessly horizontal. (170)

Though she may not realize its full ironic implications, Katrina sums up her dispassionate judgment of the scene in a single line: "He makes me cleverer than I am" (171). Although the solipsism of this remark attests to how little she concerns herself with others, it also reiterates the image projected by the photograph of her: lasting impressions of Katrina derive from poses that she has initiated and that others have captured.

At the same time, whether an accurate view of Katrina's intellectual ability or not, this portion of the drama provides readers with additional insight into the dynamics surrounding Edward's adultery. His decision to give his wife the most powerful lines in the play—despite her opinion that it subverts reality—demands our reconsideration of the impact his promiscuity has had on his consciousness. Further, the stunning condemnation of this dialogue underscores his view of how unreflective Melissa is, even as it glosses her liaison with his son Martin, described in *Billy Phelan's Greatest Game*, as far more complex than it might initially have appeared.[7]

By the time Katrina returns home, the retrospective tone of the day has created a detached sense of herself. Questioning her life takes the form of a perspective already set in the past. "What, really, was my destiny?" (172). This suggestion of closure, of finality, has an important bearing on how one interprets the final moments of Katrina's life. Her actions stand out clearly, but her motivations remain opaque. When she notices that the Christian Brothers school next door is on fire, the conscious choice she makes to remain in the house seems almost instinctual: "She went to the window of the office and parted the curtains to see the Christian Brothers school next door in flames. It was clear to her that the fire would make the leap to this room in a matter of minutes. She went back to Edward's chair and put her head down on his desk. The smoke was familiar in her mouth. She had breathed fire before" (175). For readers, the most intriguing feature of this selection is not Katrina's decision to allow the flames to consume her but the question of how to judge her passive acceptance of death. On the one hand, readers might see her as a victim of conflicting social forces that she could neither foresee nor control. Conversely, they might view her as a perverse manipulator, dying in a gesture of disdain for all who cared for her. The strength of this account lies in its willingness to allow readers to make that choice.

Edward's response to her death is equally ambiguous. He has her funeral mass said in Sacred Heart Church and then buries her privately in Albany Rural Cemetery. This evocation of alternating denominational rituals—public Catholicism and private Protestantism—neatly captures the ambivalence of their relationship. Edward knows that Katrina was never part of his society, yet a Catholic mass allows him to thumb his nose once more at her side of the family (though only her mother remains alive). By interning her at the Albany Rural Cemetery, he denies her link to his family and returns her to the place where they consummated their relationship twenty-seven years earlier. A further twist to this behavior comes in the chapter's final lines when Edward makes clear his belief that she is a suicide by telling his son "[w]e will regret forever that she has willfully left us" (177). Again, it remains for readers to decide if conscience or callousness shapes his decision not to bury her in the hallowed ground of a Catholic cemetery. (Those inclined to a hasty judgment either way should recall the marvelous contrast of veneration and sacrilege in the scene at Saint Agnes Cemetery that opens *Ironweed*.)

Accounts of the completion, production, and closing of Edward's play follow in rapid succession, inextricably linking that drama and Katrina's life (or at the very least her death). *The Flaming Corsage* folds after a single performance, condemned by Thomas Maginn not as immoral but simply as bad drama.[8] In a gesture that presages the novel's conclusion, Edward returns to his art to comprehend the experiences that have overwhelmed him. He composes a fragment of a play, set at Sing Sing and detailing the execution of Maginn for unspecified crimes, with Giles and a deceased Edward present as witnesses. The scene has the aura of magic realism that has hovered about Kennedy's writing since *The Ink Truck*, but putting such a slant in a play avoids the problems of continuity that arose from this approach in his earlier works.

The narrative now increasingly mirrors Edward's desultory search for meaning. It shifts to a description of his reclusive life in his parent's home. As he strolls the streets he knew as a child, he thinks of his dead father, perhaps unconsciously comparing their lives. On his walk, he meets Cappy White, whom he and Katrina had encountered with his wife Mamie on the day that Edward brought Katrina to meet his parents. Mamie is long dead, and Cappy now leads the life of a hermit. The exchange between the two desolate men shows the stunning power of Kennedy's economic language.

> "Hi ya, Cappy," Edward said.
> "Who's that?"
> "Eddie Daugherty."
> "Eddie, yeah, you're back. I heard you lost everything."
> "That's right, Cappy."
> "So did I."
> "I know."
> "How you livin'?"
> "Best way I can."
> "You still got your son," Cappy said.
> "I guess you could say that."
> "I lost my son."
> "I know you did. I hate that, Cappy."
> "So do I."
> "You get out much, Cap?"
> "Nope. No reason to."
> "Maybe it'll get better."
> "No, it won't get no better. You oughta know that."
> "I keep wondering whether it's finished."
> "It's finished."
> "How do you know?"
> "They ain't nothin' worth doin'."
> "It seems like that, all right." (190–91)

Though both men find themselves in the same situation, their language traces their diametrically opposed views in terse but eloquent phrases: Edward's timid optimism and Cappy's exhausted nihilism. The scene represents the emotional conclusion of the novel, but the narrative continues in deference to Edward's perhaps unrealistic determination to impose meaning on the events that have shaped his life.

As the novel moves toward its end, a more conventional narrative pattern struggles to impose a kind of closure. It leads Edward to confront Maginn in a whorehouse where the latter is now residing, with the seediness of the place serving as an ironic commentary on the consequences of living the life of venereal obsession that Maginn had always claimed he sought. As a locus of adult fantasies, the bordello is an apt backdrop for Edward's explanation of the complex scheme—involving the hotel shooting and the death of Cully Watson—that Maginn hatched to bring about Edward's destruction and to avenge himself for the humiliation that he suffered through the fireman's wife joke. Maginn counters with his own version of the story that adds another level of deceit to the actions of almost every character involved, and the only truth that emerges in the telling and retelling of the events surrounding the shooting at the Millerton House is the breadth of human venality—from the banal to the purely evil. Multiple layers of deceit have made the truth all but irrecoverable, and violence becomes the only way to bring this bitter disquisition to an abrupt halt. One of the whores knocks Edward unconscious with a lead pipe. When Edward comes to, Maginn's flight serves as a way of forcing an explanation of the ambiguities that muddled perceptions of the events described in the opening of the novel.

The final pages, however, revert to a form that undermines any inclination to draw a clear conclusion from the experiences of any of the characters. Returning home, Edward engages in two dramatic dialogues with Katrina that articulate his view of what undermined their marriage. The conversations might seem biased to any reader with sympathy for Katrina, for they highlight both her mania and her frigidity. In that regard, they do her an injustice, for in the end it is solipsism more than anything else that characterizes her. Edward's own failings escape him, but they do not necessarily get past the reader. Near the close of the chapter, Edward speaks rhetorically to his father: "Did you ever consider . . . that I never was the Irishman on horseback? It may be I was free of racial and social destinies, and that what I wanted was altogether different from what had gone before" (207). Although all this may be quite true, he fails to grasp the significance of what he has said. Being "free of racial and social destinies" and wanting something "altogether different from what had gone before" mean simply being cut off from his community and living outside the structure afforded by its ethical system. Such an isolation may have no effect on a character who moves from that community. (Arguably, Peter Phelan's life demonstrates that possibility.) But no one who chooses to remain in Albany can sustain himself alone without becoming another Cappy White.

CHAPTER NINE

The Siege of Vicksburg and the Battle at *Grand View*

As the efforts of Henry James, another author with Albany connections, amply attest, for accomplished novelists the transition to composing drama has not always been easy or successful. Fortunately for readers interested in William Kennedy's writing, his full-length play *Grand View* runs counter to that experience. It shows all the skills at evoking place, developing character, and examining issues that distinguish his other works, and it stands as a wonderful complement to the novels of the Albany cycle.

Grand View was first staged in Albany in the spring of 1996 and was presented four years later, after extensive revisions, at the Pegasus Players Theatre in Chicago. Kennedy wrote the play while working on his novel *Roscoe*, and the two form a sharp portrait of the men who animate the McCall political machine that governs Kennedy's novelistic Albany from Prohibition through the New Frontier. These parallel examinations of Patsy McCall and his cronies represent a marvelous extension of the unique environment of the novels of the Albany cycle, animating figures and illustrating mores that have characterized Kennedy's writing since the appearance of *Legs*.

In a fashion more sustained and detailed than in any of Kennedy's previous fiction, *Grand View* takes up the topic of politics and explores its impact on individuals from the working-class, ethnic society that has served as the focal point of so many of his works. As in *The Flaming Corsage*, the play traces the uneasy relationship between an Irish American community determined to enjoy its share of the wealth and power in American society and a Yankee/Dutch infrastructure resistant to efforts to divide the spoils further. The play, however, gives one a much sharper sense of the political forces that continuously shift between an uneasy equilibrium and the violent attempts

167

at dominance that inform connections between these groups. Although many of the figures who appear in the play are new to the Kennedy canon, the ambitions and urges that drive them reflect the motivations that have propelled his characters throughout the Albany cycle.

The action of *Grand View* centers on a prominent Albany Democratic politician, Patsy McCall, who has appeared in various supporting roles in Kennedy's earlier fiction. Throughout the Albany cycle, Patsy has been a symbol of the political power that affects the lives of so many in the city. In order to explore the emotional and spiritual consequences of dedicating one's life to the accumulation and cultivation of power, Kennedy goes beyond Patsy's emblematic role and looks at him as an individual.

As in several other works—*Billy Phelan's Greatest Game, Ironweed,* and *Very Old Bones*—the action of Kennedy's play unfolds over a relatively short period of time, the Tuesday following Labor Day in 1944. Nonetheless, through recollections, allusions, and direct references, its characters draw on the experiences of a lifetime as they struggle with issues familiar to Kennedy's readers: sex, love, loyalty, and friendship. Like several earlier works, *Grand View* shows Kennedy's fascination with the ethical codes and communal ties that shape the environment of his fiction. More specifically, however, as in earlier works, he uses this play to explore the ability of an individual to survive without those props.

Kennedy bases the action of his play on a series of historical events, already detailed in *Riding the Yellow Trolley Car,* marking the high point of the political struggle between Dan O'Connell, boss of the Albany Democratic machine from the 1920s to the 1960s, and Tom Dewey, governor of New York and Republican candidate for president in 1944. During that election campaign, both as a matter of principle and as a way to curry favor with national voters, Governor Dewey unsuccessfully attempted to indict key members of the O'Connell machine on charges of political corruption. Kennedy's dramatic account of this effort, *Grand View,* highlights the way that Patsy McCall—the Albany cycle's counterpart of Dan O'Connell and the head of the clan that at the time of the play has run Albany politics for two decades—frustrates Dewey's attempts to break the machine and garner headlines that will boost the popularity of his political campaign.

At the same time, *Grand View* takes a close look at the relation of private and public values, primarily by examining the diverse elements that constitute the nature of Patsy McCall. Throughout the play, Kennedy's dialogue makes it clear that Patsy is a man adept at deflecting any criticism that threatens the public perception of his respectability. At the same time, more often than not his language incriminates him as someone who lets pragmatism rather than values govern his behavior. As in other Kennedy works, this attitude in itself does not doom an individual as long as he retains a sense of community. However, by the end of *Grand View*, Kennedy has made it clear that Patsy, a man who frequently criticizes others for a failure to listen, has cut himself off from any meaningful connection with the world he claims to inhabit. Betrayal and indifference mark him as oblivious to the feelings of everyone around him and leave him trapped in a cramped, isolated space of his own creation.

This alienation at first appears difficult to discern, for Patsy possesses all of the abilities of a master politician, skilled at projecting an aura of good fellowship that makes him adept at building and sustaining the alliances necessary to maintain power. As the dialogue quickly makes clear, however, self-interest dominates his every action. He operates as a predator, able to read the strengths and weaknesses of others and quick to set his own plan of attack based on that knowledge. Further, Patsy's fascination with Civil War history, first noted in *Billy Phelan's Greatest Game*, reinforces the audience's sense of his skill as a tactician. It recurs specifically in *Grand View* through repeated references to the account, in the memoirs of Ulysses S. Grant, of the siege and capture of the city of Vicksburg. Short passages read to Patsy by Richard Maloney, the Albany district attorney and the lieutenant in the McCall machine, or by Patsy to Alice Shugrue, the owner of the resort that lends the play its title, give an account of the strategy, at the same time both ponderously methodical and stunningly daring, that captured the city, split the South, and marked the turning point in the War between the States. These allusions to Grant's maneuvering form an ironic counterpoint to the political chess game that Patsy plays with the governor of New York, Thomas Dewey, and with Dewey's representative, Patsy's longtime rival Corbett Atterby.

The play opens with a strident monologue that lays the groundwork for understanding the political struggle animating the action. Corbett Atterby, who is later introduced as Patsy's former friend, delivers a vitriolic speech predicting the demise of the McCall machine. "Regardless of the McCall Machine's well-known ability to pack juries with sympathizers, we now have enough proof to indict and convict its leaders" (Kennedy 2000,9).[1] In both its tone and its language, Atterby's diatribe introduces the deep hostility that informs the public struggle between the Republican governor and his supporters and the Albany Democratic machine. It also sets up the contradiction between that animosity and the cordiality that simultaneously obtains between Patsy and Corbett.

Immediately after that speech, which serves as a prologue, the primary action of the play opens with Alice Shugrue tidying the parlor of the Grand View Lake House on the morning after a raucous Labor Day party. The play unfolds on a single September day in 1944, and the date captures a range of diverse feelings that counterpoint the opening action. The transition that marks the move from the summer holidays to the approach of fall is quite evident. Also apparent is the country's anticipation of a change from the hardship of conflict to the benefits of peace based on a sense that the war in Europe will soon be over. Finally, the ripening of the harvest parallels Patsy's sense of achievement in his twenty-year reign as political boss of Albany.

Later in the play, Patsy calls this period the best time of year, with the summer people gone and the lake still warm. In fact, the emptiness of a resort in the off-season emerges as the perfect representation of the hollow state of the principle characters. Each struggles with conflicting impulses toward both community and isolation, and the tragedy that unfolds marks the mistakes made by both those who place too much faith in their sense of community and those who assume too quickly their own ability to live without the support of society.

Necessarily, a great deal of exposition dominates this scene between Patsy, Alice, and later Richard Maloney, but Kennedy masterfully uses his dialogue to suggest more than he actually reveals. One sees this feature at work in a scene that at first seems to offer little more than harmless flirtatious banter with Alice but that gradually foregrounds Patsy's lascivious nature.

PATSY

God, you're a ravishing creature in the morning,
Alice. Your body drives me crazy. . . . How's your love
life? Does Willie satisfy you?

ALICE

None of your dirty business.

PATSY

Everything's my business. When's Willie coming
home?

ALICE

Thursday.

PATSY

If you find yourself frantic for some red hot love,
slip a note under my door.

ALICE

Hang by your thumbs, you maniac. (Pause)
How's *your* love life, Mr. Red Hot?

PATSY

scandalous.

ALICE

So I've heard. (6)

As Patsy escalates and personalizes his probing, the dynamics of the exchange shift from the easy give-and-take between a man and a woman to the cold reflection of Patsy's solipsistic appetites.

When Richard Maloney enters, the topic shifts, but the attitude that dominates McCall's behavior remains the same. Richard, through his curiosity about accounts of recent burglaries in the *Albany Post-Dispatch* and accounts of Corbett Atterby's speech, gives the audience hints of the crisis that serves as the fulcrum on which events of the play turn. The self-possessed Patsy seems more concerned with stories of Bing Crosby and his chances of winning an Academy Award for *Going My Way*, and the contrast in this exchange establishes the way that the two interact throughout the play. With news from Albany that members of the Democratic machine may be indicted, Richard is noticeably edgy and voices concern about the willingness of Governor Dewey to use prosecution of the Albany machine as a stepping stone to boost his efforts at winning the presidency. Patsy responds with an equanimity that reflects the self-confidence of a man who has controlled events for two decades and who rarely finds himself unprepared for any contingency.

RICHARD

I'll worry for both of us. I think the Governor's
really got something cooking.

PATSY

He smears us and he's a hero, same as when he
put [Lucky] Luciano in Sing Sing. The great racket-
buster. The big-city hero of the upstate shit-kickers.
Votes is what this is all about, Richard. You know that.
The Governor wants to be President.

RICHARD

And he might get to *be* President.

PATSY (Suddenly testy.)

Let him! Then he won't be in Albany any more.
(Beat) The people won't elect him. Break the record,
Richard, we're on vacation. We'll go fishin' this afternoon with those new flies you tied. Now let's do Vicksburg. (10)[2]

Patsy, however, cannot ease the tense atmosphere at the Grand View simply
by willing it away. A woman phones to book a room for Corbett Atterby and
his wife for the evening, claiming that the Atterbys wish to stay at the hotel
because they plan to pick up their daughter, Faye, who has been acting in
summer stock in Saratoga Springs. Though Patsy has reserved the entire resort, he encourages Alice to accommodate the request. The political instincts
of both Richard and Patsy tell them that the call is far from coincidental.
Rather, they see it as a sign that a deal of some sort may be forthcoming from
Dewey. As Richard says, "The Governor wants something and Atterby's
coming to get it" (14). Like Grant before Vicksburg, Patsy feels far from awed
by the prospect of a confrontation. On the contrary, he is intent on arranging
the encounter to his best possible advantage, and as the scene ends, the passage he reads from Grant's memoirs underscores this determination: " 'This
battle,'—Vicksburg—'more than any other, illustrated the character of the
man who planned and executed it against the advice of his own generals.
Ulysses S. Grant, an unlikely military giant, would fight many battles, but
this one—whose aim was to sever the Confederacy—was his greatest' " (16).

When the Atterbys arrive later in the day, all concerned, save the truculent Richard Maloney, achieve a neat balance between the overt conviviality of old friends reuniting and the barely concealed contentiousness of
longtime rivals. Kennedy quickly adds a sexual dimension to the conflict. In
a private moment after Corbett has gone upstairs with the luggage, Patsy re-

minds Mabel of their love affair of two decades past. When they kiss, the audience is left wondering how far either will go in pursuing the other.

Though Patsy seems here the sexual aggressor, Mabel quickly reveals a willingness both on her part and on her husband's to use old attractions to arrange this meeting with Patsy. "Corbett wanted to see you, but he thought you might not want to see him. I told him, 'Patsy'll want to see me.' Corbett thought about that, and here we are" (26). Nonetheless, through dialogue and gesture Kennedy is careful to leave ambiguous how far either Corbett or Mabel is willing to go to get to Patsy.

When Corbett returns to the parlor, the three of them engage in a series of seemingly nostalgic reveries that in fact continue to assert their competitiveness: Patsy and Corbett vying for Mabel, and Mabel asserting her independence from both. In the midst of this exchange, the Atterbys' daughter, Faye, appears. She has a brittle, tightly wound quality evocative of Laura in Tennessee William's *The Glass Menagerie,* though she covers her vulnerability with a bravado that immediately endears her to Patsy.

Faye's high-strung attitude heightens the general tension. It is clear from her parents' reactions to her every word or gesture that something is deeply wrong with Faye, yet Kennedy takes care to leave ambiguous the precise source of her anxiety. Mabel and Corbett try to prevent Faye from drinking, but alcoholism serves as a symptom rather than as the source of her problem. A general reticence about what is disturbing her intensifies the mystery surrounding her behavior.

Coincidentally, the scene begins to develop Faye's function as a catalyst, a role that she will play for much of the action. When Faye probes Patsy to learn more about her parents, cordiality becomes increasingly difficult to sustain, with the animosity that Patsy and Corbett feel for one another standing out as all too apparent. Faye's questions about the lives her parents lived before they were married expose the old scars of past slights and put her recollections in uneasy juxtaposition with her vulnerability. Over the course of the play, the degree to which all three are drawn to Faye becomes clearer, but even at this early stage she is obviously the focus of their mutual concern.

At the same time, Kennedy endows Faye with a powerful if deeply wounded nature. She combines a fierce strength of character with a deep self-loathing, making her both formidable and fragile. In a telling instance of self-analysis, she moves from being an actress referencing lines from Chekhov's *The Sea Gull* to being an interpreter applying those lines to her own life.

Chekhov was writing about me in those lines. I want to fly free like that sea
gull. Yes, you're insipid and worthless, but you love someone, and you
think they love you. They don't shoot you. They take you out under the
pine trees and, just to pass the time, they try to screw you. Then they
leave. "Show's over, Honey." I know nothing about the kind of love my
mother had. (Beat) Patsy, may I *please* have that drink now? (42)

The seamless shift from Chekhov's words to her own shows both her talent
at improvisation and her tenuous grip on her own sanity.

The sparring in company, however, is only the preliminary to the real
struggle. Shortly after Faye and Mabel go to their room, Corbett presents
Patsy with the choice of going to jail or betraying a number of his cronies in
the Albany machine. The threat, however, is short-lived, for, after Corbett
leaves, Jimmy Gill, a policeman working for Richard Maloney, appears.
Jimmy relates in great detail how he has successfully burglarized Republican
offices at the state capitol, and he presents Patsy with evidence of corruption in the form of canceled checks to political cronies of the Republican
Party that can be used to counter the indictment threats from Dewey.

The act ends with Richard reading from Grant's memoirs, once again
offering the audience hints of what will come through reference to the campaign around Vicksburg. "Grant's plan was to attack Vicksburg from the
rear, but he could do this only if his generals fought several diversionary battles, if he could ferry ten divisions across the Mississippi River, and then suffer a long siege without supplies or reinforcements. This seemed impossible"
(51). The reader obviously knows how the struggle turns out, belying the
pessimism of the prose and suggesting that Patsy's situation is by no means
as bleak as Corbett Atterby assumes it to be. The scene is set for a confrontation after dinner.

The second act of the play begins after the evening meal. In ironic replication of the initial banter between Alice and Patsy, it opens with an exchange in which Jimmy Gill clumsily tries to impress Faye. Unlike Patsy's
calculated suggestiveness, Jimmy's talk reveals his failure to understand the
complexity of Faye's nature. She is neither awed nor offended by the young
man's allusions to the rigors of his job as a policeman, but rather seizes on
them as a goad. Rather than allowing Jimmy a measure of esteem derived
from the secondhand knowledge of violent behavior, Faye confronts him
with a series of questions about his own actions.

Did you ever arrest somebody and take them into the back room of the
police station and beat them until their eyes popped out of their sockets?
(Beat) Did you ever shoot anybody in the chest and watch them bleed to
death and listen to them try to scream while they strangulate on their own
blood? (Beat) Did you ever kick a man in the face until his mouth was as
wide as your shoe and half the shoe went inside his face when you kicked
it? (Beat) Did you ever beat up a crazy woman? Did you ever punch a
woman in the tits? (54)

As her interrogation becomes increasingly pointed, Jimmy can respond
only by admitting that she is far different from anyone he has ever encountered. "Christ, you are weird" (55). He tries to regain control of the situation
by making reference to what really happened at the execution-style murder
of Jack Diamond. All he succeeds in doing, however, is make Richard and
ultimately Patsy uneasy over his loquaciousness.

Faye's fascination with violence and her determination to make Jimmy
see the implications of this sort of behavior offer a useful demarcation between individuals in this world. Although menace stands out as a common
weapon employed by most characters in the play, only a few show themselves willing to accept the full consequences of the behavior they seem to
advocate. What Faye understands and Jimmy does not is that threats will
carry one only so far and that the truly successful individual must have a
ruthless willingness to carry them out.

As the play progresses, events make it clear to the audience that few of
the characters are capable of that behavior. Indeed, as the dialogue shows
what the results of such single-mindedness will be, this ability to take a confrontation to its conclusion no matter what the consequences becomes a
formidable attribute. To the surprise of no one familiar with *Billy Phelan's
Greatest Game*, Patsy never waivers in his commitment to such a course of action. The other characters' determination to hold to a position no matter
what might arise remains unclear, however.

Jimmy and Faye leave to go for a walk along the lake, and a false conviviality surfaces when Patsy and Mabel sing some of the songs that were popular
when they were young. Despite this aura of amiability, attentive members of
the audience will infer an undertone of bitterness from the dialogue, and Corbett takes advantage of the conflicted mood to present Patsy with the situation as he sees it. The Dewey administration has incriminating wiretaps that

Corbett now plays. It quickly becomes clear that the evidence on the record-
ings can put Patsy and his cronies in jail for a long time. Corbett also tells Patsy
that the governor has arranged a change of venue so that the corruption cases
will be tried in Manhattan, where the political influence of the Albany machine will have no impact. For a moment, this state of affairs seems a clear-cut
triumph for governmental reform, but events quickly reveal that Dewey is as
much a political animal as Patsy. Corbett offers Patsy a deal: if Patsy will stand
by while Richard Maloney is run out of office and if he will cooperate with the
prosecution of other machine figures, his prison sentence will be reduced.

Patsy, knowing full well why the governor is willing to bargain, scorn-
fully dismisses the offer and presents a counterproposal. He shows Corbett
the results of Jimmy's burglary: stacks of canceled checks that incriminate
members of Dewey's administration, including Corbett, in kickback
schemes that have bilked the state. If Dewey does not scale back his prose-
cutions, Patsy will give copies of the checks to the newspapers, thus ending
any chance Dewey might have of winning the presidency.

The subplot of a domestic tragedy reasserts itself when Faye returns
from her walk outraged that Jimmy has made advances to her. Jimmy, baffled by her mercurial nature, only responds in a tone of wounded pride, feeling that Faye led him on. When Patsy hears what has been going on, he too
becomes outraged, in a clear signal of a deeper emotional involvement than
seems justified by his recent introduction to Faye. Jimmy's crude efforts at
seduction have exposed more than he, or the audience for that matter, realizes. As will shortly become clear, Patsy genuinely believes Faye to be his
daughter, and he responds to the situation with the feelings of an angry father, ordering Jimmy out of the lodge.

Despite this outburst, however, Patsy remains the politician, and he
quickly and coolly returns to the business at hand. With coldhearted metic-
ulousness, he recounts the various cronies of the governor who have bene-
fitted from kickbacks, and he ends by producing a check made out to Malco
and Associates, a company held by Corbett. Faye is scandalized and begs
her father to deny the charges. Corbett is desperate to retain his daughter's
respect but unable to rebut Patsy's charges. Instead, he counters with a story
of Patsy and his brother beating a pimp to death. Faye repeatedly urges her
father to defy Patsy's threat to give the checks to the newspapers, but in a
desperate, self-incriminating gesture Corbett can respond only by ordering
her upstairs. Faye runs off, and Corbett follows, obviously aware of the
tremendous damage done to her psyche.

This moment, however, is hardly one of triumph for Patsy, and for the first time the play shows him miscalculating his position. In an effort to alienate Mabel from her husband, he continues the conversation with her, driving home the point of Corbett's involvement. Mabel, however, is tougher than Patsy has anticipated. She makes it clear that she is the one who will be implicated by the evidence that Patsy has produced, for it is her name on the checks' endorsements. The choice is equally clear to Patsy. Making good on his threats to expose Dewey will send to prison the woman whom he has claimed to love for years.

Just as Corbett moments earlier had responded to his daughter by trying to deflect the conversation to another topic, Patsy, aware that he may have gone too far, seeks to redeem himself by testifying to his devotion to Mabel. He talks of spending the past twenty years hovering at the edge of her life: "I had you followed every step of the way, every time you got your picture in the papers, some fancyassed party, some charity ball. I went to Faye's high school graduation. I saw her *Sea Gull* show twice last week. I got movies of you buyin' a hat on Fifth Avenue. I watched you comin' outa gettin' your hair done. I watched your life, Mabel. I watched your life" (77). Finally, Patsy reveals why he has so doggedly followed the lives of the Atterby family: "Faye is my daughter" (78).

This declaration of paternity, however, only pushes Mabel farther from him. What seem to Patsy to be acts of devotion leave both Mabel and the audience with the uneasy image of him as a voyeur. Rather than affirming his credentials as a concerned parent and lover, this behavior underscores a dominant feature of the play: most of the characters are always being watched, often without their knowledge, and this intense scrutiny only emphasizes the isolation many of them feel.

Nonetheless, Patsy remains oblivious to the effect of his speech, for even after this exchange he believes himself to be still very much in control of the situation. He launches into a long disquisition that gives his view of how things are going to be run in Albany for the foreseeable future:

> Corbett and the Governor, a pair of reformers. Reformers botch everything. They're out to change people like me and that can't be done, because I'm not just *me*, Mabel. I'm something even *I* don't understand all the way. But do I have to? How much you gotta know about electricity to plug in a lamp? I know in my bones how to get power and keep it—you do what's necessary. And that's who I am—the keeper of the power. (79)

In another monumental miscalculation, Patsy ends his diatribe with the threat that unless Mabel comes back to him, he will tell Faye that he is her father. He scarcely realizes how far away he has already driven Mabel.

Corbett's return to reveal that he has put in a call to Dewey and expects instructions telling him not to make a deal defers immediate resolution of the conflict, though it does not diminish the tension in the scene. Patsy repeats his threat to tell Faye that he is her father, which in turn forces Mabel to admit to her husband that she does not know which of the two men made her pregnant. When Corbett attempts to call Patsy's bluff, Mabel forcibly stops him from getting Faye. Without further dramatics, Patsy sums up the situation: "The game's over Corky. (Beat) Isn't that so Mabel" (84). Although correct in sensing a conclusion, he has again misjudged the results.

Before the consequences become clear, Dewey calls the resort. While Corbett goes to take the call, Jimmy tries to make peace with Patsy. The older man will have none of it and roughly orders Jimmy to return with the checks to Albany.

When Corbett returns, it is with the news that Dewey is now offering a much different deal to Patsy. It is finally obvious to Corbett that Dewey knew from the start that Patsy had stolen the checks, and yet the governor had sent Corbett to the confrontation with no knowledge of the weakness of his position. Now Corbett attempts to wring concessions out of Patsy so that the Dewey administration can save some face in the matter.

At first, Patsy's behavior seems to fit the unvoiced code of ethics on which the machine relies. He agrees to give up Cooley, the informant who first went to the Dewey camp with evidence of corruption, but will see no others go to jail. He demands that Dewey rescind plans to supplant Richard Maloney and appears immovable in terms of further concessions. When Corbett presses for someone else to be arrested, Patsy unexpectedly shifts his ground. He allows personal animosity to override political loyalty. He agrees to give them Jimmy. He goes so far as to tell Corbett that Jimmy is now driving back to Albany with copies of the stolen checks and can easily be arrested by state troopers. The deal is sealed with this betrayal.

Richard, who for all his machinations still follows the moral system of the political machine, which is founded on fidelity to the group, is aghast at what Patsy has done. Jimmy, though crude and of limited intelligence, has always behaved with loyalty. Richard cannot stand by while Patsy gives this man up for prosecution, and he storms out of the room. Patsy, oblivious to all that he has done, makes a final effort to win Mabel from Corbett, but Mabel chooses her husband: "Mabel loves Corbett" (89).

After the Atterbys have left the parlor, Richard reappears, packed and ready to leave. He tells Patsy pointedly that their friendship is over. He declares his intention to go to Florida and spend his time fishing. Patsy can respond only with an empty threat that ironically mocks his sense of omnipotence: "I'll sink your goddamned boat" (90).

As the Atterbys leave, Patsy makes one last effort to take control of the situation. He tries to make good on his threat to tell Faye of his belief that he is her father. Corbett, however, steps in. As his wife and daughter walk out the door, he proves himself as willing as Patsy to use violence. The two men wrestle, and the stage direction gives a lightning conclusion to the scene. "CORBETT picks up standing ashtray, holds it like a club. PATSY stops moving, stares at empty doorway. CORBETT tosses ashtray to floor, goes out" (91–92).

Patsy remains in the parlor, and Alice reenters. As he sits there absorbing what has occurred, his mind turns again to the Battle of Vicksburg, thinking of Grant's behavior when he had defeated the Confederate forces: "After the surrender he let 'em march out with their sidearms and clothes. The officers took their horses. (Beat) Grant coulda stripped 'em naked—left 'em for the dogs to eat. But he let 'em go with dignity" (92). The lines have a powerful poignancy for the audience, for they reveal Patsy as the antithesis of Grant; he is a man overcome by hubris and by his mistaken belief that he could win his struggle with the Atterbys by threatening to strip them of all dignity.

For a moment, it seems that Patsy has realized the foolishness of his own behavior and has in fact learned, if only belatedly, from the example of General Grant. That possibility is quickly dispelled when the phone rings, and Alice takes a message from Richard: "The state troopers stopped Jimmy Gill's car half a mile from here. He went whacky and yelled at them, then he tried to outrun them and they shot him twice. His car ran into a tree. He's alive, but not by much. They're taking him to Saratoga Hospital. (Beat) Richard said to tell you, 'You do championship work, Patsy' " (93). Patsy registers no emotion and shows no regret. His only response is to call the bishop who has a cottage across the lake and to ask that a priest go to the hospital to give Jimmy the last rites of the Catholic Church.

Patsy's obliviousness to all that he has done becomes eminently clear when he launches into a diatribe against Mabel as Alice slips away. The play closes with Patsy alone on stage, showing neither regret nor self-doubt. He remains defiant and in this posture becomes much more than the typical tragic figure. Patsy, indeed, is one of the few people in the play able to employ violence, no matter what the cost, to achieve his ends. His willingness to sacrifice all others, including both the woman whom he professes to love and the girl he claims as a daughter, sets him apart. It also enforces the image of what one must do to maintain the kind of political control that he has held for two decades.

Grand View revisits themes of power, appetite, and loyalty that have dominated Kennedy's writing throughout the Albany cycle. It also shows his profound insight into the complex relations of the political world of his city. With a sensitivity displayed by few others, he can trace the elements of machine politics, evoke its impact on the lives of ordinary people, and lay out its complex social function. In the end, he neither celebrates nor condemns this political phenomenon. Rather, he retains a confidence in his audience's ability to judge it from his finely etched portrait.

Coda

Though I have come to end of this study, it strikes me as both presumptuous and pointless to attempt to write a conclusion to an analysis of the works of William Kennedy. As Kennedy himself demonstrated so vigorously at the writers' conference in his honor held in Albany in April 1999, he remains very deeply committed to developing the Albany cycle and indeed to refining every aspect of his craft. I fully expect the appearance of a number of subsequent works that will fill out the histories of his flamboyant characters—the Phelans, the Daughertys, and the McCalls—and that will introduce a range of new individuals whose stories will continue to exert a profound impact on readers of his fiction.

I have in the preceding pages endeavored to explain this impact by highlighting the stylistic and thematic features distinguishing Kennedy's work from that of his contemporaries. Kennedy writes in the clear, direct style that calls to mind what he most admires in Hemingway's prose. His training as a journalist has given him a deft ability to offer powerful descriptions in crisp, precise language that never lapses into the trite or predictable. His sense of place conveys both the uniqueness and the universality of Albany, making it both familiar and fascinating to first-time and repeat readers alike. His profound interest in humanity translates into a relentless exploration of the characterizing features of human identity, and in his fiction he conveys the complexity of the flawed state of so many individuals without ever losing respect for the uniqueness of each character. And his own deeply grounded belief in the metaphysical importance of our lives, balanced by a healthy skepticism for organized systems of belief, leads to a heightened spirituality informing the ethos of his novels.

At the same time, Kennedy's deep love of the craft of writing prevents his work from becoming programmatic or predictable. From *The Ink Truck* through *Grand View* and on to *Roscoe,* even the casual reader can see in his writing a continual striving for new effects, different impressions. Kennedy will never become a popular writer in the sense of being an author whose formulaic approach produces a familiar product every time he publishes a new work. Rather, he remains an artist deeply committed to developing his craft with every creative effort, and therefore one who will continue to attract and inspire intelligent readers for generations to come.

Overall, Kennedy stands as a writer who continues to engage our interest because he has never lost the joy he experiences in practicing his craft. His writing attests to a deep love of his work and a profound respect for those who read it. He will continue to delight, exasperate, amuse, enrage, and awe us for as long as he continues to write.

Notes

Introduction

1. For a different perspective on how these features have shaped Kennedy's writing, see Van Dover 1991, 5–18.

2. *The Ink Truck* as Prelude

1. Kennedy features Albany in everything that he writes, but the cycle itself comprises the fiction that traces the lives of interrelated Irish American families—the Quinns, the Phelans, the Daughertys, the McCalls—from the mid-nineteenth century to the mid-twentieth century.

2. For a synopsis of the historical inspiration for the novel, see Van Dover 1991, 27.

3. For a detailed look at how this process functions in Joyce, see Gillespie 1989, 81–103.

4. The echoes of the headlines that punctuate the Aeolus chapter of Joyce's *Ulysses* seem unmistakable when one reads the section titles of *The Ink Truck* in succession.

5. Lest that comment seem too dismissive, one would be hard-pressed to find examples in modern literature—beyond Stephen Dedalus, Quentin Compson, and Houlden Caufield—of characters who are able to instill a universal appeal into their self-absorption.

6. For a detailed description of how Free Indirect Discourse functions, see Bally 1912, Chatman 1975, Cohn 1966, and McHale 1978.

3. *Legs* and the Pursuit of Knowledge

1. For an interesting discussion of the challenges that arise in using an attorney to tell the story of Jack Diamond's life, see Wittaker 1985.

2. For a summary of the parallels between the historical Jack Diamond and Kennedy's creation, see Van Dover 1991, 46–48.

3. The novel itself fosters this ambivalence. It opens with a declaration from Marcus that both announces the book's conclusion and calls it into question: "I really don't think he's

dead" (11). In the final lines of *Legs*, Marcus imagines Jack echoing these sentiments: " 'Honest to God, Marcus,' he said going away, 'I really don't think I'm dead' " (317).

4. For an interesting look at this aspect of Jack Diamond, see Fanning 1990.

5. The run-on quality of these lines is just one example of Kennedy's subtle invocation of Joyce. Just as Molly Bloom, in her chapter-long soliloquy at the end of *Ulysses*, offers a rambling, unpunctuated disquisition on her life and loves, Kiki Roberts captures the same rhythm of discourse in her abbreviated description of intercourse with Jack Diamond.

6. Like the previously noted passage that mimics the style of James Joyce, this one calls to mind another of Kennedy's literary antecedents, Borges. Although the connection seems a bit forced here, it presages later associations that appear with much greater skill.

7. As I noted in the introduction, I do not see the need for such completion as a weakness in the novel. Rather, it reflects what the critic Roland Barthes (1977) has outlined as the way that skillful writers draw readers into full engagement with the text.

8. Somewhat perversely, Jack does seem to have a limited awareness of modernist writers. Kennedy uses Marcus's narrative in a deft maneuver that avoids cloying parallels: "It took me forty-three years to make the connection between Jack and Gatsby. It should have been quicker, for he told me he met Fitzgerald on a transatlantic voyage in 1926, on the dope-buying trip that got him into federal trouble" (Kennedy 1975, 73). The glancing connection Jack himself makes underscores his own limited sense of resistance to the social institutions that the modernists decried.

4. The Emergence of Self in *Billy Phelan's Greatest Game*

1. Although the subject of this study precludes taking up the topic in detail here, ethnicity forms an important feature in the composition of all of Kennedy's characters. For a thoughtful examination of its function in both *Billy Phelan's Greatest Game* and *Ironweed*, see L. Kennedy 1993.

2. This will become more evident in *Ironweed*, the novel that immediately follows *Billy Phelan's Greatest Game*. There, the narrative's prevalent concern for Francis Phelan centers around his reestablishing connections with place and thus regaining a sense of self. No matter how alienated Francis may feel, his old North Albany neighborhood evokes powerful memories and retains an irresistible attraction. Returning to that world expands his identity, for it draws the impressions of family members and friends into the conception he holds of himself.

3. For an alternative perspective of the way games and gaming shape the novel, see Michener 1995.

4. For a correction of the scoring of Billy's game, see Naparsteck 1992.

5. Martin's dual need to become both a father and a son might remind some readers of the similar plight of Leopold Bloom in *Ulysses*—a novel that Kennedy has himself often identified as an important influence on his works. For an examination of the various father-son relationships in *Billy Phelan's Greatest Game*, see Van Dover 1991, 73–75.

6. Implications of this relationship are touched on throughout the Albany novels, but they are not fully explained until *The Flaming Corsage* (1996).

7. Billy's attitude calls to mind a sentiment ascribed to Jimmy the Greek, a well-known

gambler of the 1970s, who said that next to gambling and winning, the best thing in the world was gambling and losing.

8. One might argue that the deficiency in the comprehension of women is as much a fault of Kennedy's writing as it is of Martin's nature. Whatever the source, it is not until *The Flaming Corsage* that readers see in the person of Martin's father, Edward Daugherty, a character with a deep understanding of the nature of the women who appear in Kennedy's fiction.

9. Like so many other events incorporated into his fiction, Kennedy bases this blackout on an actual incident that occurred in Albany when Thomas Dewey decided to attack the O'Connell machine. For further details on Kennedy's use of this incident, see Lynch 1999, 88.

10. As elsewhere in Kennedy's work, the analogues to Joyce are all too apparent. As the darkened Albany becomes an unreal city, the pilgrimage that Billy and the others make evokes a similar trip that Stephen Dedalus and Leopold Bloom make to nighttown in *Ulysses*.

11. Again Joyce's presence becomes apparent when one considers how close these musings come to those of Stephen Dedalus in the National Library during the "Scylla and Charybdis" chapter of *Ulysses*.

12. It is in this chapter that Kennedy anachronistically has Martin remembering his father making reference in 1921 to Yeats's "Sailing to Byzantium," a poem written in 1927 (cf. Kennedy 1978, 232 and 234).

5. *Ironweed* and the Consequences of Resurrection

1. For the most detailed study of *Ironweed* yet to appear, see Giamo 1996.

2. See, for example, Tierce 1988.

3. For a detailed examination of the quest for male identity in *Ironweed*, see Yetman 1991.

4. One aspect of this connection appears in Griffin 1988b.

5. For a detailed examination of the associations between Dante, Halloween, and *Ironweed*, see Reilly 1987.

6. For an assessment of the roles of gender and personality in *Ironweed*, see Griffin 1988a.

7. With a deft nod to popular culture, Kennedy also integrates into the exchange between Francis and Rudy an oblique reference to the October 30, 1938, broadcast by Orson Welles's Mercury Theater on the Air of an adaptation of H. G. Wells's *The War of the Worlds*: "Hey, what the hell was all that about the man from Mars last night? Everybody was talkin' about it at the hospital. You hear about that stuff on the radio?" (11).

8. For an examination of the way that baseball shapes this process, see Yetman 1990.

9. For a detailed examination of this theme, see Novelli 1992.

10. For a discussion of the impact of Francis Phelan's alcohol addiction, see Taylor 1992.

6. The Consequences of Time in *Quinn's Book*

1. Of course, the similarities in name and profession invite readers to see Will Canaday as the near homophonic equivalent of Bill Kennedy, the novel's author. Given Canaday's detachment from events in the latter half of the work, however, this connection seems little more than a bit of cleverness Kennedy shares with his more attentive readers.

2. Here the link to Faulkner becomes more apparent as the Plums suggest a variation on

the pattern of mendacity leading to a measure of material success, much like the Snopes, whom Faulkner sketched. Admittedly, the Plums are more degenerate and perhaps for that reason ultimately less successful than the Snopes family.

3. For an interesting account of a figure who may have served as a model for John the Brawn McGee, see Reilly 1989.

7. The Centering of *Very Old Bones*

1. Just as Will Canaday in *Quinn's Book* shows noticeable echoes of a middle-age William Kennedy, the life of Daniel Quinn shows parallels to that of Kennedy as a younger man: army service in Europe, an interest in journalism, and marriage to a Hispanic woman. Kennedy himself acknowledged this connection in a 1997 interview with Tom Smith.

2. Van Dover identifies George Quinn as the grandson of the Daniel Quinn of *Quinn's Book* (1991, 63). This supposition comes from information that appears in two short stories Kennedy wrote in the mid-1980s, "The Secrets of Creative Love" (1983c) and "An Exchange of Gifts" (1985–86). However, because these stories construct a life for Daniel Quinn, the nephew of Billy Phelan, that is very different from the family affiliations that appear in the chronology in *Very Old Bones*, I have followed the information supplied in the novel.

3. Christian Michener has noted this similarity in structure (1998, 197).

4. Again Joyce comes to mind with his opening to the Sirens chapter of *Ulysses*, though Kennedy's overture-like approach is by no means as abbreviated as Joyce's.

5. The clearest example of how an author can set up and manipulate this perspective occurs in Joyce's *A Portrait of the Artist as a Young Man*.

6. In my opinion, the less than satisfying aesthetic response generated by *Quinn's Book* comes in part from its failure to sustain this inquiry into the development of human identity. Of course, its role as a transition piece, a work that provides background information that will be used in a number of other novels, may also preclude it from operating at this level.

7. Readers such as Christian Michener, however, will not go even this far in criticizing the technique. In "A Magical Time in Albany," a paper delivered at a symposium on Kennedy's work held in Albany, April 16–17, 1999, Michener calls the shift an example of magic realism.

8. Kennedy glosses the various allusions to very old bones in the interview with Tom Smith (1997, 208).

9. Again one sees an echo of Joyce in the way Orson's failed novel mimics the ending of *Finnegans Wake*.

10. In *The Flaming Corsage* (Kennedy 1996, 179), the narrative says that the play closed after one performance, which seems one of the few times when contradictory information slips into the complex series of details that inform Kennedy's Albany cycle of novels.

11. As Christian Michener has noted, Francis's actions also inspire Edward Daugherty's play *The Car Barns* and, to a lesser degree, *The Flaming Corsage* (1998, 234–35, n. 8.

12. In describing Claire Purcell crossing the lobby of the hotel, the narrative notes both her age—fifty-eight, nearly the same as Peg Phelan Quinn in the contemporary narrative—and the sexual effect that she has on men. Time and again in the narrative, sexuality asserts a strong pull, though generally for men and women who need the attention that it provides as

an alternative to family support (cf. Jack Diamond, Billy Phelan, all of the Daughertys, the young Francis Phelan, Peg Phelan Quinn, Maud Fallon, Magdalena Colón).

13. The description is sure to call to some readers' minds the Viking-Penguin Press, Kennedy's own publisher.

14. The film buff Kennedy may also be evoking a similar scene from *The Graduate* in which Benjamin, seeking to shock Catherine, takes her to a strip club.

15. The description of Orson's stay in the woods, complete with quotations from *Finnegans Wake*, parallels Kennedy's own description of going to the Adirondacks to write *Legs*. See *Riding the Yellow Trolley Car* (Kennedy 1993, 41). In an interview in *Salmagundi*, Kennedy also describes how this experience came about (Kennedy 1994).

8. The Cyclical Impulse of *The Flaming Corsage*

1. The bordello is made up of four tents located on the State Fairgrounds just past the Bull's Head Tavern, the scene of one of John the Brawn McGee's boxing triumphs described in *Quinn's Book* and a name that here has a proleptic double entendre.

2. Here, the analogue between sex organs and cameras first adduced in *Very Old Bones* recurs, with the female-camera association replaced by the male camera.

3. This scene may recall for some readers a similar incident in *Billy Phelan's Greatest Game* in which Billy cows a rowdy teenager with a hot cup of coffee.

4. For a very different assessment of this exchange, one that gives a much kinder view of Edward's motivations, see Michener 1998, 241–45.

5. The Delavan fire episode is based on an actual Albany hotel fire of the period. See Sheppard 1996.

6. The narrative confirms that the affair between Edward and Melissa Spencer lasts no more than a year and is over when Giles bursts in on them in the hotel. Though *Billy Phelan's Greatest Game* may leave the impression that Melissa and Edward have a prominent and long-running affair, it is really Martin Daugherty who will have the more sustained relationship with her.

7. Needless to say, the entire chapter sheds new light on why, in 1938, Melissa will have such a keen desire to play the Katrina character in a revival of the drama.

8. In *Very Old Bones*, the narrative claims the play lasted for two performances.

9. The Siege of Vicksburg and the Battle at *Grand View*

1. I am very grateful to William Kennedy and to Alex Levy of the Pegasus Players Theatre of Chicago for providing me with a copy of the working script for the Pegasus production of *Grand View*, which ran from April 18 to May 28, 2000. All subsequent quotations are from this draft.

2. Throughout the play, Kennedy uses the term *Beat* to indicate a pause in the speech of one of his characters.

Works Cited

Bally, Charles. 1912. "Les Style indirect libre en françias moderne." *Germanisch-Romanische Monatsschrift* 4: 549–56.

Barthes, Roland. 1977. *Image, Music, Text.* Translated by Stephen Heath. New York: Hill and Wang.

Chatman, Seymour. 1975. "The Structure of Narrative Transmission." In *Style and Structure in Literature: Essays in the New Stylistics,* edited by Roger Fowler, 213–57. Ithaca, N.Y.: Cornell Univ. Press.

Cohn, Dorrit. 1966. "Narrated Monologue: Definition of a Fictional Style." *Comparative Literature* 18 (spring): 97–112.

Dumbleton, Susanne. 1996. "William Kennedy: Telling the Truth the Best Way I Can." In *The Eye of the Reporter,* edited by Bill Knight and Deckle McLean, 3–16. Macomb: Western Illinois Univ. Press.

Fanning, Charles. 1990. *The Irish Voice in America: Irish-American Fiction from the 1760s to the 1980s.* Lexington: Univ. of Kentucky Press.

Giamo, Benedict. 1996. *The Homeless of Ironweed.* Iowa City: Univ. of Iowa Press.

Gillespie, Michael Patrick. 1989. *Reading the Book of Himself: Narrative Strategies in the Works of James Joyce.* Columbus: Ohio State Univ. Press.

Griffin, Paul F. 1988a. "The Moral Implications of Annie Phelan's Jell-O." *San Jose Studies* 14 (fall): 85–95.

———. 1988b. "Susan Sontag, Franny Phelan, and the Moral Implications of Photographs." *Midwest Quarterly* 29 (winter): 194–203.

Iser, Wolfgang. 1978. *The Act of Reading: A Theory of Aesthetic Response.* Baltimore and London: Johns Hopkins Univ. Press.

Jauss, Hans Robert. 1982. *Towards an Aesthetic of Reception.* Translated by Timothy Bahti. Minneapolis: Univ. of Minnesota Press.

Joyce, James. 1939. *Finnegans Wake.* New York: Viking.

———. 1964. *A Portrait of the Artist as a Young Man.* Edited by Chester Anderson. New York: Penguin.

————. 1986. *Ulysses*. Edited by Hans Walter Gabler. New York: Random House.

Kennedy, Liam. 1993. "Memory and Hearsay: Ethnic Identity in *Billy Phelan's Greatest Game* and *Ironweed*." *Melus* 18: 71–82.

Kennedy, William. 1969. *The Ink Truck*. New York: Penguin.

————. 1975. *Legs*. New York: Penguin.

————. 1978. *Billy Phelan's Greatest Game*. New York: Penguin.

————. 1983a. *Ironweed*. New York: Penguin.

————. 1983b. *O Albany! Improbable City of Political Wizards, Fearless Ethnics, Spectacular Aristocrats, Splendid Nobodies, and Underrated Scoundrels*. New York: Penguin.

————. 1983c. "The Secrets of Creative Love." *Harper's* 267 (July): 54–58.

————. 1985–86. "An Exchange of Gifts." *Glen Falls Review* 3: 7–9.

————. 1988. *Quinn's Book*. New York: Penguin.

————. 1992. *Very Old Bones*. New York: Penguin.

————. 1993. *Riding the Yellow Trolley Car*. New York: Penguin.

————. 1994. "Gifts from Joyce." *Salmagundi* 103 (summer): 35–50.

————. 1996. *The Flaming Corsage*. New York: Penguin.

————. 2000. "Grand View." Unpublished working script of play produced by the Pegasus Players Theatre of Chicago, 18 April to 28 May 28.

Lynch, Vivian Valvano. 1999. *Portraits of Artists: Warriors in the Novels of William Kennedy*. San Francisco: International Scholars.

Magalaner, Marvin. 1959. *Time of Apprenticeship: The Fiction of Young James Joyce*. London: Abelard-Schuman.

McHale Brian. 1978. "Free Indirect Discourse: A Survey of Recent Accounts." *PTL: A Journal for Descriptive Poetics and Theory of Literature* 3 (April): 249–87.

Michener, Christian. 1995. "Martin Daugherty's Victories in *Billy Phelan's Greatest Game*." *Papers on Language and Literature* 31 (fall): 405–29.

————. 1998. *From Then into Now: William Kennedy's Albany Novels*. Scranton, Ill.: Univ. of Scranton Press.

Naparsteck, Martin. 1992. "Kennedy's *Billy Phelan's Greatest Game*." *The Explicator* 55 (winter): 104.

Novelli, Cornelius. 1992. "Francis Phelan and the Hands of Heracles: Hero and City in William Kennedy's *Ironweed*." *Classical and Modern Literature* 12 (winter): 119–26.

Reilly, Edward C. 1987. "Dante's *Purgatorio* and Kennedy's *Ironweed*: Journeys to Redemption." *Notes on Contemporary Literature* 17 (May): 5–8.

————. 1989. "John the Brawn McGree [sic] in *Quinn's Book*: A Probable Source." *Notes on Contemporary Literature* 19 (May): 4–5.

Royko, Mike. 1971. *Boss: Richard J. Daley of Chicago*. New York: NAL/Dutton.

Seshachari, Neila C., ed. 1997. *Conversations with William Kennedy*. Jackson: Univ. of Mississippi Press.

Sheppard, R. Z. 1996. "Living with the Ashes." *Time* (13 May): 92–93.

Smith, Tom. 1997. "Very Bountiful Bones: An Interview with William Kennedy." In *Conversations with William Kennedy*, edited by Neila C. Seshachari, 190–213. Jackson: Univ. of Mississippi Press.

Taylor, Anya. 1992. "*Ironweed*, Alcohol, and Celtic Heroism." *Critique* 33 (winter): 2, 107–20.

Tierce, Michael. 1988. "William Kennedy's Odyssey: The Travels of Francis Phelan." *Classical and Modern Literature* 8 (summer): 247–63.

Van Dover, J. K. 1991. *Understanding William Kennedy*. Columbia: Univ. of South Carolina Press.

Wittaker, Stephen. 1985. "The Lawyer as Narrator in William Kennedy's *Legs*." *Legal Studies Forum* 9, no. 2: 157–64.

Yetman, Michael. 1990. "Mythologizing the Personal Past: Baseball as Symbolic Self-Redemption in *Ironweed*." *Aethion* 8 (fall): 1–9.

———. 1991. "*Ironweed*: The Perils and Purgatories of Male Romanticism." *Papers on Language and Literature* 27 (winter): 84–104.

Index